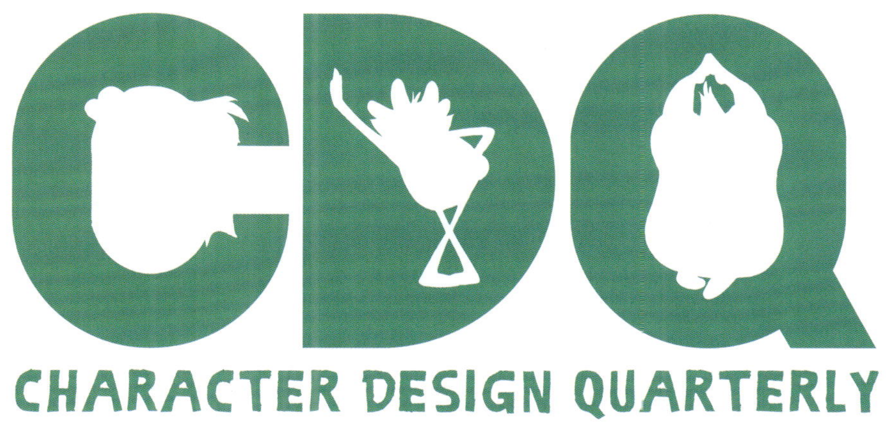

CDQ
CHARACTER DESIGN QUARTERLY

CONTENTS

Images by individual artists as credited throughout the book

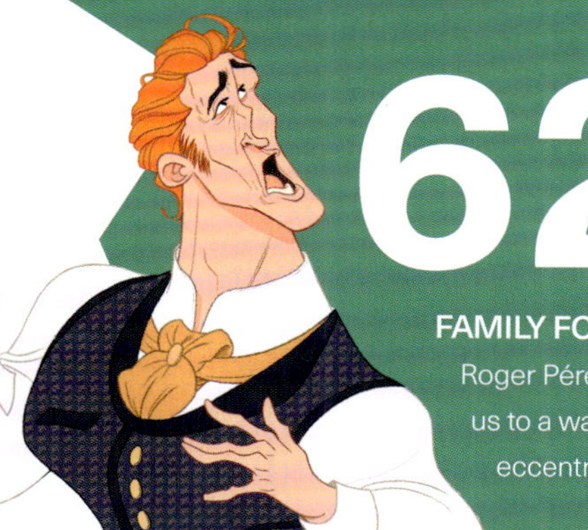

WELCOME TO
CHARACTER DESIGN QUARTERLY 31

One of the many creative fields where character design plays a huge part is video games, and in this issue we have interviews with two artists who have thrived within the medium. We were delighted to be able to speak to Rex Crowle, the BAFTA award-winning creative director of games such as *Tearaway* and *Knights and Bikes*, and David Ardinaryas Lojaya, the art director of the indie smash-hit *Coral Island*. We spoke to Rex about his fantastic work updating classic designs in *Return of Monkey Island*, and David shared his process for creating the many inhabitants of *Coral Island*.

We are also thrilled to welcome Linnea Kikuchi (aka Feefal) to *CDQ*, who's nature-inspired art should need no introduction. A long-time collaborator of 3dtotal, we spoke to Linnea about her career, inspirations, and how she created this issue's stunning cover illustration.

We have in-depth tutorials from Roger Pérez and Teo Skaffa, who both share their own unique way of creating characters, Yaroslava Apollonova gives her tips for using Procreate, and our new development gallery continues to be a great way to quickly see how artists put together some of their favourite character designs.

Whether you want to create characters for video games, animation, or even just for fun, there's plenty to inspire you packed into this issue of *CDQ*.

SAM DRAPER
EDITOR

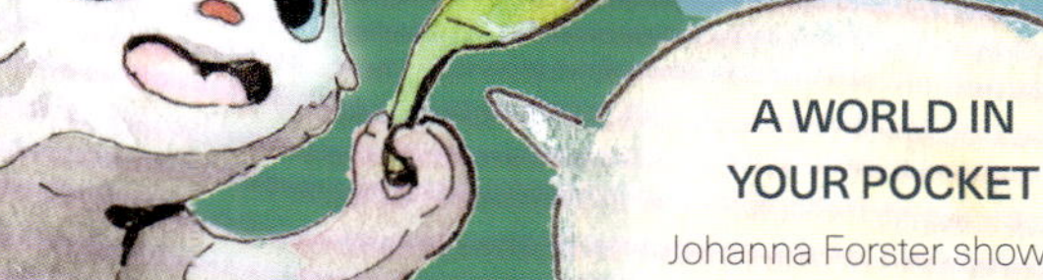

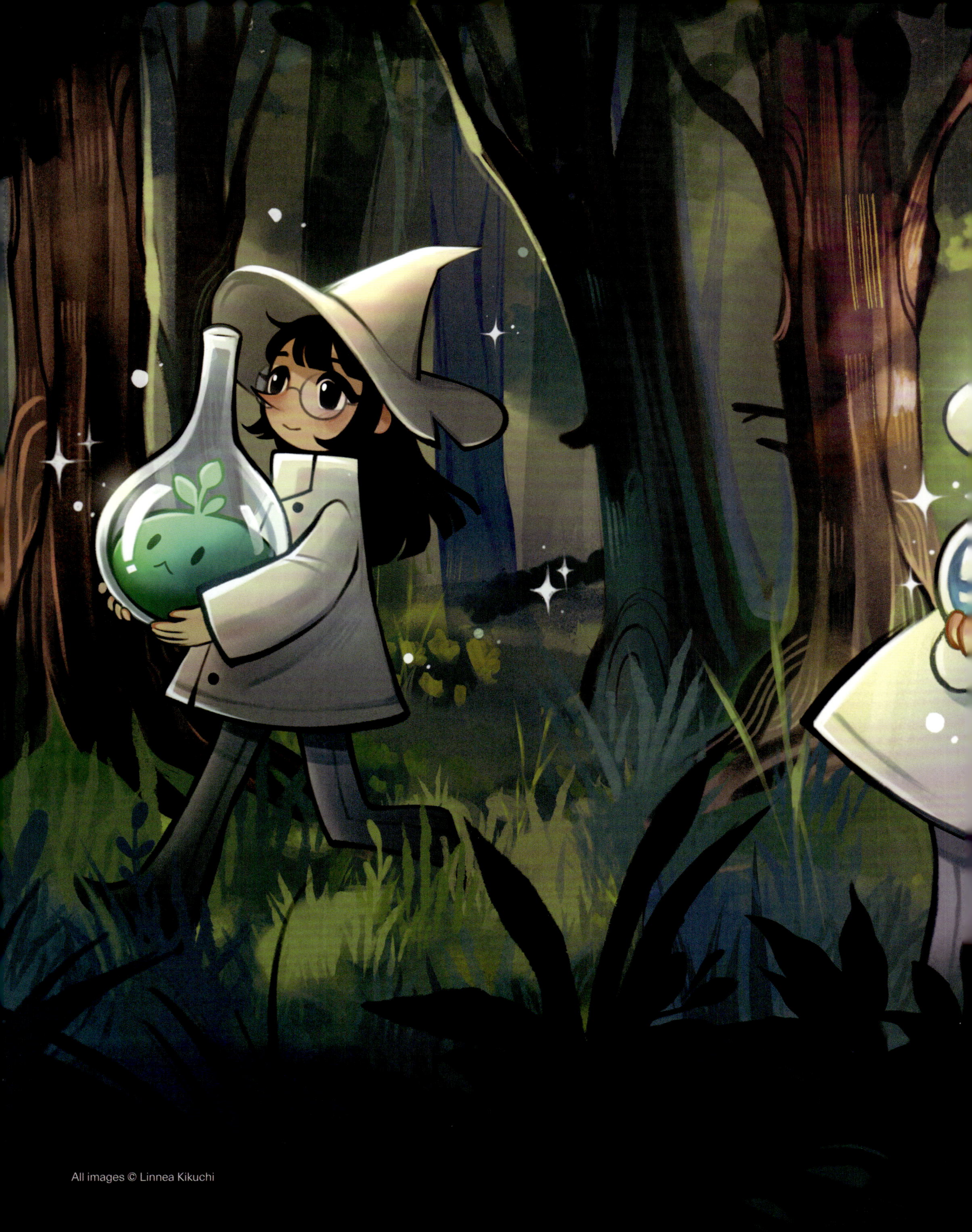

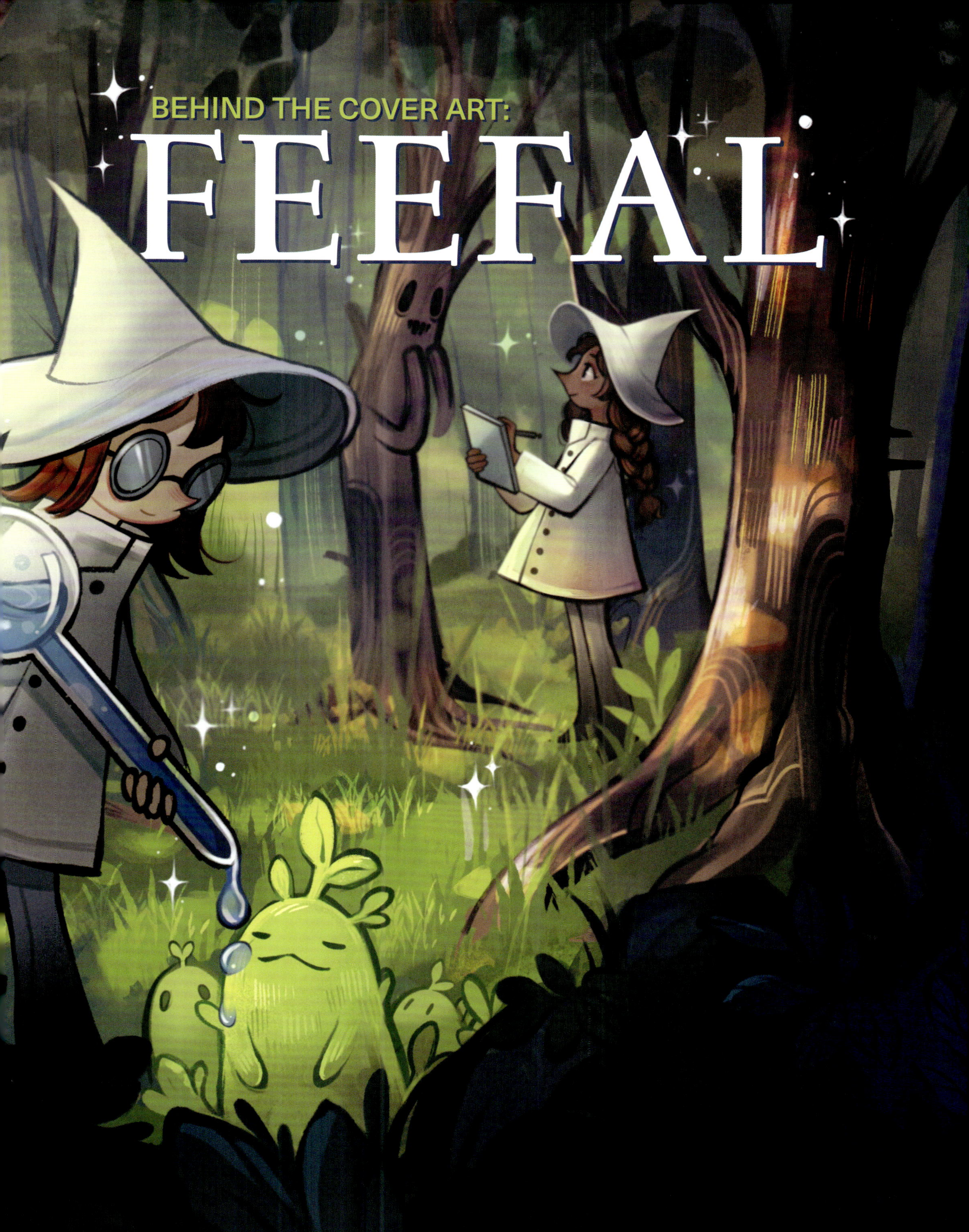

BEHIND THE COVER ART:
FEEFAL

Hi Linnea, welcome to *CDQ*! Can you tell us a little about your career in art so far?

My art journey began when I first made my Instagram account back in 2016. I had dreamt of being an artist since the dawn of time, but it always seemed like such an abstract goal – it's just so difficult to know how to get started when there's no clear guide on how to make your passion into a career! My hometown is very biased towards modern art, so I got the impression that the sort of artwork I gravitated towards wasn't of much value. It wasn't until I started posting my artwork online and reached an international audience that I realised I was capable of creating work that resonated with others.

As of today, I mainly make my living through my Patreon and selling artwork directly to people via conventions and my web shop. I have done my fair share of freelancing these past few years, and it's always exciting to be part of a bigger project. But most of all I love the freedom of being able to explore my own hyper-fixations for a living.

My biggest and proudest achievement is the art book I published with 3dtotal in 2022, titled *The Art of Feefal*. Oh man, I love that book so much! It's my biological baby in book form.

A character inspired by pixie-cup lichen, a fungus that grows in high moisture environments in soil and dead wood

Held back by the ghost of you

The cover art for this issue is so interesting – what was the inspiration behind the illustration?

I started thinking about all the similarities between lab scientists and witches. Laboratory experiments almost seem like real magic to someone like me who doesn't understand the science behind them. And there's a bunch of other similarities, too, like how they both brew potions and concoctions contained within funny-shaped flasks, surrounded by shelves of mysterious ingredients – and let's not forget that many years ago you were likely to be accused of performing witchcraft if you were too familiar with the use of medicinal herbs. These two worlds were simply meant to collide in a balanced mix between fantastical fiction and science.

Once I had my initial idea down, I had to map everything into a setting. I decided on a lush forest, with these cute witches in lab coats performing experiments on the flora surrounding them. They grant plants life using their magic-infused chemicals. I wanted the illustration to showcase an uplifting and joyous scene, so all the plants and trees are happy about their newly acquired sentience. If I was a shrub basking in the sun, whose only concern in life was photosynthesis, I'm not sure if I'd react so positively to being cursed with cognitive thought!

'I had dreamt of being an artist since the dawn of time, but it always seemed like such an abstract goal'

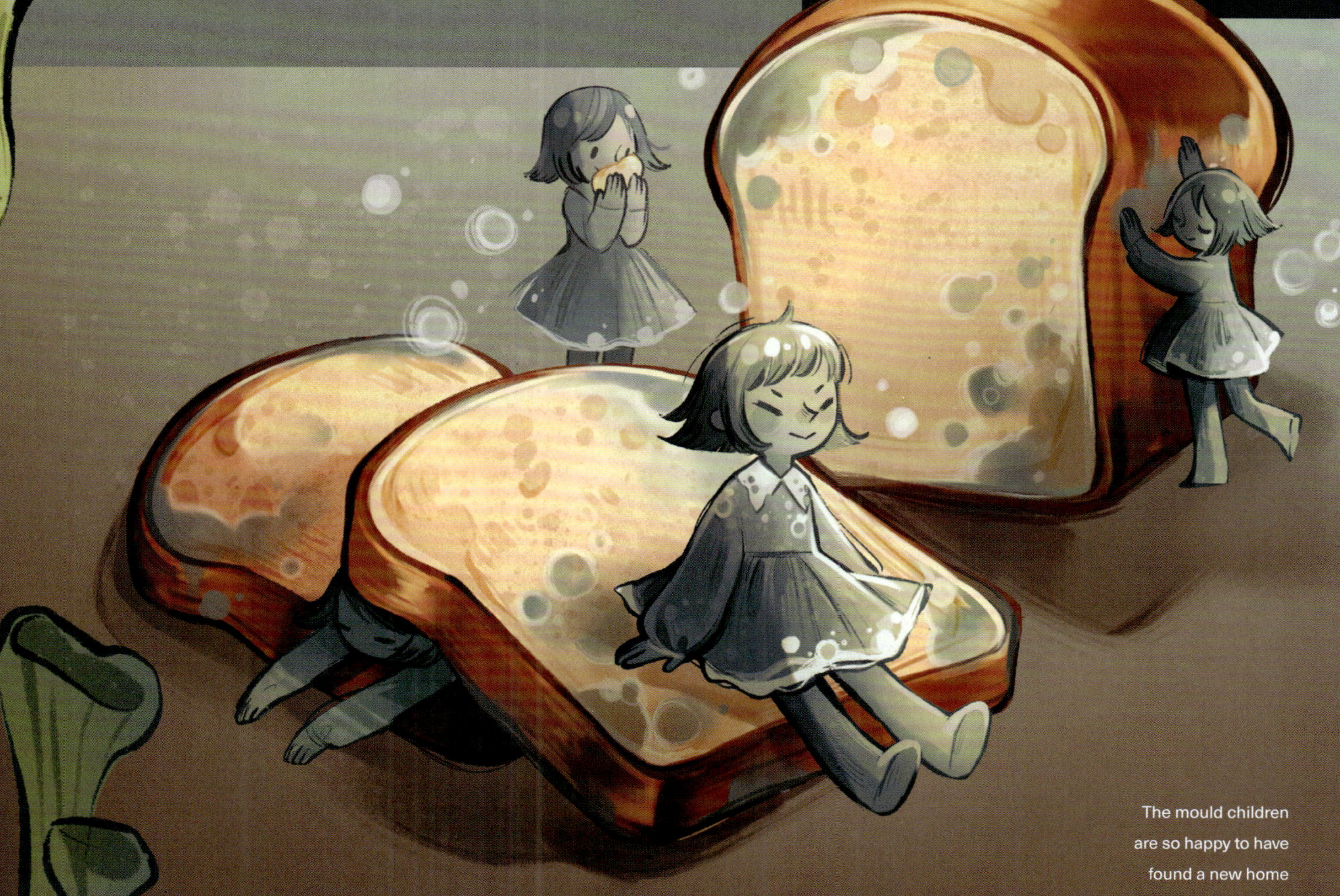

The mould children are so happy to have found a new home

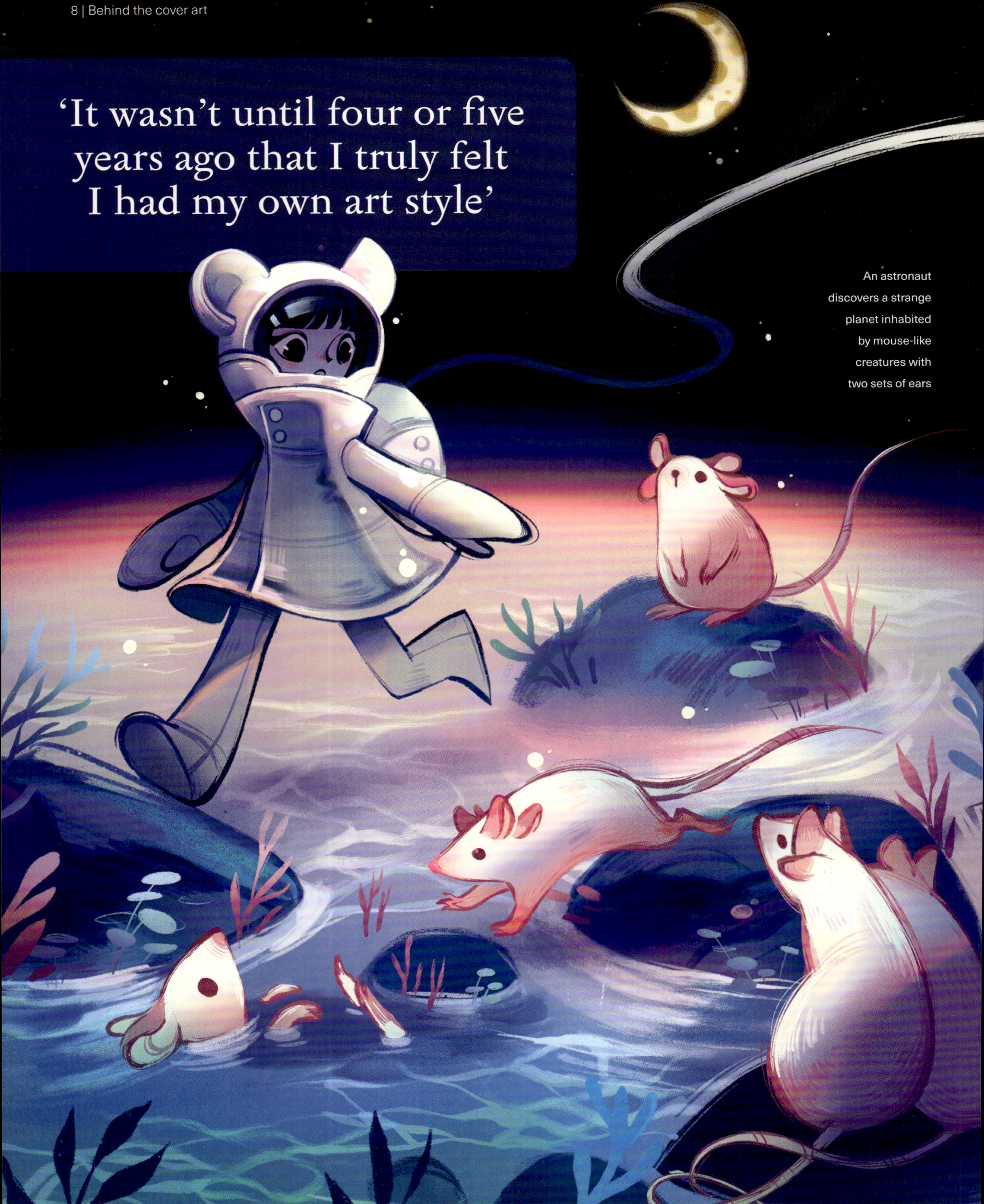

'It wasn't until four or five years ago that I truly felt I had my own art style'

An astronaut discovers a strange planet inhabited by mouse-like creatures with two sets of ears

Your style is so unique – a Feefal character is instantly recognizable! How long did it take for you to develop your own distinct style?

Thanks! I'd say it wasn't until four or five years ago that I truly felt I had my own art style. It's still evolving, and I find myself changing up my style ever so slightly each year. As I journey through life on this planet my interests and way of viewing life starts to shift, which is then reflected in my way of drawing, whether I want it to be or not.

I draw a lot without reference, and by doing so my brain starts to make little connections and preferences on how I approach different shapes. I'll work on a character and accidentally make the lines a bit too billowy and thick, but then step back and realize it actually looks cooler that way. Gradually, your style seems to shift and before you know it, you've taken another step into conjuring up your own weird way of shaping things.

Below: A play on cosmic bodies (planets), but it's literally a cosmic body. Despite its silly origins, this is currently my favourite painting

Light and shadow play a big part in making your characters look so compelling. Do you have any tips for lighting characters effectively?

First step is always to determine a set light source – you need to have a concrete idea of where the light hits, since this will determine where you place the shadows. I like to make a Layer Mask, set the mode to Overlay, and use a bright yellow to paint over the desired areas. This will give your characters a nice, warm, sunny glow. If you prefer a cooler tone and a 'moonlight-esque' light source, try a light cyan or blue instead.

You must also have an understanding of volume to be able to shadow everything correctly. Think of the shape, which parts protrude from the whole, and how this will affect the shadows being cast. For my base shadows, I clip a new layer to my current one and set it to Multiply. I then place my shadows on the desired areas using a light blue, grey, or light brown, depending on if I want a cooler or warmer shadow.

As a final touch I add highlights. The viewer's eye will be drawn towards the lightest points of your drawing, so I like to focus the highlights on places where I want more emphasis.

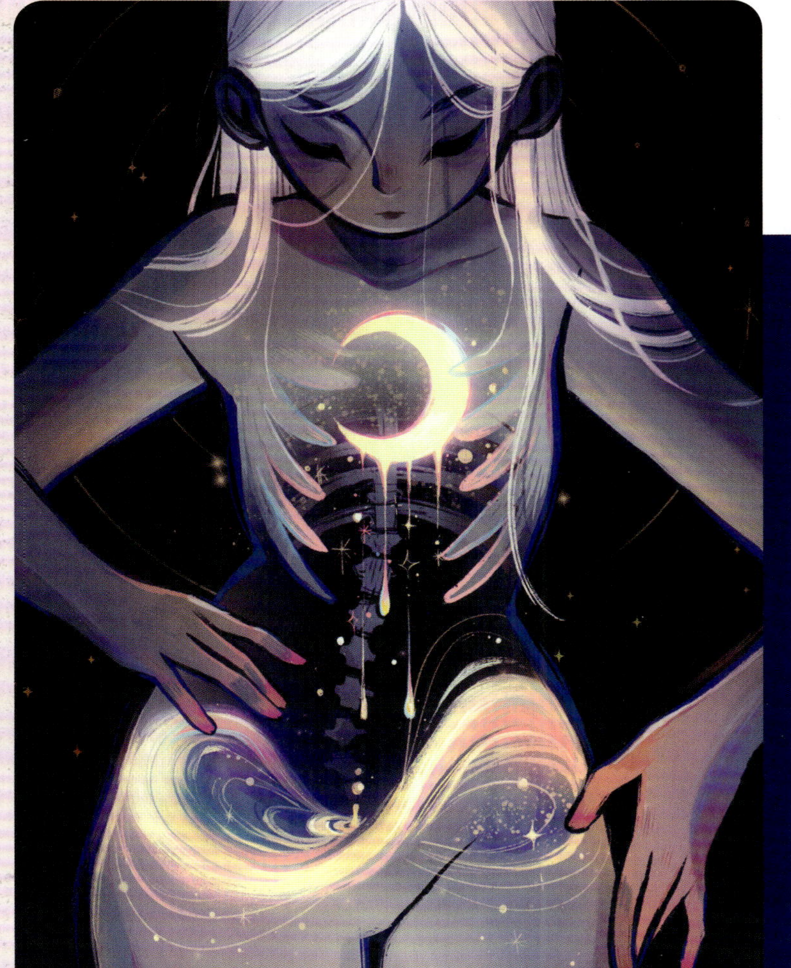

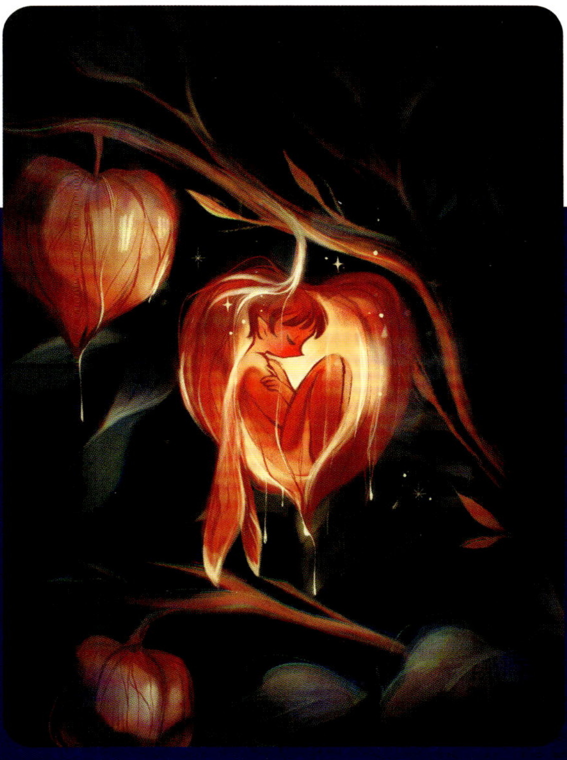

Above: Be careful when eating the berry from a physalis plant – it might just be a fairy cocoon in the middle of metamorphosis!

What do you think are the key elements of creating unique and interesting character designs?

I think the best recipes for character designs can be sourced directly from the earth. I take heavy influence from nature, but I enjoy taking it a step further and using references that lie outside the typical topics, like mould, different types of cells, and most recently tooth anatomy.

I regularly become extremely invested in some niche topic and start mulling over how I would translate all the properties of said topic into a unique character. How would their components work if viewed through an anthropomorphic lens? What would their personality be like? Asking these questions is a key part of the process. If you want your character to have depth and feel like an accurate portrayal of the source material, it's so important to take the time to understand all the building blocks that make up its creation. I strive for my characters to fully represent their origins, rather than just look visually similar to them.

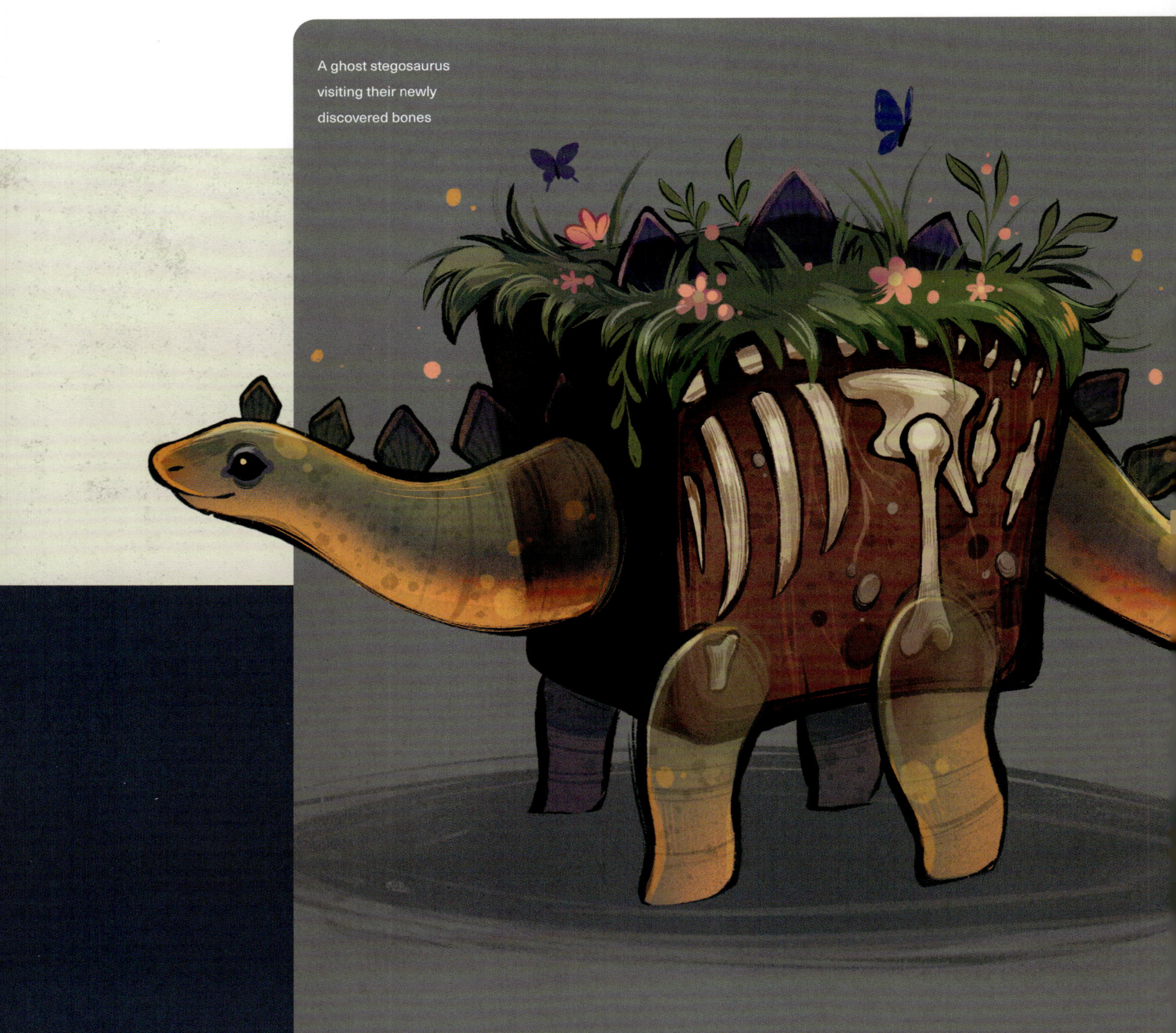

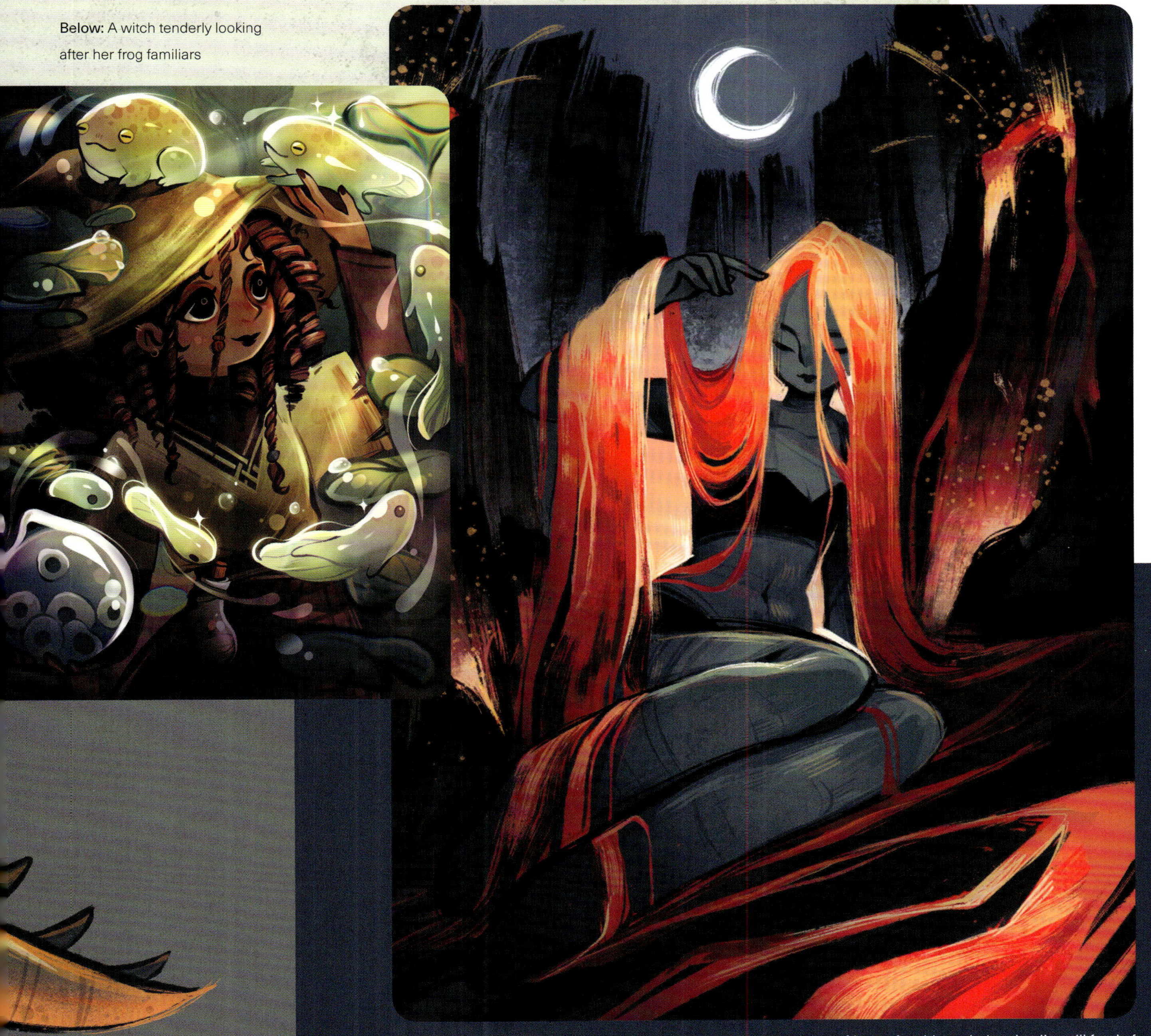

Below: A witch tenderly looking after her frog familiars

Above: An older painting that I'm still fond of

Finally, have you got any upcoming projects we should be looking out for?

Every February I host a drawing challenge called Funguary that's centred around designing characters based on mushrooms. I always release a zine featuring all my artwork from the challenge at the end. 2024 was my third year hosting the challenge and I've accumulated quite a few drawings by now, so my plan is to produce a small art book dedicated to the project. So, if you're someone who is also interested in anthropomorphic fungi, be on the lookout!

CRAFTING THE COVER

Feefal shows us how she brewed up this issue's cover illustration

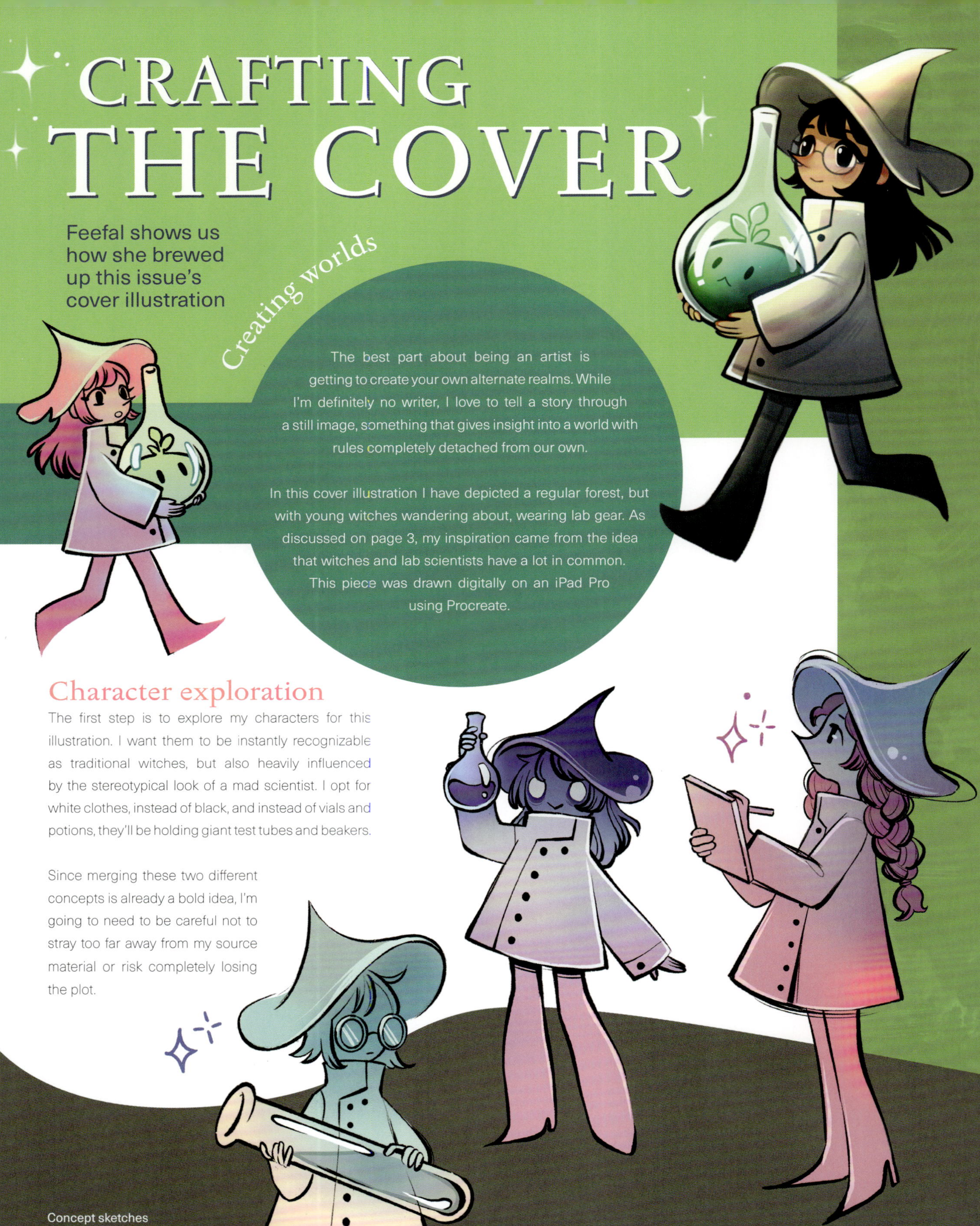

The best part about being an artist is getting to create your own alternate realms. While I'm definitely no writer, I love to tell a story through a still image, something that gives insight into a world with rules completely detached from our own.

In this cover illustration I have depicted a regular forest, but with young witches wandering about, wearing lab gear. As discussed on page 3, my inspiration came from the idea that witches and lab scientists have a lot in common. This piece was drawn digitally on an iPad Pro using Procreate.

Character exploration

The first step is to explore my characters for this illustration. I want them to be instantly recognizable as traditional witches, but also heavily influenced by the stereotypical look of a mad scientist. I opt for white clothes, instead of black, and instead of vials and potions, they'll be holding giant test tubes and beakers.

Since merging these two different concepts is already a bold idea, I'm going to need to be careful not to stray too far away from my source material or risk completely losing the plot.

Concept sketches for the characters

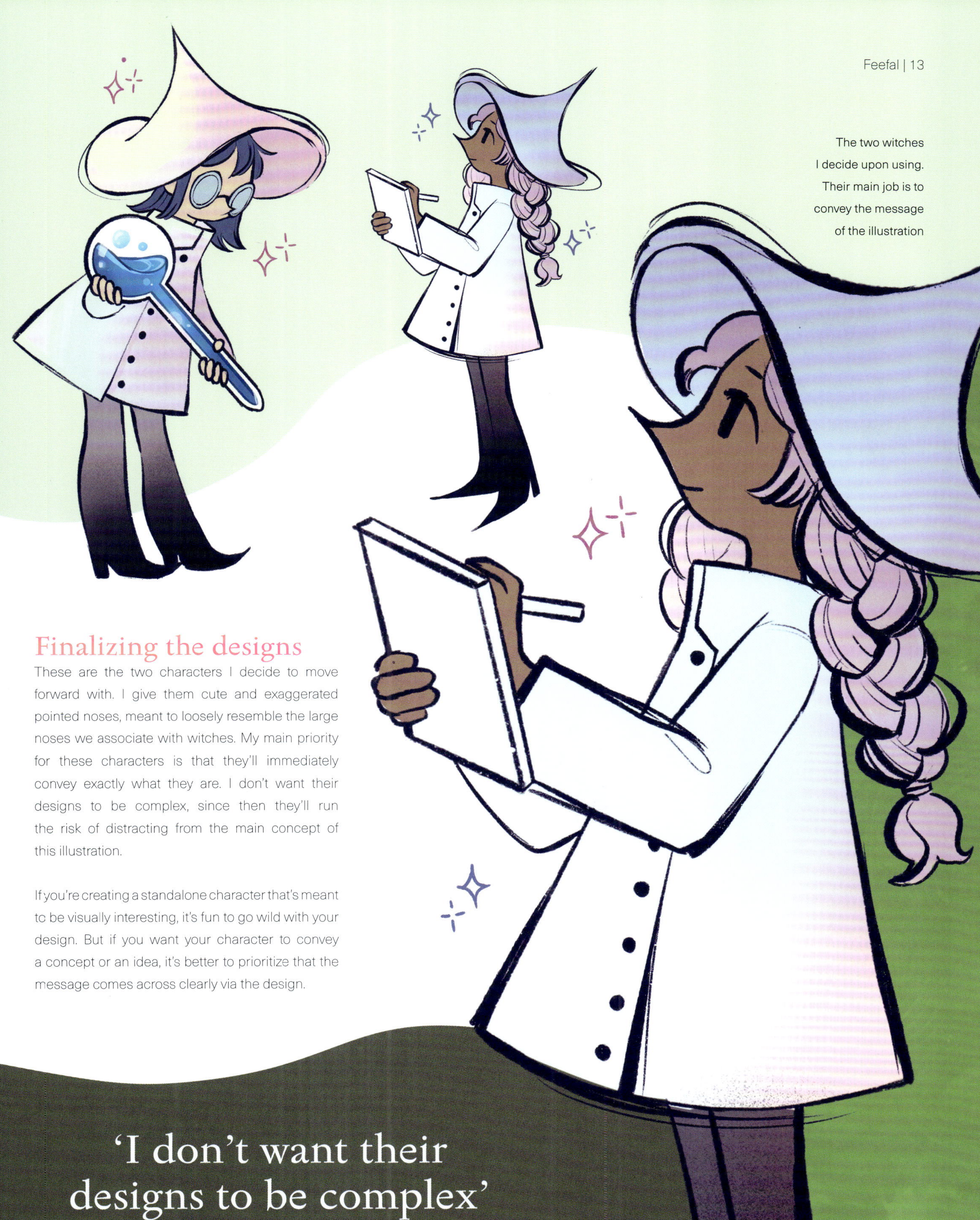

The two witches I decide upon using. Their main job is to convey the message of the illustration

Finalizing the designs

These are the two characters I decide to move forward with. I give them cute and exaggerated pointed noses, meant to loosely resemble the large noses we associate with witches. My main priority for these characters is that they'll immediately convey exactly what they are. I don't want their designs to be complex, since then they'll run the risk of distracting from the main concept of this illustration.

If you're creating a standalone character that's meant to be visually interesting, it's fun to go wild with your design. But if you want your character to convey a concept or an idea, it's better to prioritize that the message comes across clearly via the design.

'I don't want their designs to be complex'

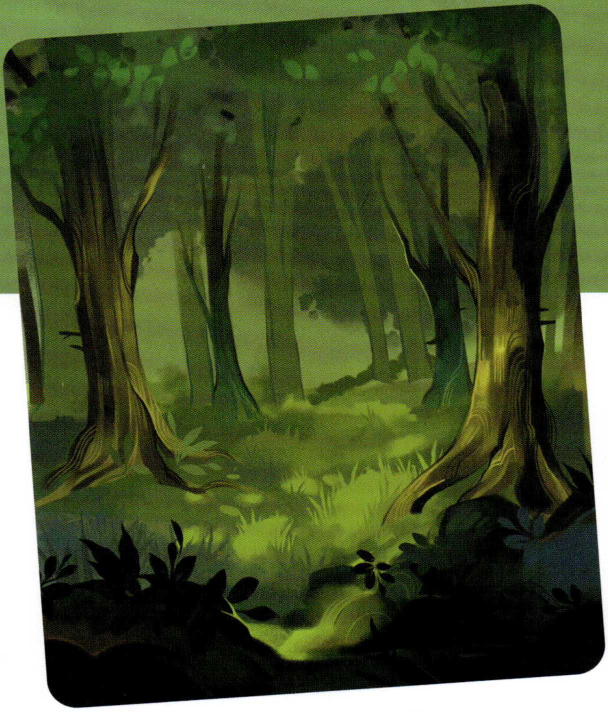

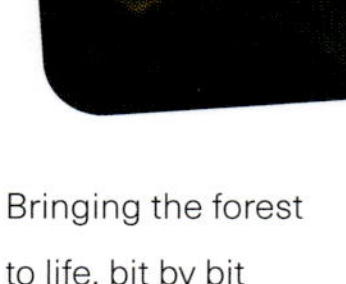

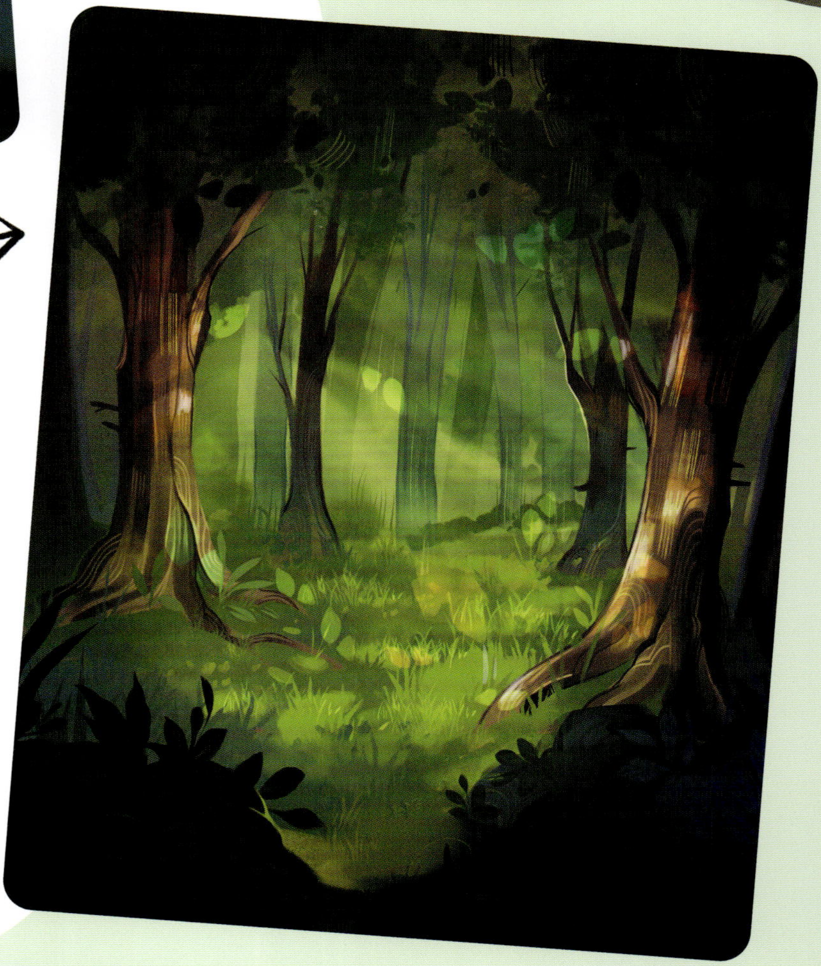

Bringing the forest
to life, bit by bit

Background development

Now onto the background. If I wanted the characters to be the focal point of this illustration, I would have opted for a more subtle design in order to not distract the viewer. But in this case, the forest will be playing a vital role as the playground for their shenanigans, so I want it to look enchanting and inviting.

I start by painting a base layer of different green colours, with a gradient from dark green in the foreground to bright green in the back, in order to indicate depth. Then I paint a few detailed trees and add a layer of grass using Devin Elle Kurtz's grass brushset. Finally, I add dark foliage in the foreground and a scatter of light across the forest using a Layer Mask set to Overlay.

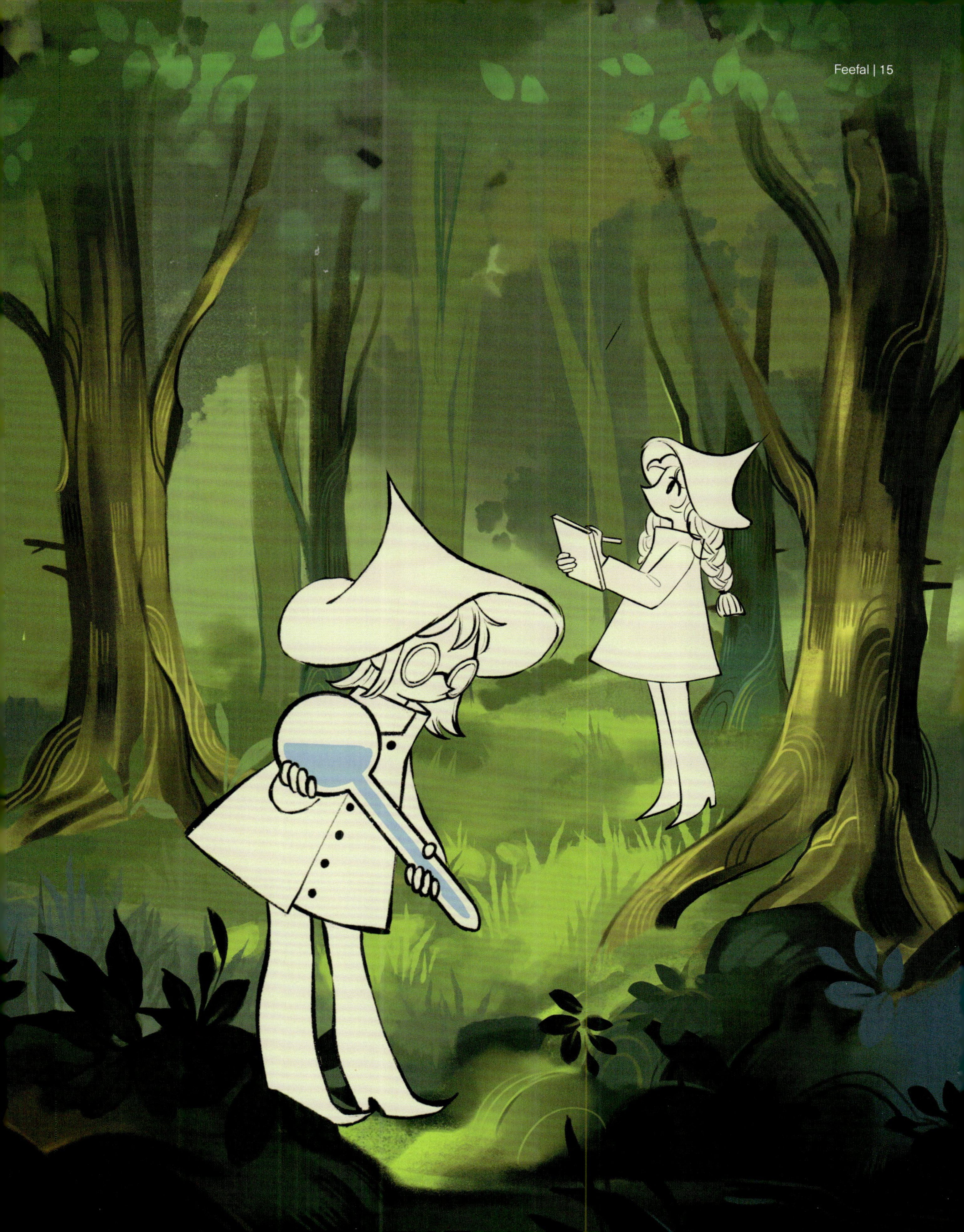

Designing the
forest creatures

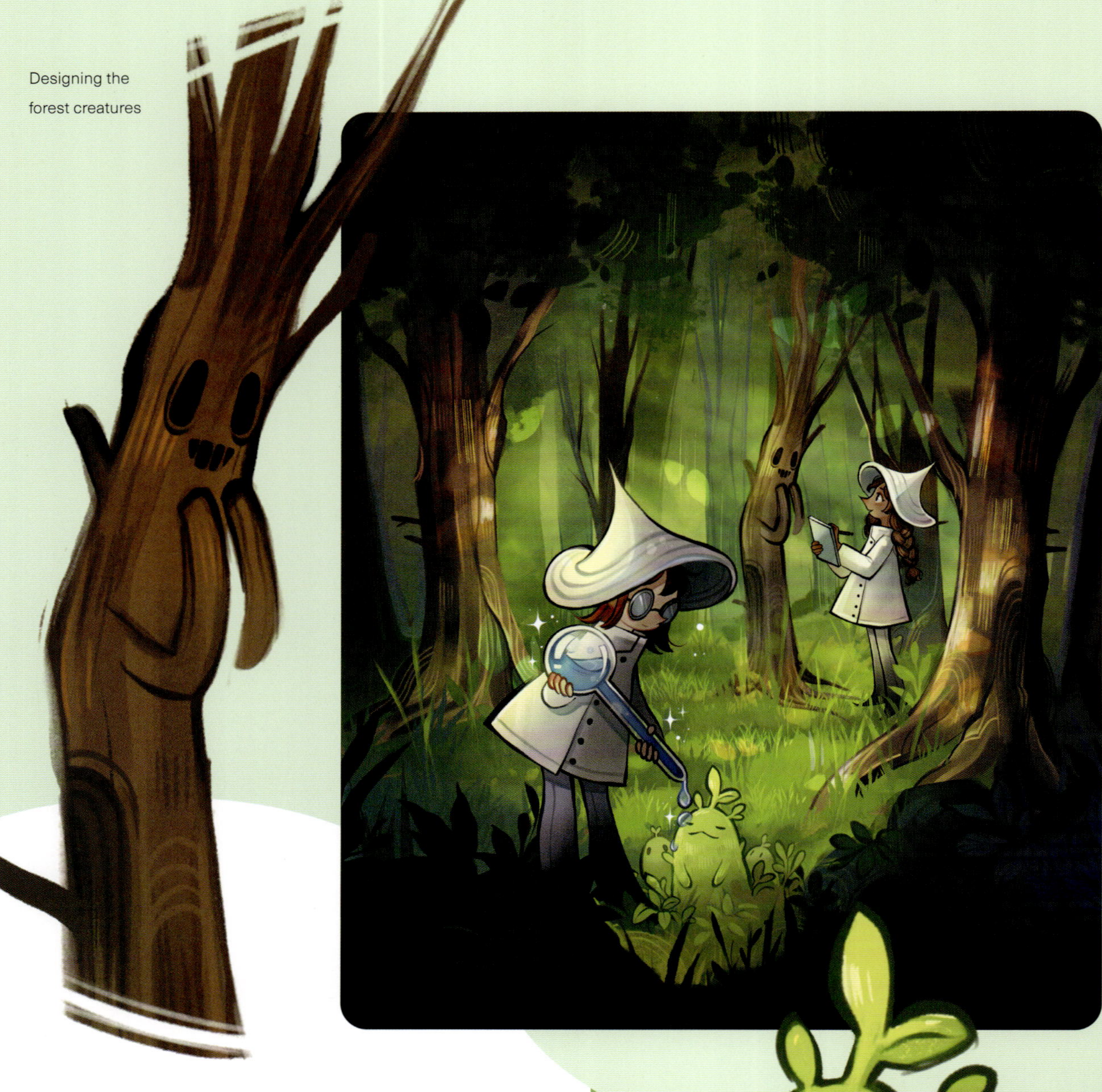

Adding additional creatures

Next, I add the the forest creatures directly affected by the
witches' experiments. Let's start with my green foliage
blob – it's a bush that has been granted sentience via the
wicked ways of the vial! I want it to be a cute character
that sprouts directly from the ground, while still distinctly
looking like a plant.

I follow the same design principle when creating
the tree, because I want it to blend in with the forest
background. I add swirls and texture to the bark design
in order to make it look more interesting.

Piecing it all together

Now that I have built up my painting, I introduce more small details and add scattered lights throughout the forest. The light is coming through from behind the trees, so I add shade on the opposite side from the light source. This is the step where the whole illustration comes together, so it's essential to check that all the characters are in harmony with each other. I add a slight blur to the back of the forest, in order to signify distance.

I also decide to change the design of the witches' hats into something a bit more 'classic'. I like the futuristic shape of the old hats, but I feel this new look more directly conveys the message of who they are.

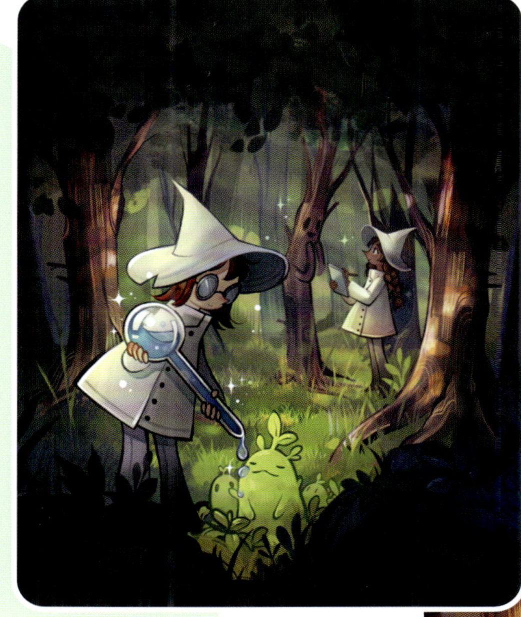

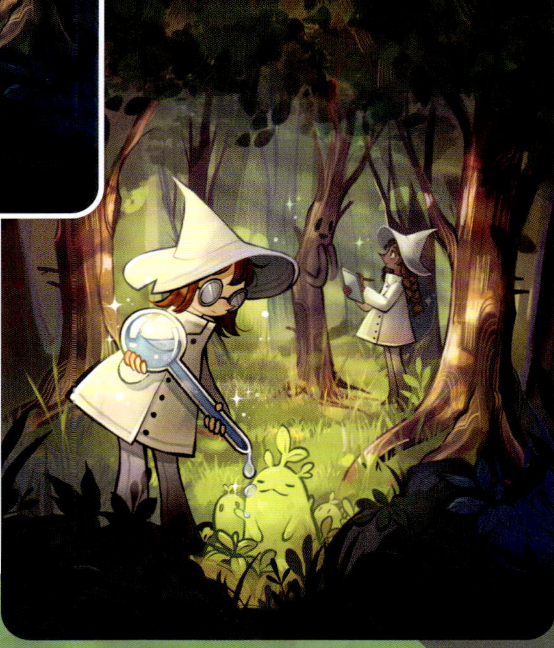

I try both warm and cool tones while adding more details and lighting

If the hat doesn't fit

The original witch hat design was very sleek, futuristic, and funnel shaped. It was loosely based on diagrams of black holes, which look like grid maps that slowly taper into a thin point as they reach the singularity. I still think it's a nice concept, but it started to feel disconnected from the rest of the illustration. So, in the end I decided to go with a more classic witch hat design instead.

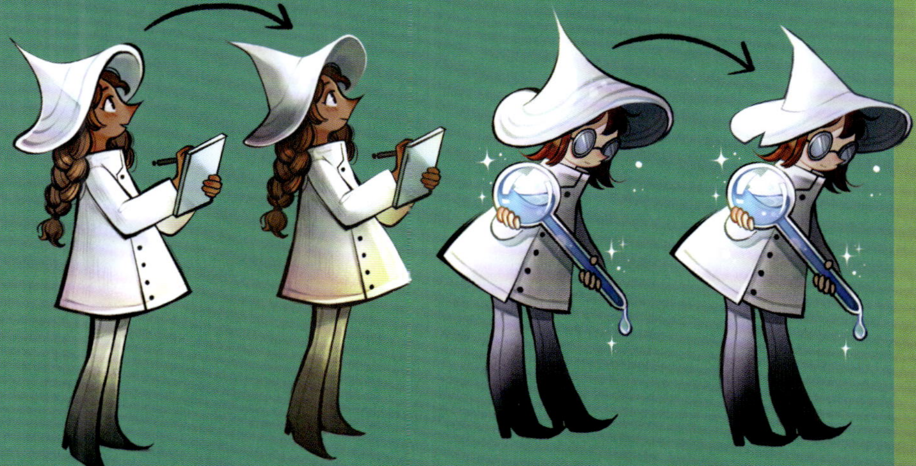

Extending the image

Finally, I need to widen the illustration so that the image will wrap around the back cover of the magazine. I start by expanding the forest background, which I achieve by following the same process we went through earlier on. Blending this additional space into the already established background proves to be a little tricky. I use colour adjustments and plants to cover up any awkward spaces and it all comes togther nicely.

With all this extra space, I can now add an additional witch into the mix. I look back at my original concept sketches and promote one of the discarded witches into an official design. This new witch is carrying a creature in a jar. The morality of a sentient creature being contained within a flask is slightly questionable, so I'm trying to avoid thinking about it too deeply!

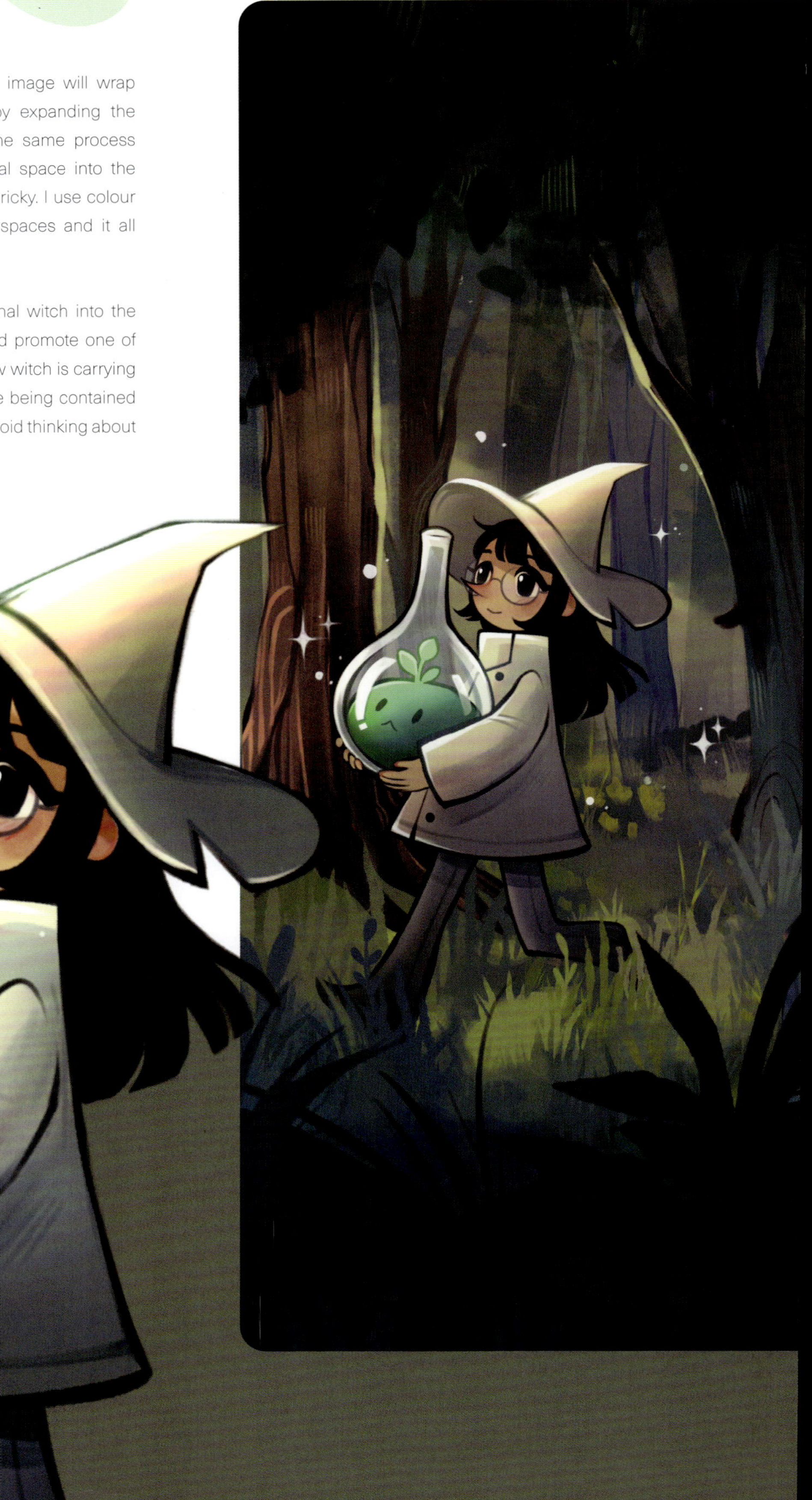

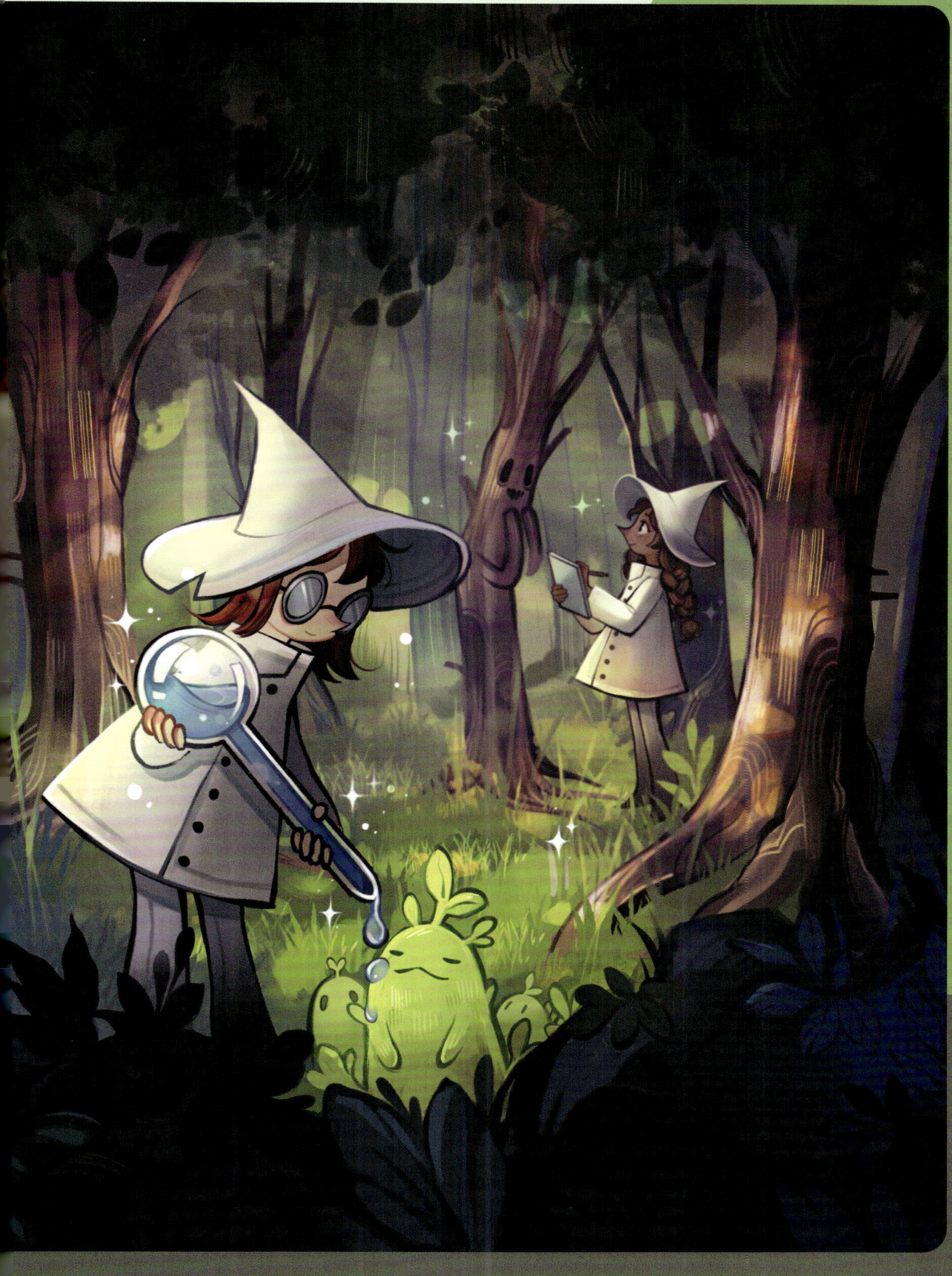

The full
illustration,
with its new
extension
attached

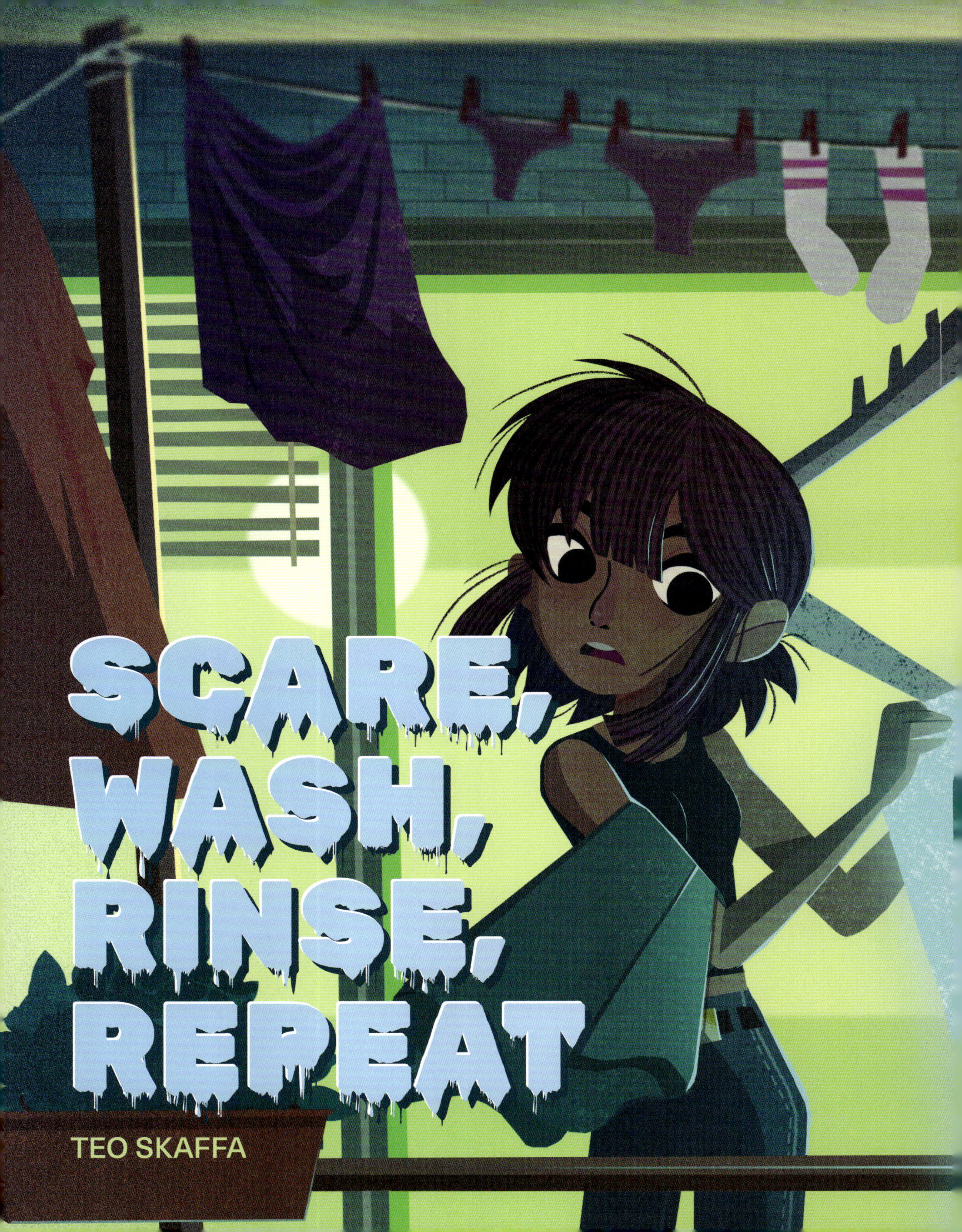

SCARE,
WASH,
RINSE,
REPEAT
TEO SKAFFA

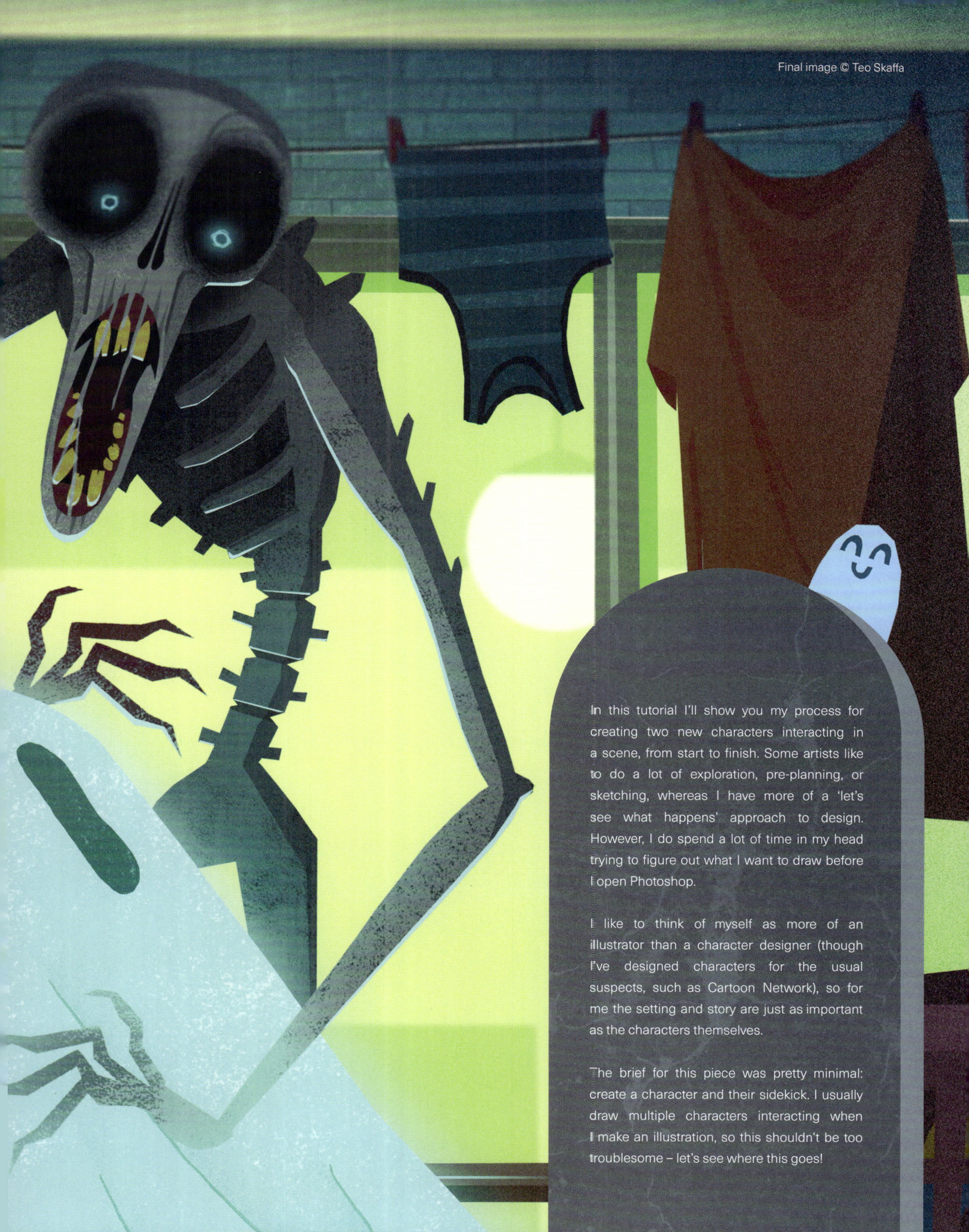

In this tutorial I'll show you my process for creating two new characters interacting in a scene, from start to finish. Some artists like to do a lot of exploration, pre-planning, or sketching, whereas I have more of a 'let's see what happens' approach to design. However, I do spend a lot of time in my head trying to figure out what I want to draw before I open Photoshop.

I like to think of myself as more of an illustrator than a character designer (though I've designed characters for the usual suspects, such as Cartoon Network), so for me the setting and story are just as important as the characters themselves.

The brief for this piece was pretty minimal: create a character and their sidekick. I usually draw multiple characters interacting when I make an illustration, so this shouldn't be too troublesome – let's see where this goes!

Whenever I create personal work, I like to give myself a few constraints to work with. I do this for several reasons: limitation drives creativity (there's endless things to draw otherwise) and ensures that whatever I draw is consistent with the rest of my portfolio. The rules are not super strict – I see them more as guidelines. Here are the design principles I always keep in the back of my head.

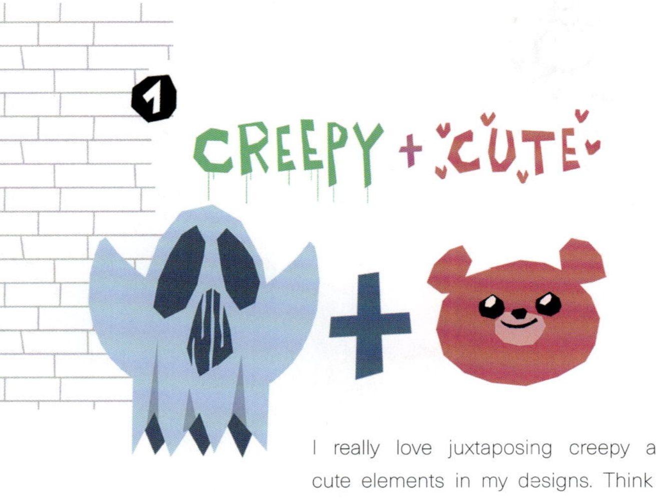

I really love juxtaposing creepy and cute elements in my designs. Think of a horrific monster doing cute things, or a cute character in a terrible situation.

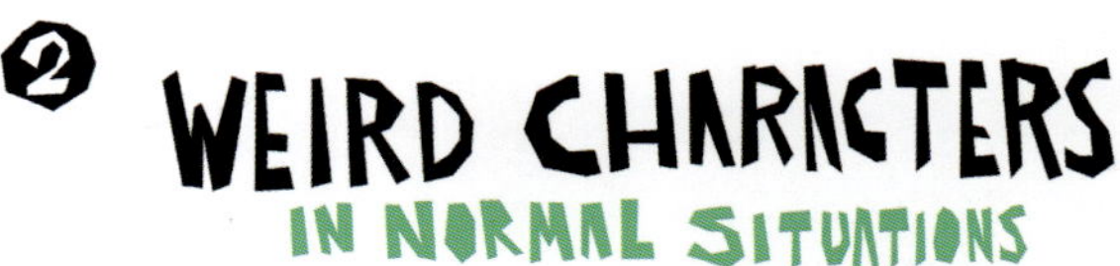

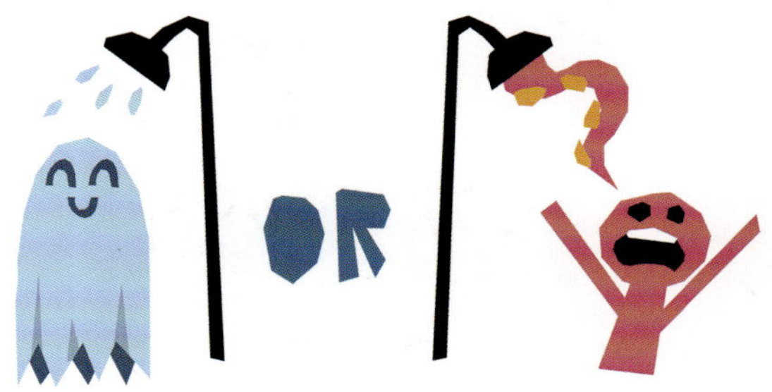

NORMAL CHARACTERS
IN WEIRD SITUATIONS

I love to draw weird monsters doing mundane things or experiencing normal situations, like a vampire going shopping, or a ghost on a date. The opposite can also work – placing a normal character in a weird situation, like a character walking their monster dog.

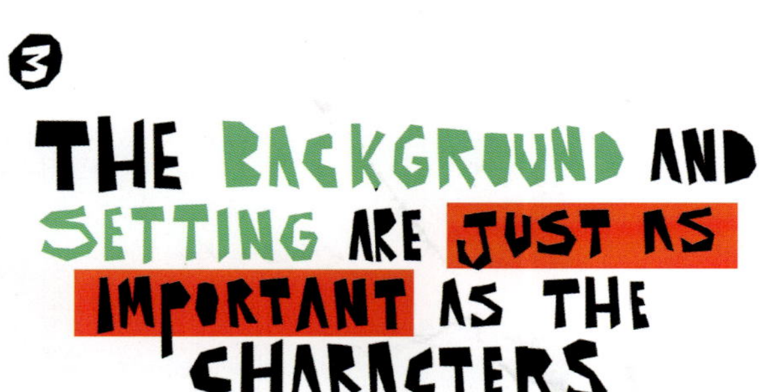

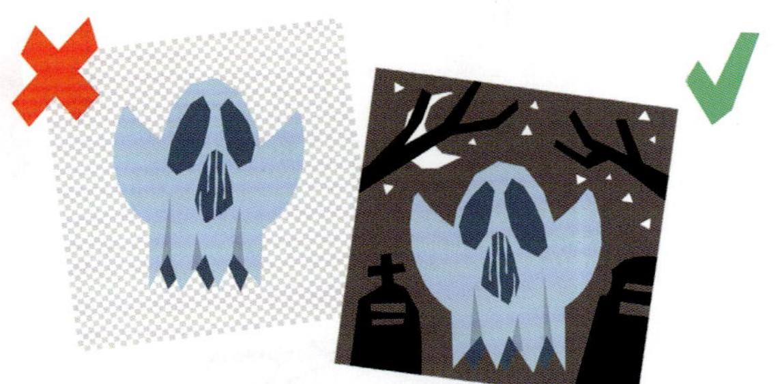

I treat the background and setting as if they are another character. A vampire going to the cinema to watch a romantic comedy is a lot more interesting to me than drawing them in in their usual spooky castle. The setting can completely change the narrative and tells you a lot about the characters themselves.

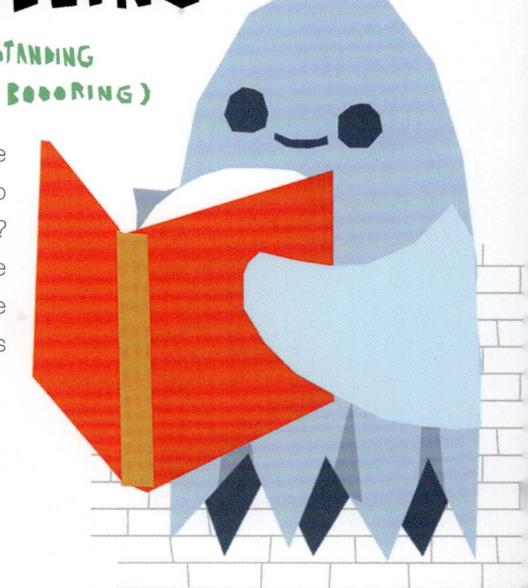

I won't draw anything until I have an idea for a small story I want to tell. What are the characters doing? Why are they doing what they're doing? I want the viewer to have more questions than answers when looking at my images.

Before we get started, let me explain my way of working, which I've been told is a little bizarre! Here are the key steps I use when creating a character.

IT'S ALL ABOUT THE LASSO

When I'm drawing I exclusively use the polygonal lasso tool. While using various lasso tools is not uncommon, I stick to the polygon tool for pretty much everything I do. Yes, I know this is insane.

SKIPPING THE SKETCHING

I don't sketch in the traditional sense – I go straight to creating shapes and colour. I start with very rough shapes and chisel them down (or add bits) until each element looks how I want it to look. I guess you could describe this process as a digital way of sculpting, rather than drawing.

REFINING THE DESIGN

Here's an example of where I start with a character and where I end up. My 'sketch' is a cruder version of the final, more detailed design.

ALL THE LAYERS

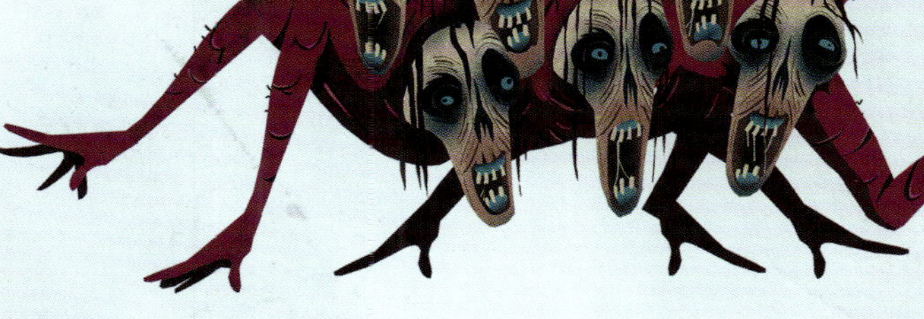

I keep pretty much everything I do on its own layer, right down to even the tiniest details. This can result in files of 300 layers or more which, I have to admit, is a little crazy! I keep the layers organized into folders so I can manage everything a little better. We'll get more into this later in the tutorial.

Coming up with ideas is the important part of the process, but also the most difficult to show you, as it mostly happens in my head! Here's the process I usually follow.

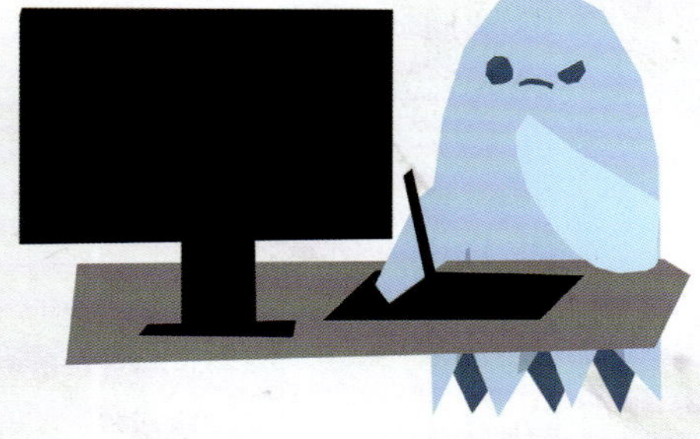

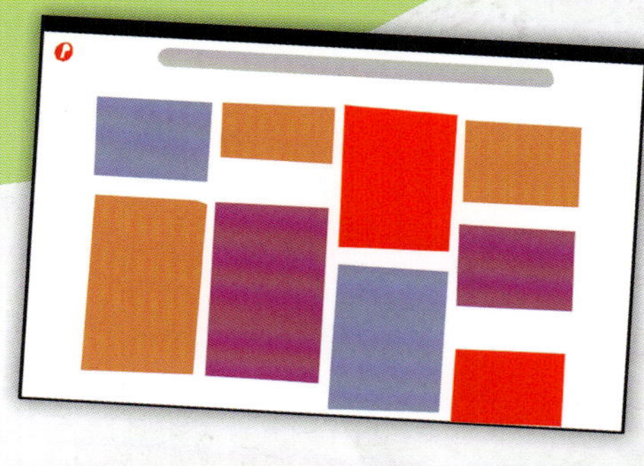

❶ THINK!

I always start by sitting down and simply thinking about what it is I want to draw. Sometimes, I'll know the setting I want to use (such as a train station, or the inside of the car) and I need to think about what sort of characters would be fun to draw in that environment. The opposite is also true – I might know I want to draw a vampire, but need to find a setting that would match my rules of design from earlier. For this tutorial, I know I want to do something more than just draw a standard character and sidekick. I decide to interpret the brief as one character helping another out – after all, isn't that what sidekicks are for?

❷ HUNTING FOR IDEAS

Next, I hit the internet, open Pinterest, and start to randomly look at images. Inspiration can come from anywhere: photographs, illustrations, graphic design, product packaging – anything that looks cool. I'm not looking for specific images, anything can spark the imagination. It could be composition, colour palette, the way light hits an object, or something else completely random.

❸ ORGANIZING THOUGHTS

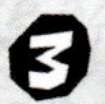

I fill up my Photoshop file with images of anything I've found that looks cool and place them around the edge of my canvas. I try to organize everything by theme (composition, colour, lighting, and so on) as this will often spark my imagination in unexpected ways.

After all this, I end up with three distinct ideas taking shape: one inspired by a photo of a girl having a birthday party, another by an illustration of someone having a bath, and a third by some vintage adverts for laundry detergent.

YOU DO YOU

There are thousands and thousands of tutorials teaching you how to draw, what techniques to use, and so on. My technique is quite unique, and while I wouldn't recommend everyone draw like I do, it can be helpful to explore different ways of working. At the end of the day, the important thing is that you find something that works for you. Remember, there's no right or wrong way to draw.

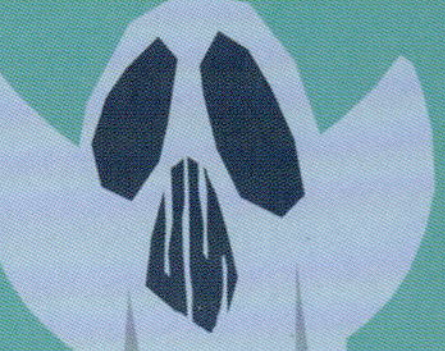

Now I have some ideas for how I want the piece to go, it's time to start drawing – and by 'drawing', I mean roughly blocking everything out so I can see if the composition works, and if the idea is clear enough. If I can make it work with choppy blocks then I should have no problem with the fully-rendered illustration. I move forward with three ideas, applying all of my self-imposed rules as I go.

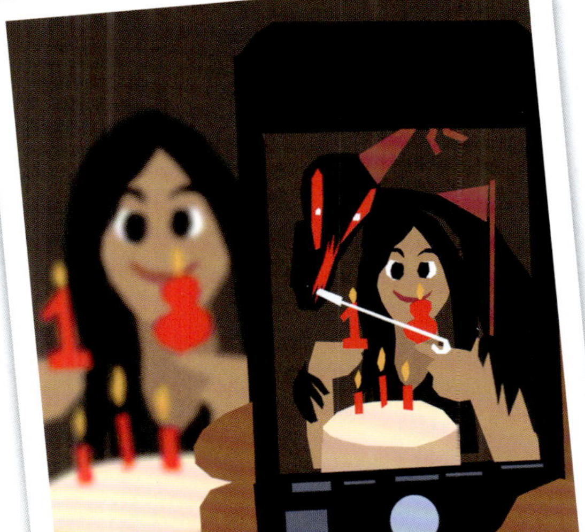

1 BIRTHDAY PARTY

I start by sketching my idea for a girl at a birthday party with her monster friend. This initial idea seems too boring (as it's just two characters posing side by side) so I think of a twist – what if we see someone taking a picture of the girl on their phone and her weird monster friend is only visible on the screen?

2 BATH TIME

I thought a funny scene would be a girl undressing a few ghosts for bath time. The naked ghosts would look horrific but the girl would seem unphased. This is perfectly in line with my earlier rule about juxtaposing creepy and cute elements. Ultimately, I decide that there's something about the composition of this image that isn't working, but the general idea of 'undressing' ghosts is cool – like a Scooby-Doo monster reveal in reverse!

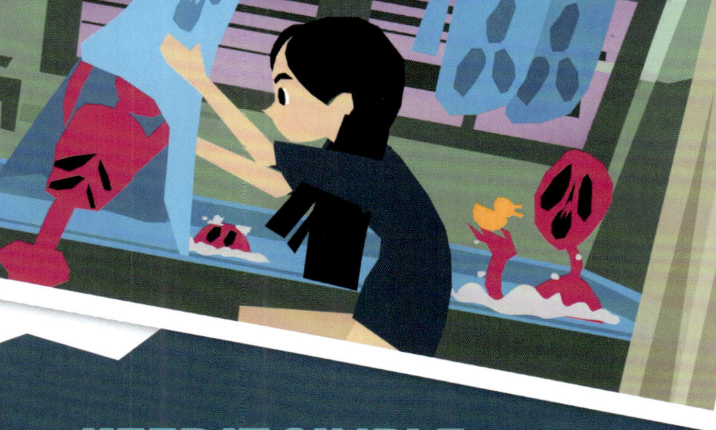

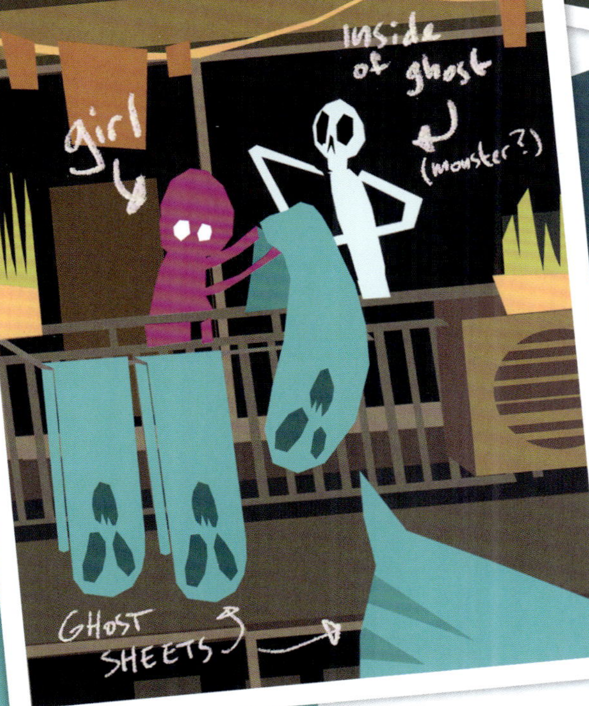

KEEP IT SIMPLE

Don't worry too much about what the characters are going to look like, or what colours you will use at this early stage – just try to get your ideas down. If you can make the composition work with blobby bits you can make it work with actual refined characters down the line. It's also a lot easier to trash your idea when you've only spent ten minutes sketching it out and it looks like garbage anyway.

3 LAUNDRY DAY

For my final idea I use the ghost 'undressing' idea again, but now the girl s hanging sheets out to dry. Maybe one of the sheets can also be flying away in the wind, to add a little more dynamism to the scene.

The next step is to give the characters a little bit more form. I still keep it pretty rough (and nowhere near the final design) so I can easily change things and won't get too attached to the characters just yet. While giving the characters a bit more shape I decide it would be funny to give the skeleton a bathrobe. Not only does it look cute, it also makes it a bit clearer that it's this particular ghost's sheets that are being hung out to dry.

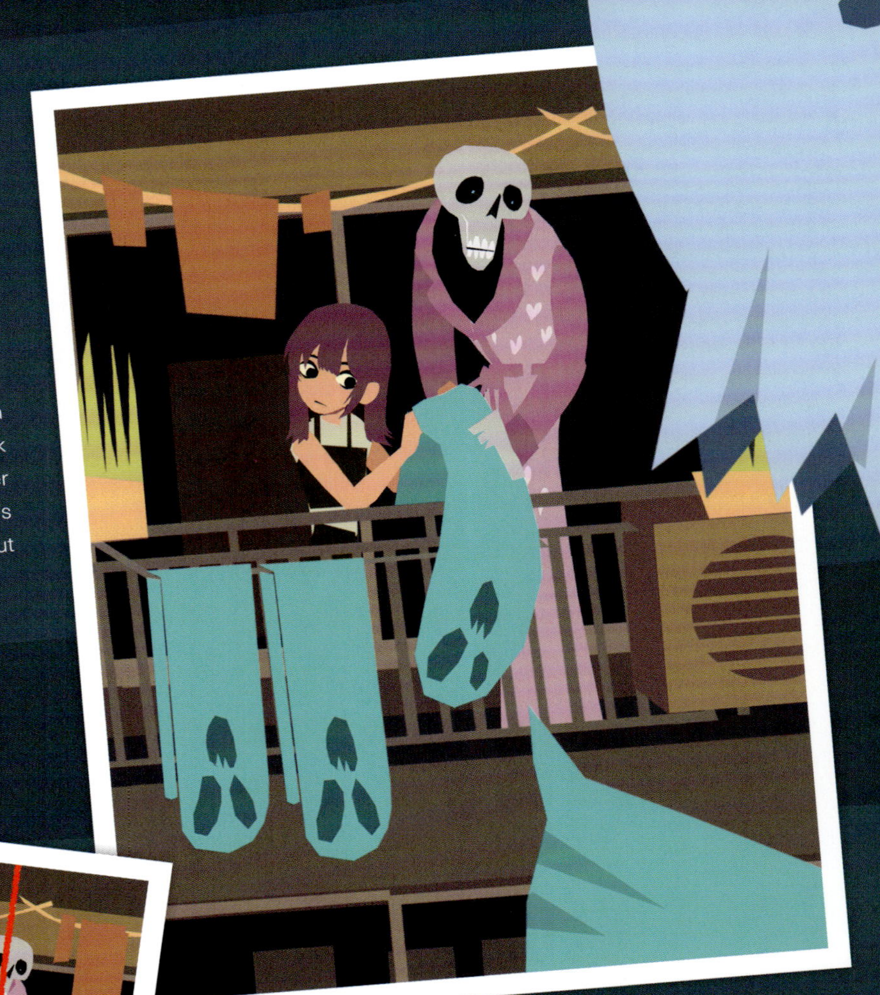

Now I've settled on an idea, the design starts to evolve

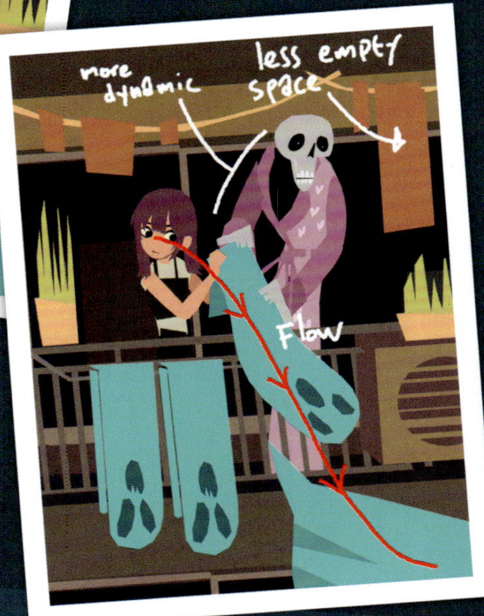

Using the rule of thirds to balance the image

Now that the characters have a bit more shape and are approximately the size they will be in the final image, let's have a look at the overall composition. Using the rule of thirds is a great way to figure out where the focal points in an image should be. I roughly tweak some of the environment details to make everything feel a bit more balanced.

I've created so many illustrations in my lifetime that this comes naturally to me now – I don't really need to use the guides anymore – but don't be afraid to just slap a few lines on your image to help you check everything looks good.

Time to start refining the colours! I'm not sure if I want this to be a day or night scene, so I create two quick 15-minute tests to see which works best. While I really like the colour and lighting of the daylight scene, I think the night version suits the overall vibe of the image a bit better. There's also more room for cool atmospheric effects, like the bright backlight, and a subtle glow from the ghost sheets. Let's go with that.

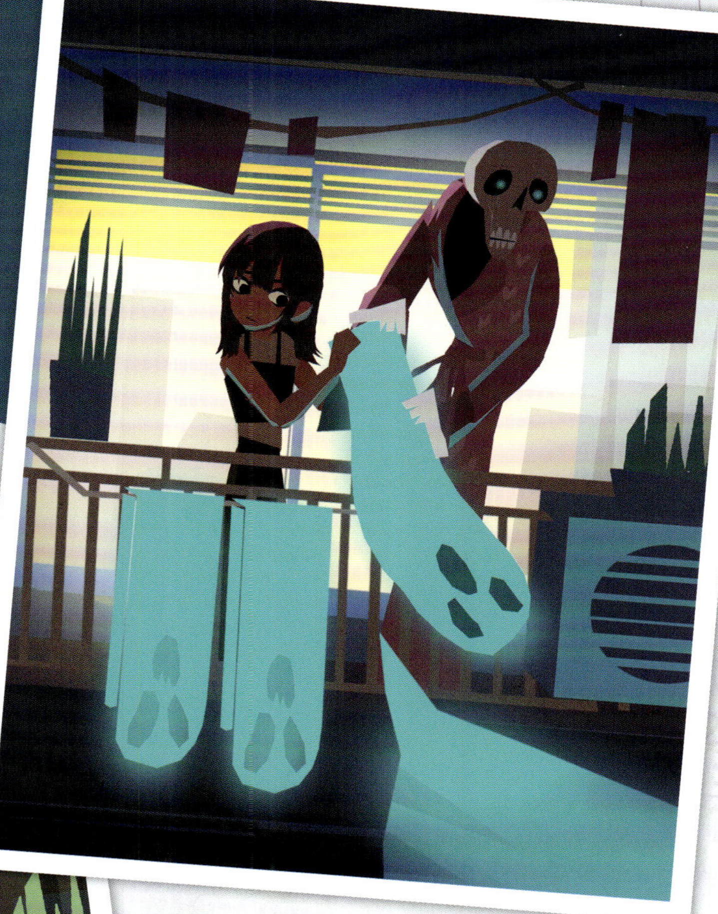

A rough attempt at a day and night version of the scene

DON'T FORGET THE FOLDERS!

I try to keep things organized even while I'm in the sketching phase. Keeping track of my layers using folders makes moving objects and adjusting colours super easy to do on the fly. The folders will come in handy once again later on in the process, too..

GET IN A SPIN!

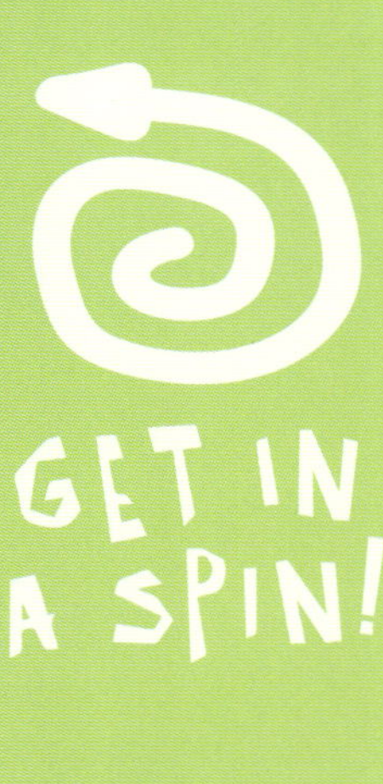

Now that I'm happy I've got the basic structure down I can start chiselling away at the characters. Let's take a look at the girl first. I always start with the face, since that's the first thing people will look at. I just keep tweaking things until I'm happy, messing around with nose and eye shapes in particular. In this case, I decide early on that I'm happy with the eyes from my sketch, so they don't change much throughout the process.

I decide it would be a good idea to give her hair some movement – it makes everything a bit more dynamic and fits in with the general idea of the image, that one of the sheets gets blown away by the wind.

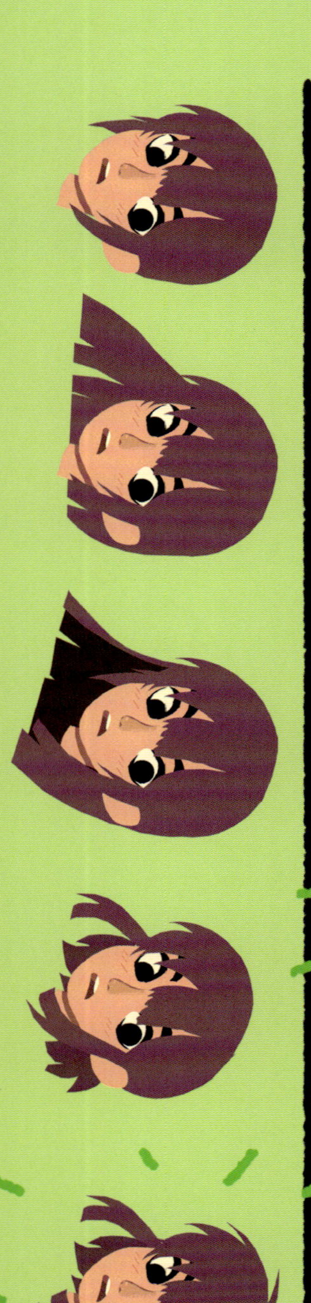

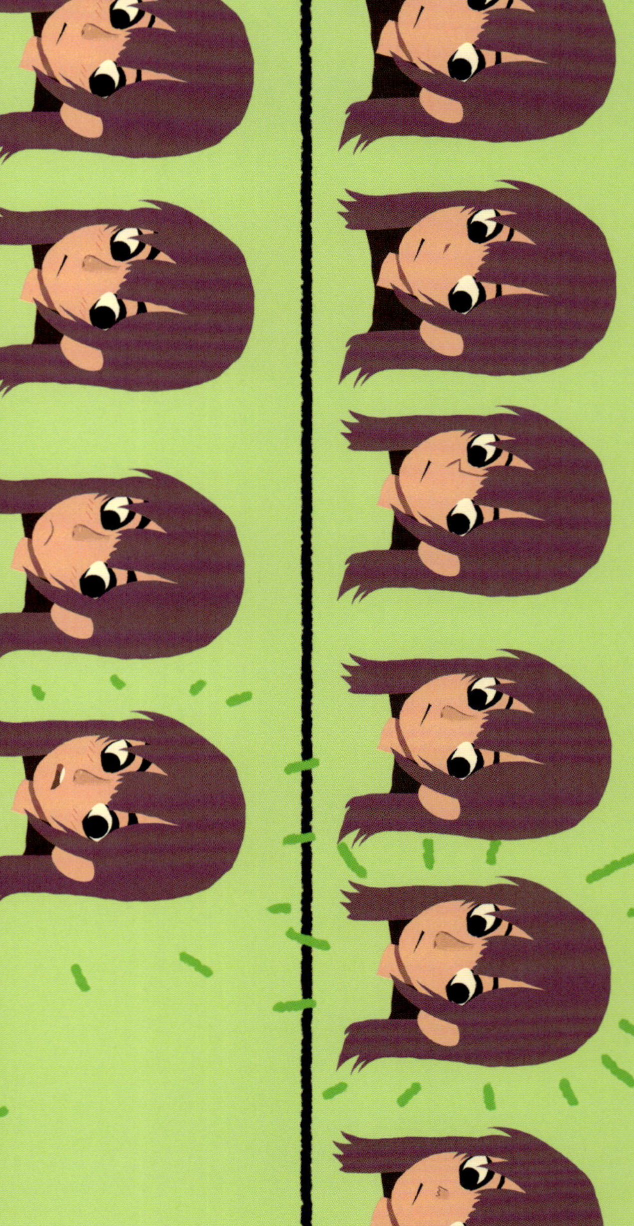

Gradually refining the girl's face until I find a version I'm happy with

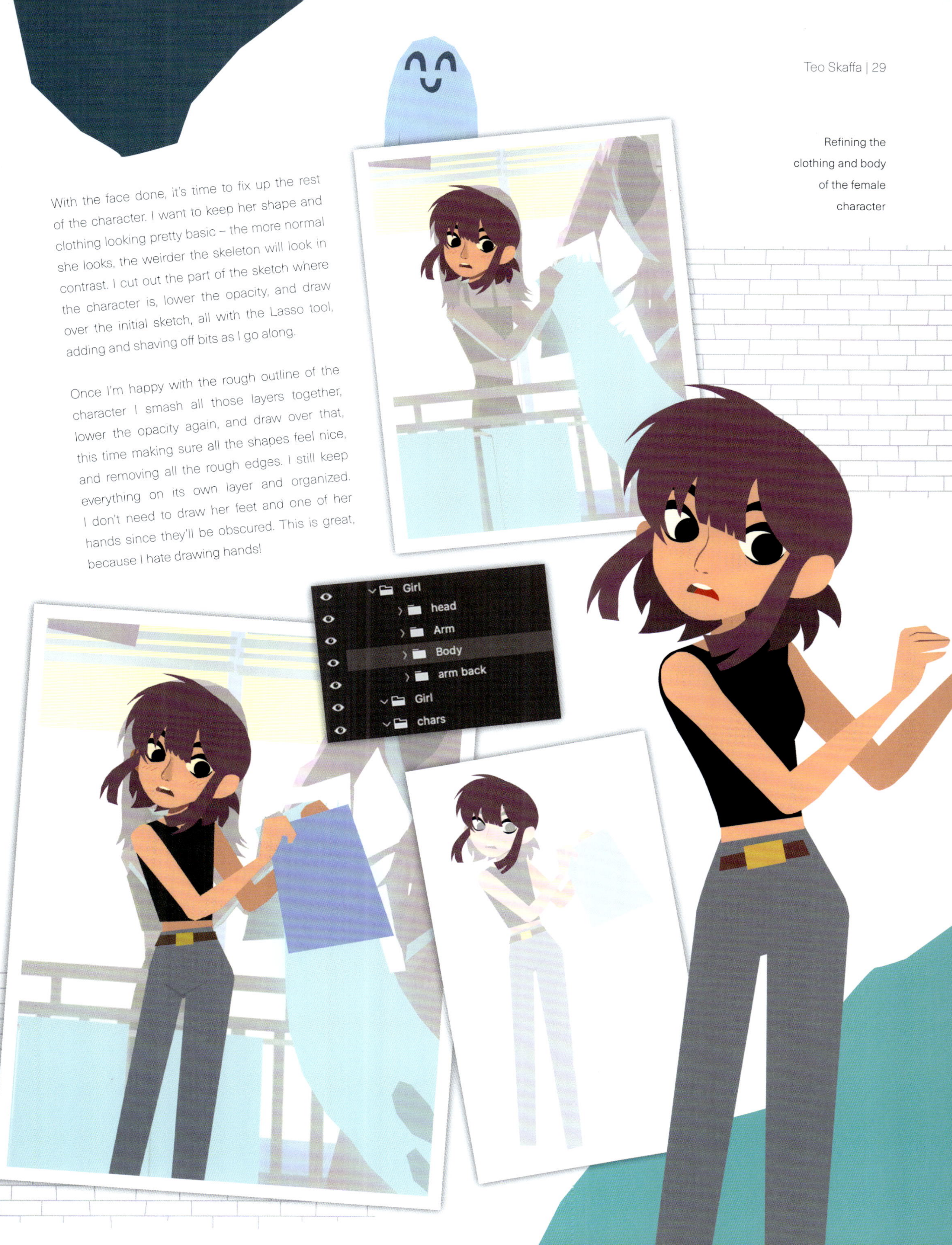

With the face done, it's time to fix up the rest of the character. I want to keep her shape and clothing looking pretty basic – the more normal she looks, the weirder the skeleton will look in contrast. I cut out the part of the sketch where the character is, lower the opacity, and draw over the initial sketch, all with the Lasso tool, adding and shaving off bits as I go along.

Once I'm happy with the rough outline of the character I smash all those layers together, lower the opacity again, and draw over that, this time making sure all the shapes feel nice, and removing all the rough edges. I still keep everything on its own layer and organized. I don't need to draw her feet and one of her hands since they'll be obscured. This is great, because I hate drawing hands!

Refining the clothing and body of the female character

The next step is to texture the character and smooth out any other kinks I find along the way. I only use a couple of brushes for most of my images (I made some specialized brushes for grass and other special effects, but we won't be needing those today). I really don't care about the lighting or atmosphere at this stage – we'll deal with those later. I colour the character how I think she would look in neutral light.

Texturing is pretty straightforward. I use the Eyedrop tool on the base colour of whichever element I want to texture, slide up (or down) the brightness, and using a textured brush, paint over the area to lighten or darken it.

For the hair I make a bunch of selections with the Lasso tool and brush in a darker or lighter colour within the selection. We've gone from a pink blob, to something that looks something like a girl, to an actually decent-looking character.

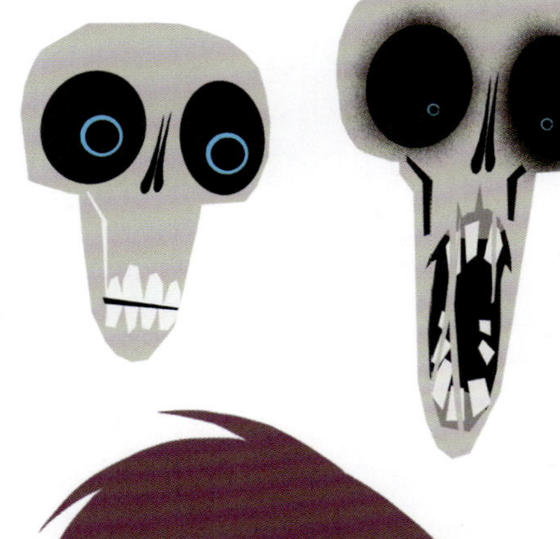

BRUSHES

TOOLS

With texturing added, our first character is complete

BRUSHES

The brushes you choose to use really don't matter, as long as you find something that does what you need. Despite what some people think, there are no magic brushes that make you draw better! The best tip I've ever received was from Rex Crowle (instagram.com/rexbox), and that is to limit your brushes. The less brushes you use, the more consistent your image will look. The brushes you see here are pretty much the only brushes I use for anything that I do.

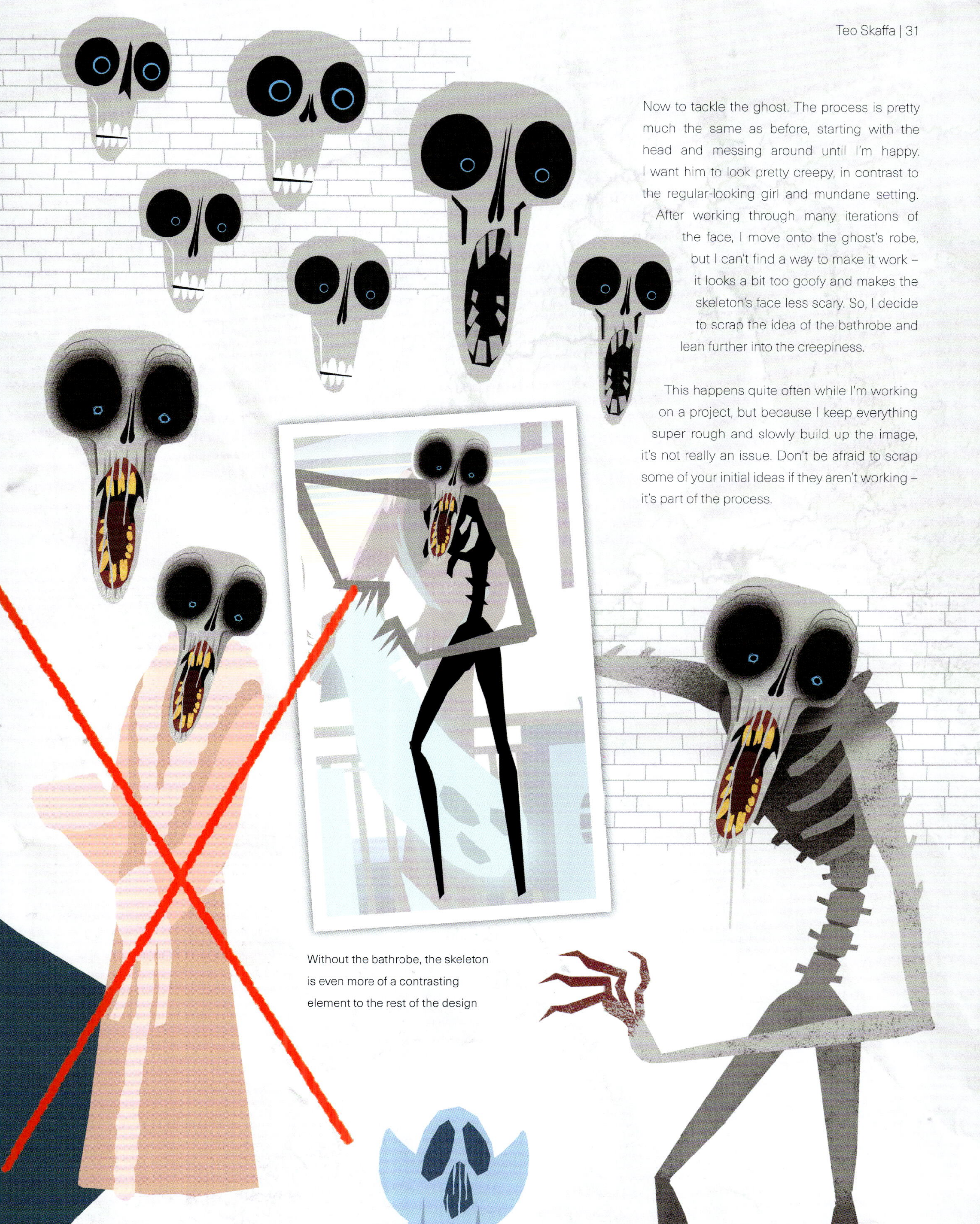

Now to tackle the ghost. The process is pretty much the same as before, starting with the head and messing around until I'm happy. I want him to look pretty creepy, in contrast to the regular-looking girl and mundane setting. After working through many iterations of the face, I move onto the ghost's robe, but I can't find a way to make it work – it looks a bit too goofy and makes the skeleton's face less scary. So, I decide to scrap the idea of the bathrobe and lean further into the creepiness.

This happens quite often while I'm working on a project, but because I keep everything super rough and slowly build up the image, it's not really an issue. Don't be afraid to scrap some of your initial ideas if they aren't working – it's part of the process.

Without the bathrobe, the skeleton is even more of a contrasting element to the rest of the design

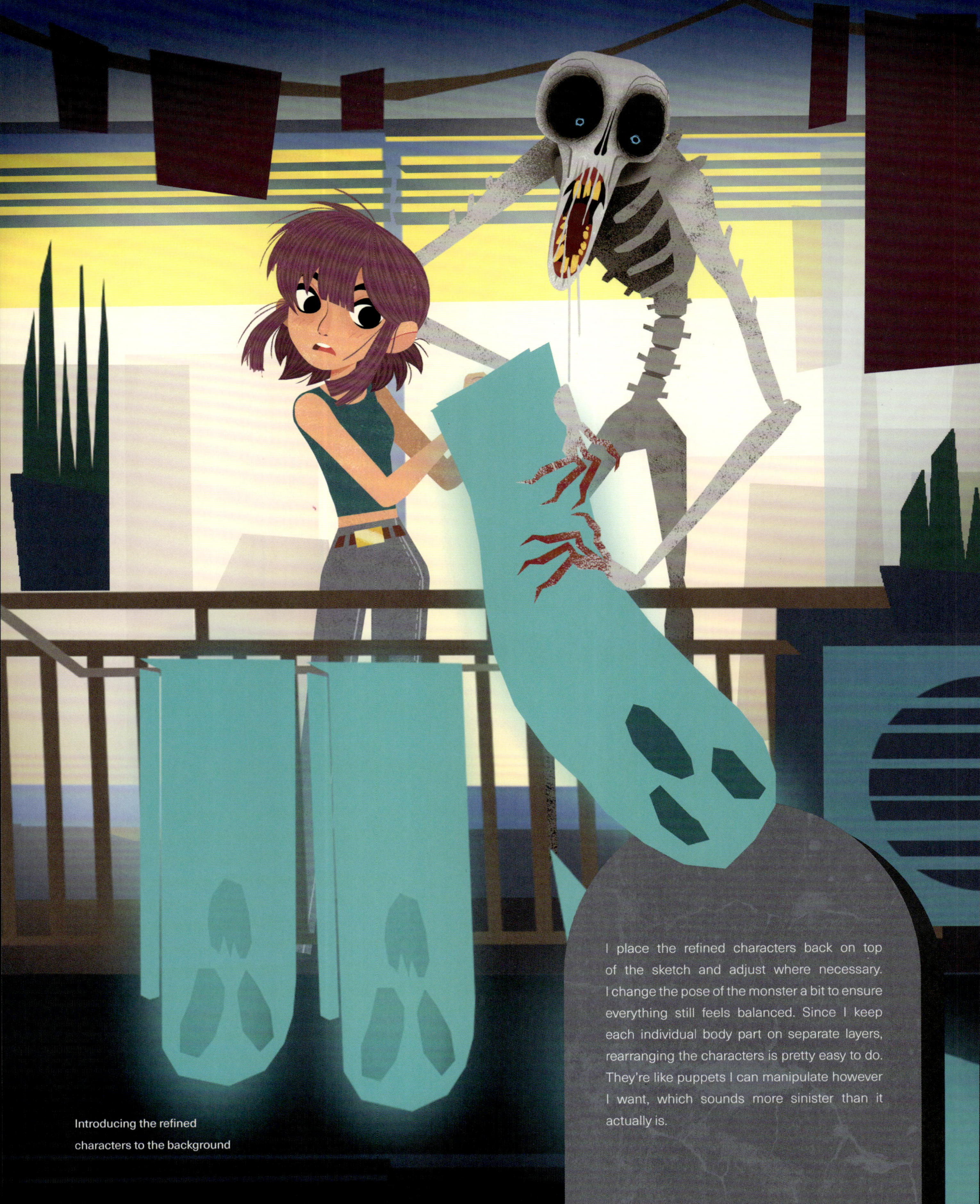

I place the refined characters back on top of the sketch and adjust where necessary. I change the pose of the monster a bit to ensure everything still feels balanced. Since I keep each individual body part on separate layers, rearranging the characters is pretty easy to do. They're like puppets I can manipulate however I want, which sounds more sinister than it actually is.

Introducing the refined characters to the background

My process for refining the background is the same as it is for the characters – gradually refining the shapes and texturing everything using the same few brushes. I keep a bunch of reference pictures next to the canvas at all times (mostly photographs), just to see how the light should affect the surroundings. This whole process is very freeform – I just start somewhere and adjust everything whenever I feel like it needs adjusting.

Once everything is textured, I throw the characters in there. The layers that make up their designs are kept in separate folders which I place within a parent folder. I then put a Clipping Mask on the folder containing both characters, set it to Multiply and lower the opacity until they feel like they fit into the scene seamlessly.

I add texture to the background and blend the characters into the scene

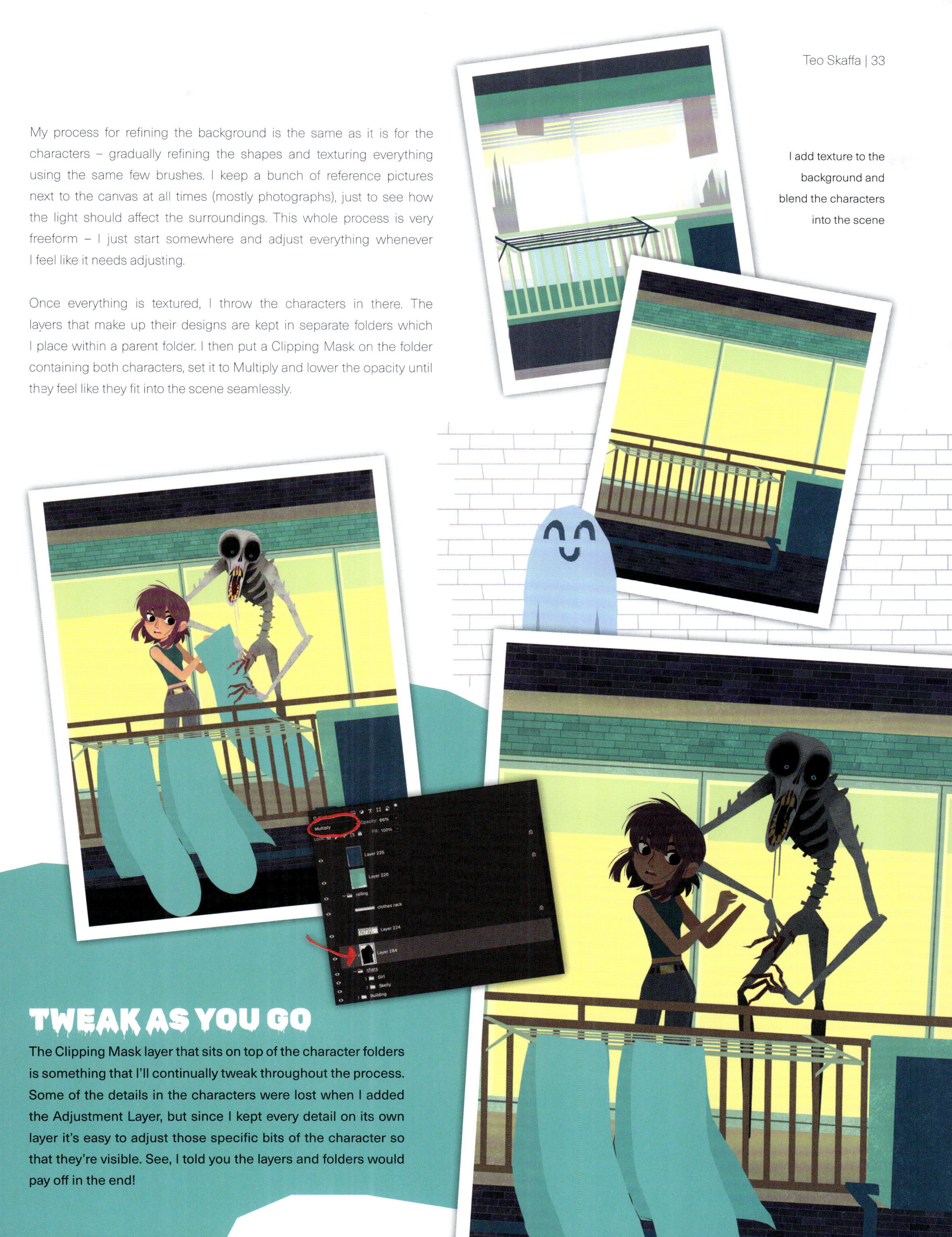

TWEAK AS YOU GO

The Clipping Mask layer that sits on top of the character folders is something that I'll continually tweak throughout the process. Some of the details in the characters were lost when I added the Adjustment Layer, but since I kept every detail on its own layer it's easy to adjust those specific bits of the character so that they're visible. See, I told you the layers and folders would pay off in the end!

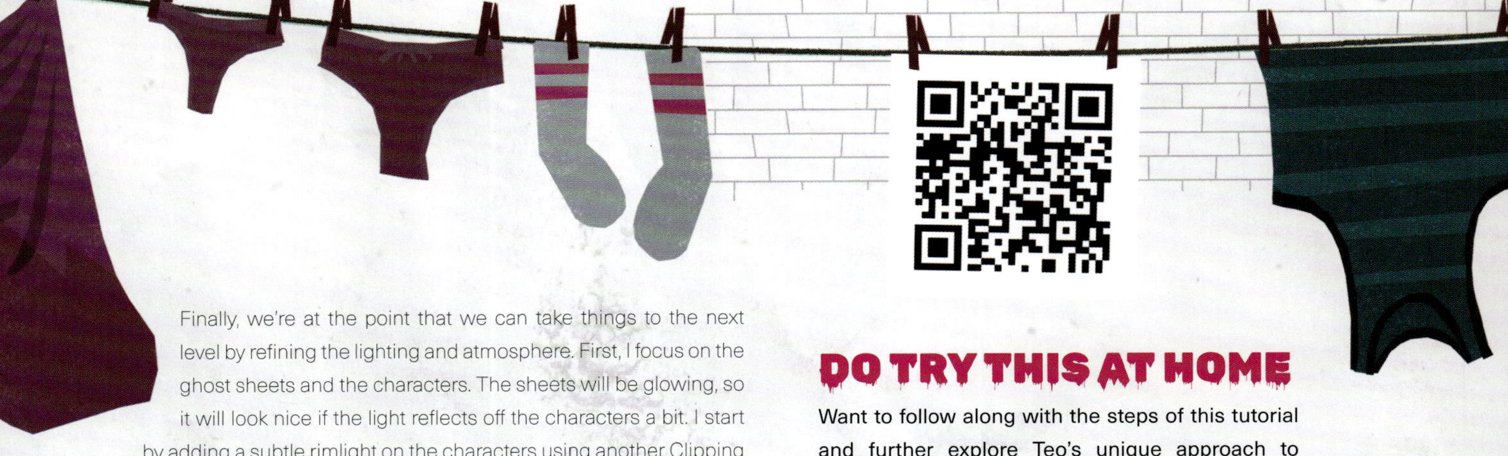

Finally, we're at the point that we can take things to the next level by refining the lighting and atmosphere. First, I focus on the ghost sheets and the characters. The sheets will be glowing, so it will look nice if the light reflects off the characters a bit. I start by adding a subtle rimlight on the characters using another Clipping Mask on top of the shadow layer (keeping in mind where the source of the light is coming from). Once I'm happy with this, I add an extra layer of shadow on the characters to give them a little bit more form – it's not much, but you can tell it's there.

With that done, I look at all the elements around the characters and make sure they're dark or light enough, adding lighting wherever necessary. Finally, I focus on the inside of the room behind the characters. I choose a slightly greener tone for the light from the windows as I feel it matches the rest of the colours better. I also add some generic shapes, indicating that there's actually stuff inside – nothing detailed, just enough to hint at objects existing within.

DO TRY THIS AT HOME

Want to follow along with the steps of this tutorial and further explore Teo's unique approach to character design? Scan the QR code to download the Photoshop file and see exactly how the design was put together.

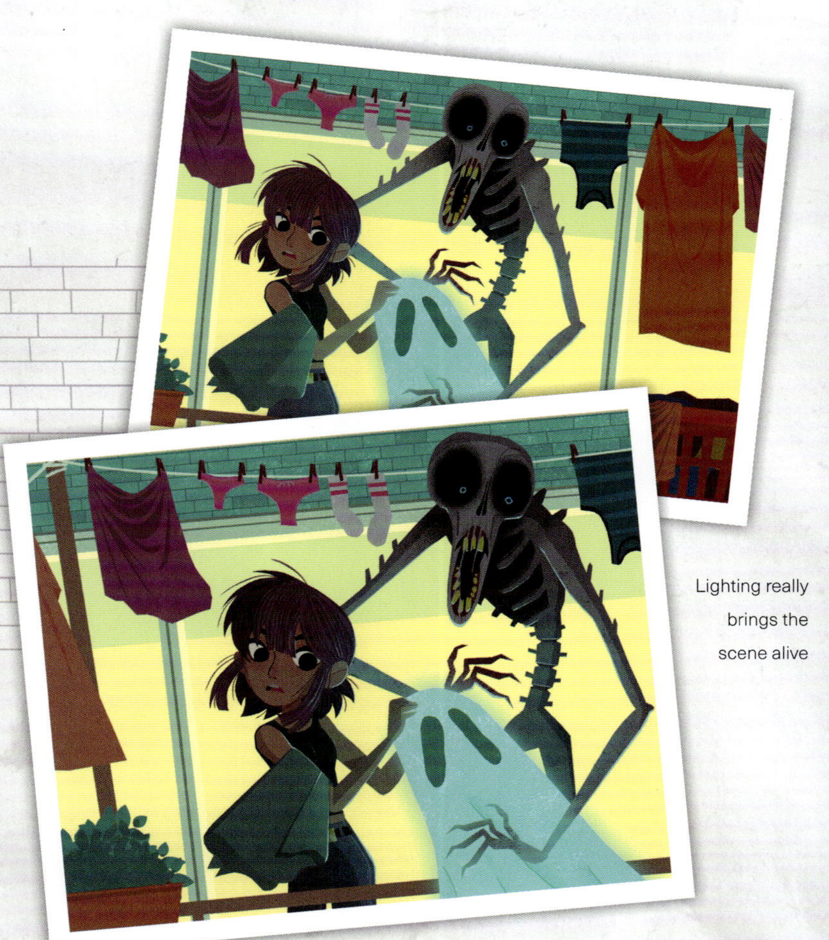

Lighting really brings the scene alive

I cut a little bit off the right and top of the canvas, to make the image slightly narrower and the composition that little bit more pleasing. I can't really explain why this works – it just feels better.

And now for one final magic trick. With everything finished, I like to throw a couple of Lookup tables (LUTs) on the image to see what they do. LUTs are used extensively in photography and film for colour-grading, but they work pretty well on illustrations, too. They can completely change the 'vibe' of an image and I find they really help to tie an image together. I encourage you to look up how to use them and experiment with them.

I play the with the LUTs until I'm happy with the final look, then add a bit of film-grain texture and blur the edges slightly, to give it a bit more of a photographic feel.

And that's pretty much it – we went from a hideous canvas with blocks and blobs, to a pretty decent-looking illustration!

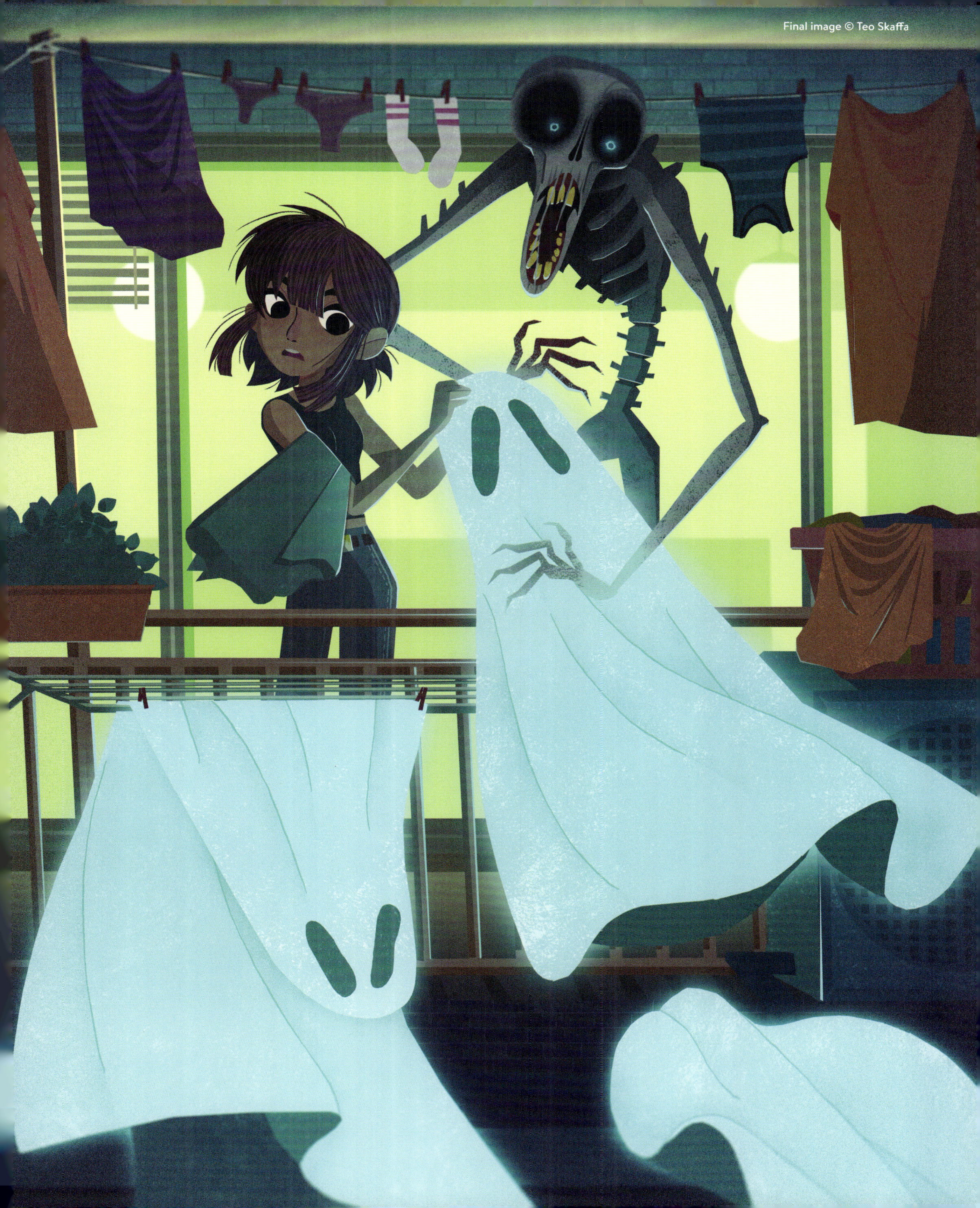

STORMS, SORCERY, AND SHRIMPS!

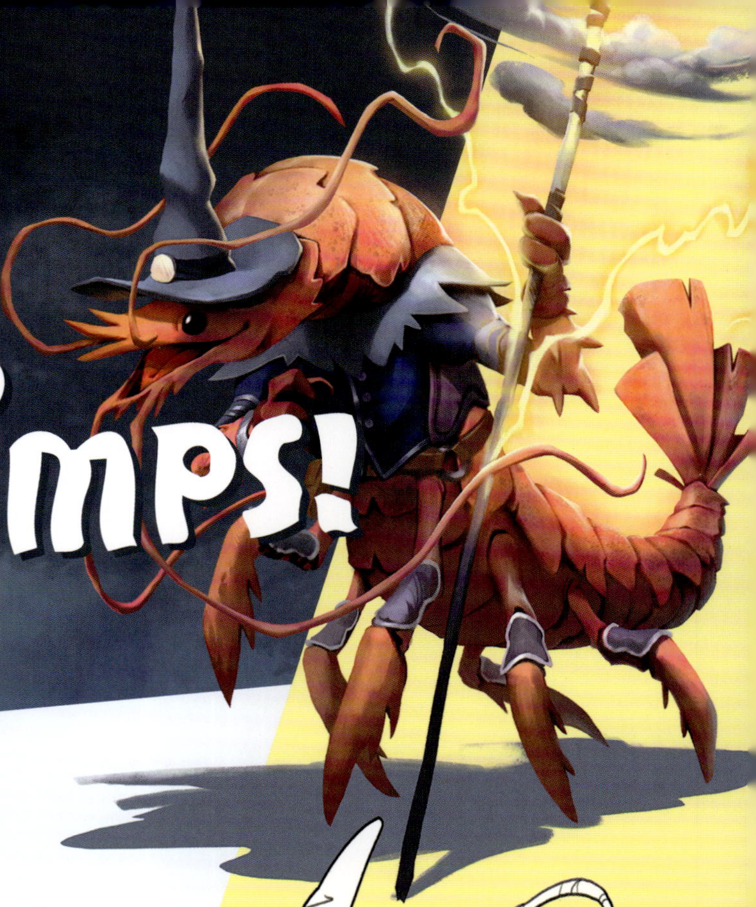

Learn how Juan Diego León uses emojis as inspiration to create unique new characters

USING EMOJIS AS INSPIRATION

Inspiration can come from anywhere when it comes to designing characters. I like to experiment with different creative techniques, and one I use often when creating art for social media is combining emojis.

Let me show you how this process works and what I take into account when creating my designs. I recommend using a sketchbook for your initial explorations and then a computer with a tablet or an iPad to digitize everything. Using this technique, you'll create characters that can inspire you to create stories and worlds beyond your initial drawing. Let's get started!

CHOOSING A DIRECTION

The first thing to do is decide on which emojis are going to form the basis of the character. For this tutorial, I decide to use these three: shrimp, mage, and storm. I look for ideas that relate to these three icons and make some quick sketches.

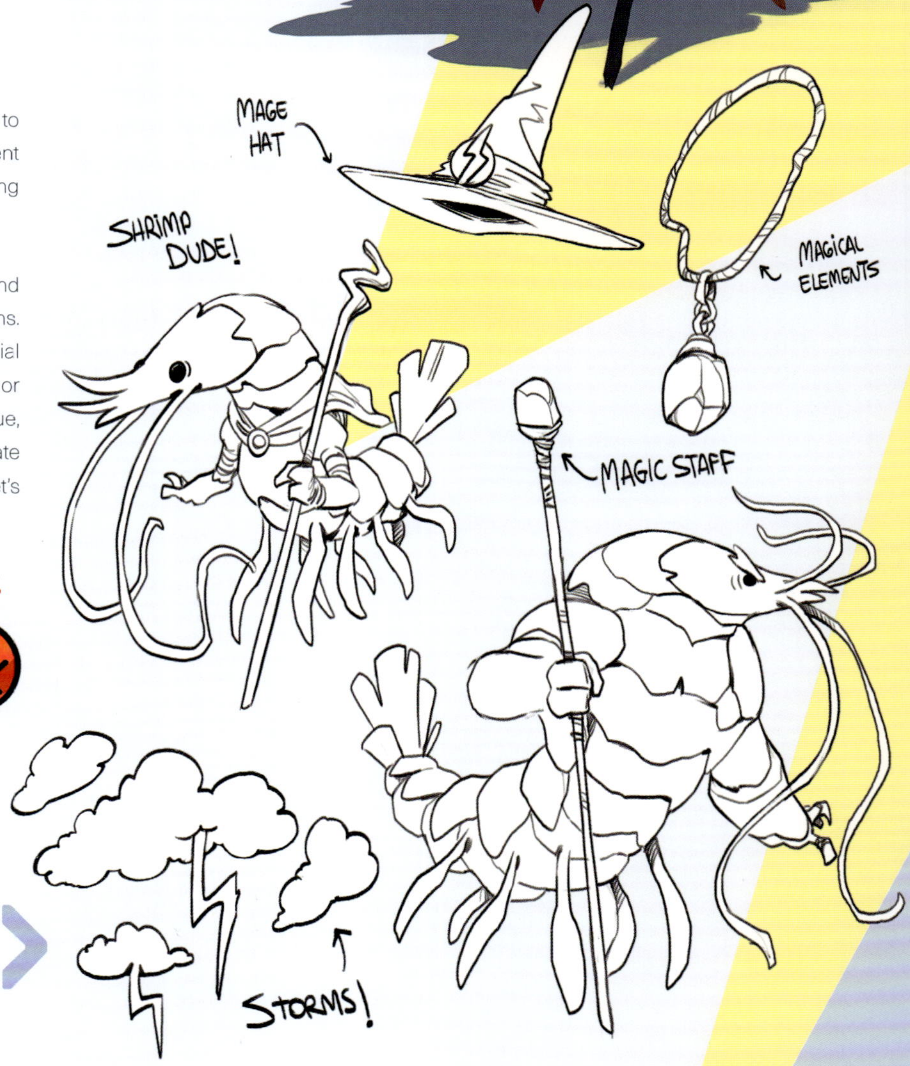

SKETCHES AND IDEAS

Next, create some rough sketches of the character, trying to include all the possible elements that will help tell their story. These sketches don't have to be perfect – just have fun!

THE SILHOUETTE TEST

Always try to test your character by painting it completely in black to see how the silhouette works. By looking at just the silhouette we should be able to clearly read the character, each element of their design, and even where they are looking.

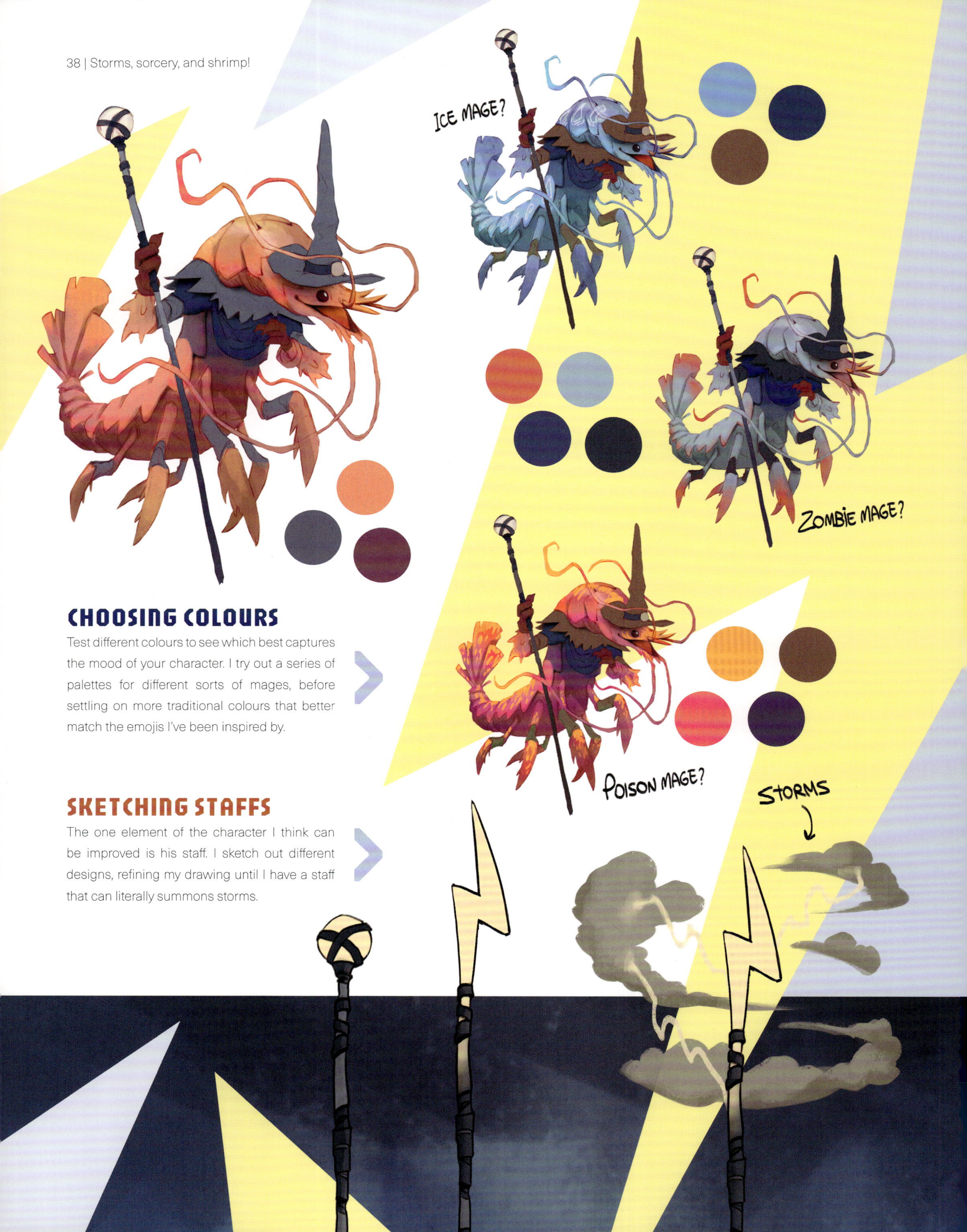

CHOOSING COLOURS

Test different colours to see which best captures the mood of your character. I try out a series of palettes for different sorts of mages, before settling on more traditional colours that better match the emojis I've been inspired by.

SKETCHING STAFFS

The one element of the character I think can be improved is his staff. I sketch out different designs, refining my drawing until I have a staff that can literally summons storms.

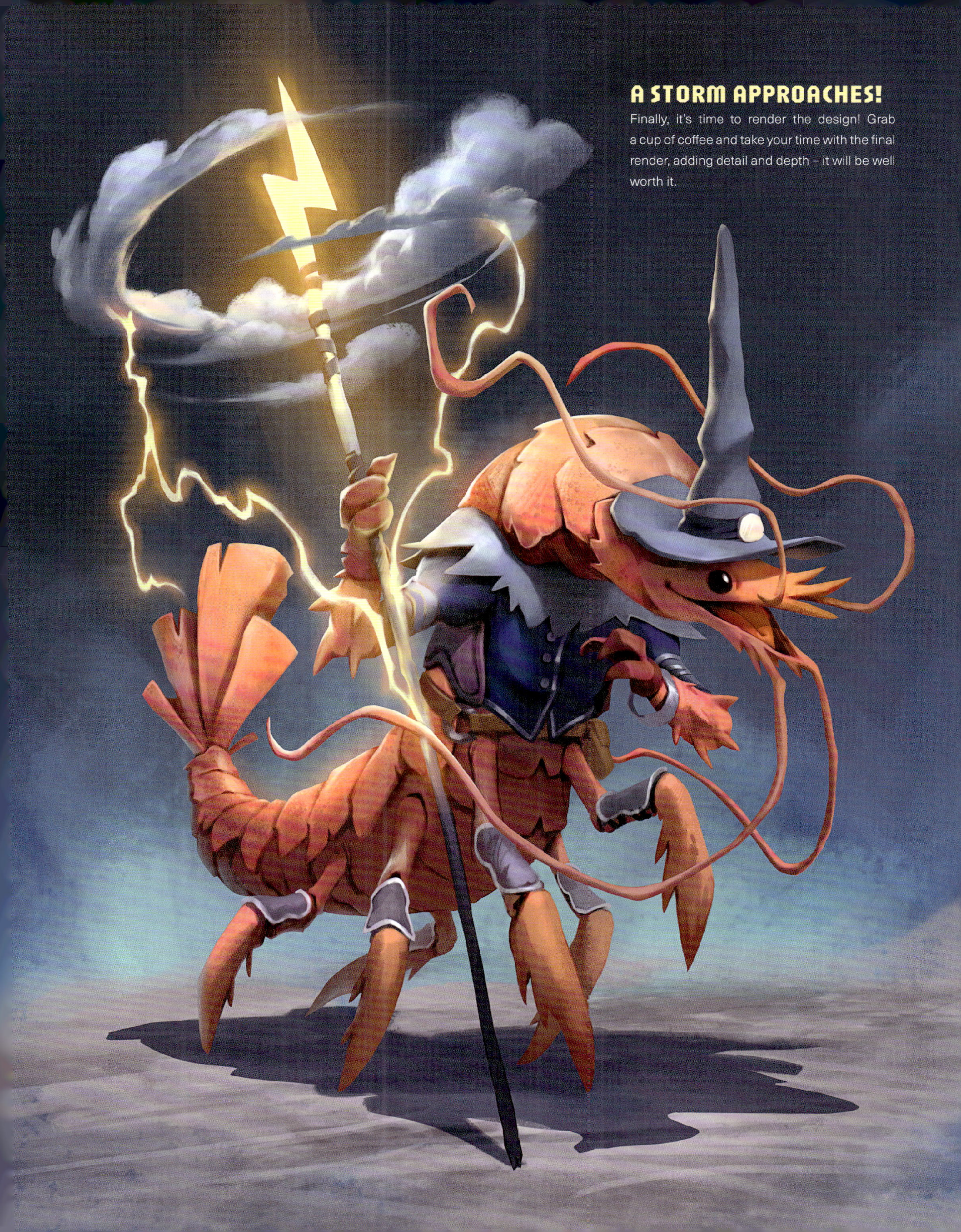

A STORM APPROACHES!
Finally, it's time to render the design! Grab a cup of coffee and take your time with the final render, adding detail and depth – it will be well worth it.

meet the artist:
REX CROWLE

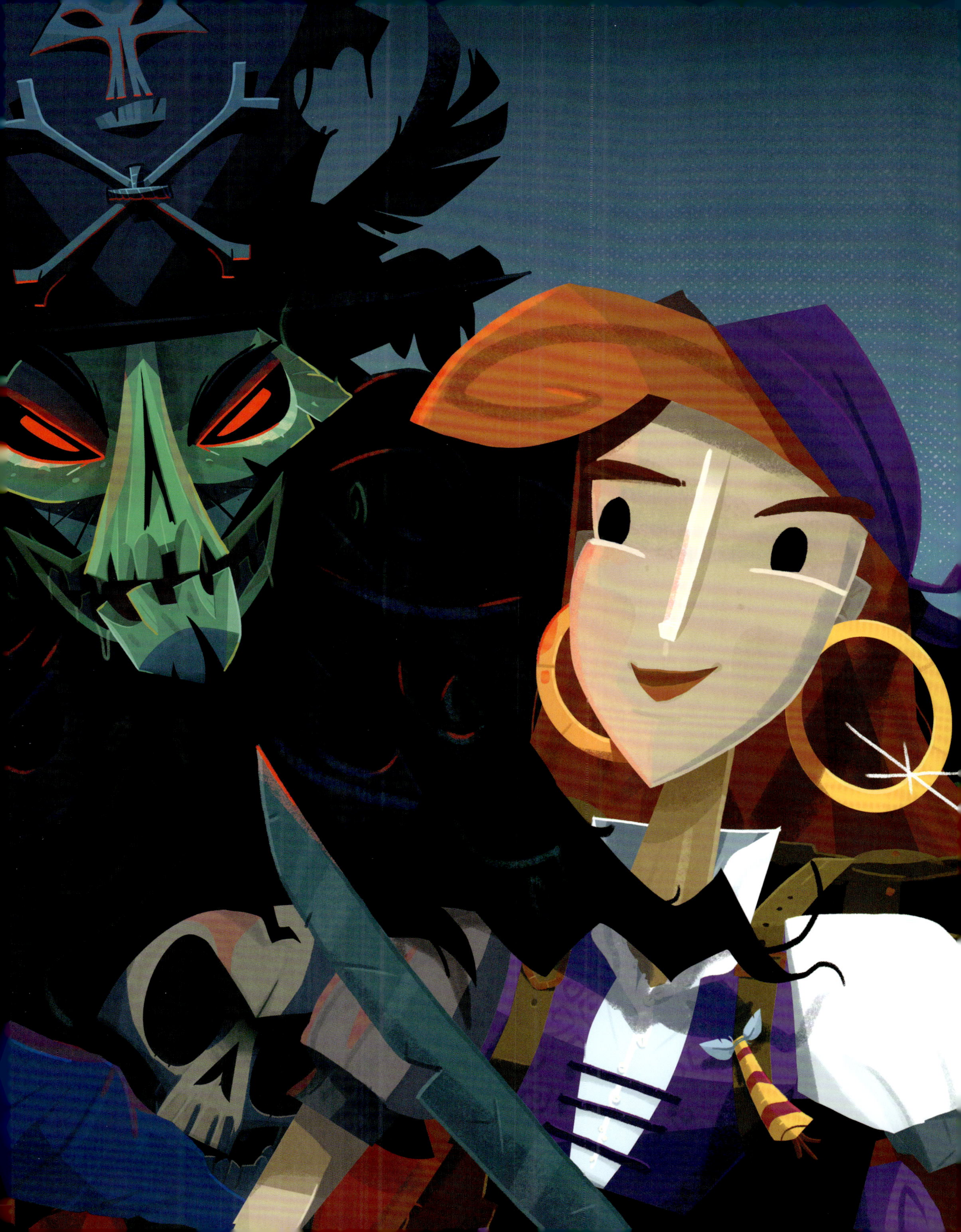

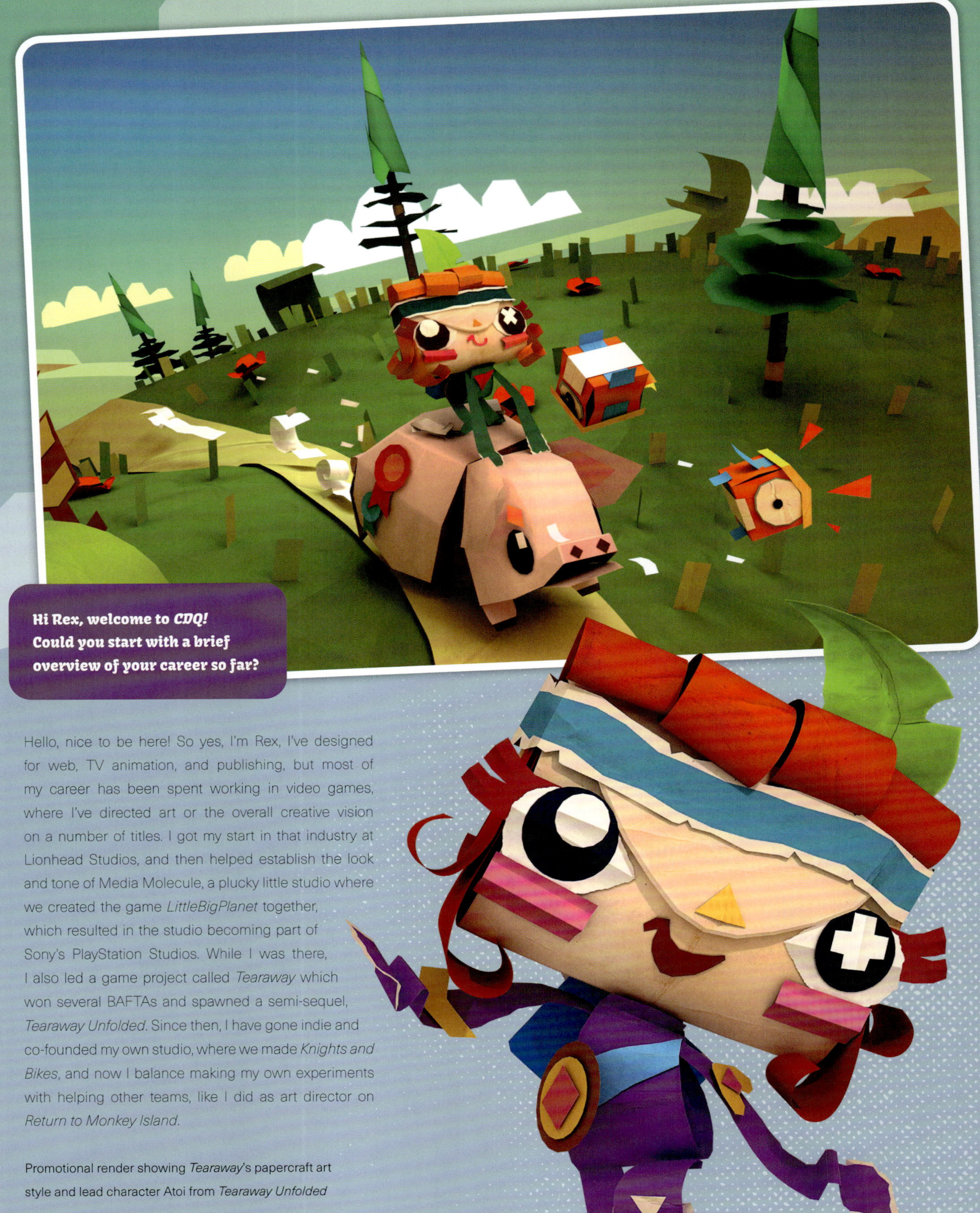

Hello, nice to be here! So yes, I'm Rex, I've designed for web, TV animation, and publishing, but most of my career has been spent working in video games, where I've directed art or the overall creative vision on a number of titles. I got my start in that industry at Lionhead Studios, and then helped establish the look and tone of Media Molecule, a plucky little studio where we created the game *LittleBigPlanet* together, which resulted in the studio becoming part of Sony's PlayStation Studios. While I was there, I also led a game project called *Tearaway* which won several BAFTAs and spawned a semi-sequel, *Tearaway Unfolded*. Since then, I have gone indie and co-founded my own studio, where we made *Knights and Bikes*, and now I balance making my own experiments with helping other teams, like I did as art director on *Return to Monkey Island*.

Promotional render showing *Tearaway*'s papercraft art style and lead character Atoi from *Tearaway Unfolded*

Early sketches
of characters
from *Knights
and Bikes*

Who and what are the main influences behind your art style?

I studied graphic design at art college and I think that still has a strong influence on me. I'm always drawn towards bold graphic shapes, stylization, and ways of presenting the world around us in new, unusual ways.

I continue to draw inspiration from the endless visual experimentation of Picasso and the aims of Cubism. I love the stylization and playfulness of Mary Blair and Javier Mariscal. The line work and humour of Ronald Searle and the characters he drew are a big influence on me as well.

Promotional poster for *Knights and Bikes*, featuring many key elements from the game

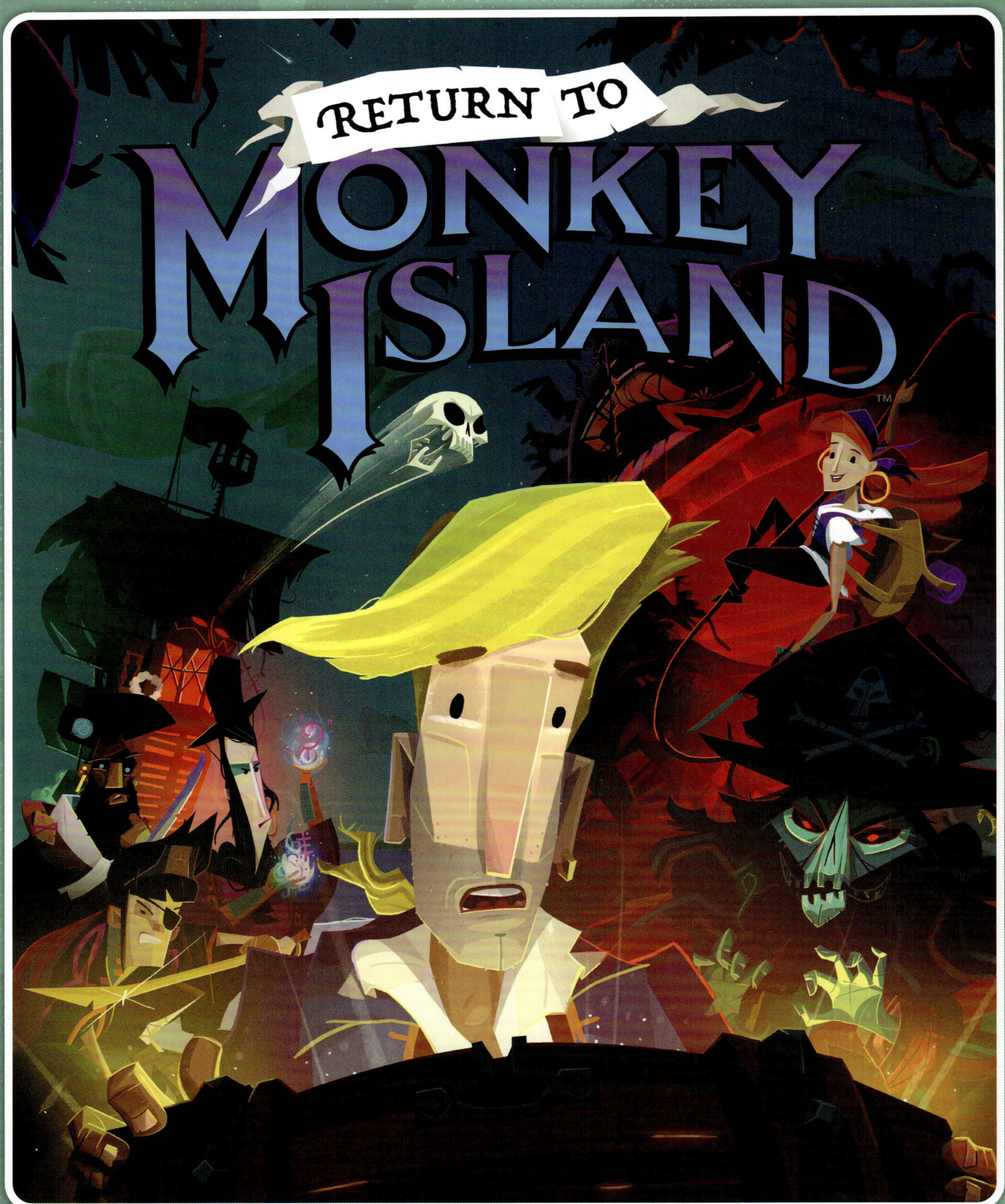

The cover for *Return to Monkey Island*

Let's talk about *Return to Monkey Island* (*RtMI*). I feel like you did a great job of updating the look while remaining faithful to the classic pixelated style of the characters (and the *Curse* versions, too). How did it feel to be working on such a revered property?

The project had an unusual start for me, as it was born out of a piece of fan art I made around sixteen years ago. At that time, the first two *Monkey Island* games had been given an HD remaster and all their original pixel art had been replaced with a modern level of detail. It was interesting to see the characters reworked like that, but it wasn't quite how I imagined them. Those early low-resolution game characters were so open to reinterpretation, which is why I think so many artists continue to redraw them for their own personal enjoyment. During a lunch break (I was still at Media Molecule at the time) I painted up a quick version of Guybrush Threepwood, the unlikely hero of *Monkey Island*, just as an experiment, but I was happy enough with my little study that I posted it on Twitter. Well, Ron Gilbert, creator of the original *Monkey Island* games, saw it, loved it, and asked me for a higher quality version to have as his desktop wallpaper. And that was the end of the story, until a dozen or so years later, in the early stages of the pandemic. Ron phoned up and asked me (after signing a stack of NDAs!) if I'd like to lead the art on a new *Monkey Island* game that he was planning with its original co-creator Dave Grossman.

My original fan-art version of Guybrush (below), and an early version from *RtMI* (left)

Obviously, I had to say yes. But I was also a little nervous about the responsibility. The first two *Monkey Island*s are my favourite games of all time, and although the series had continued in later years with many more titles by different teams (in many different art-styles), *RtMI* was to be a conclusion to the original unfinished trilogy. So this was going to be the game that the world and I had waited over thirty years for!

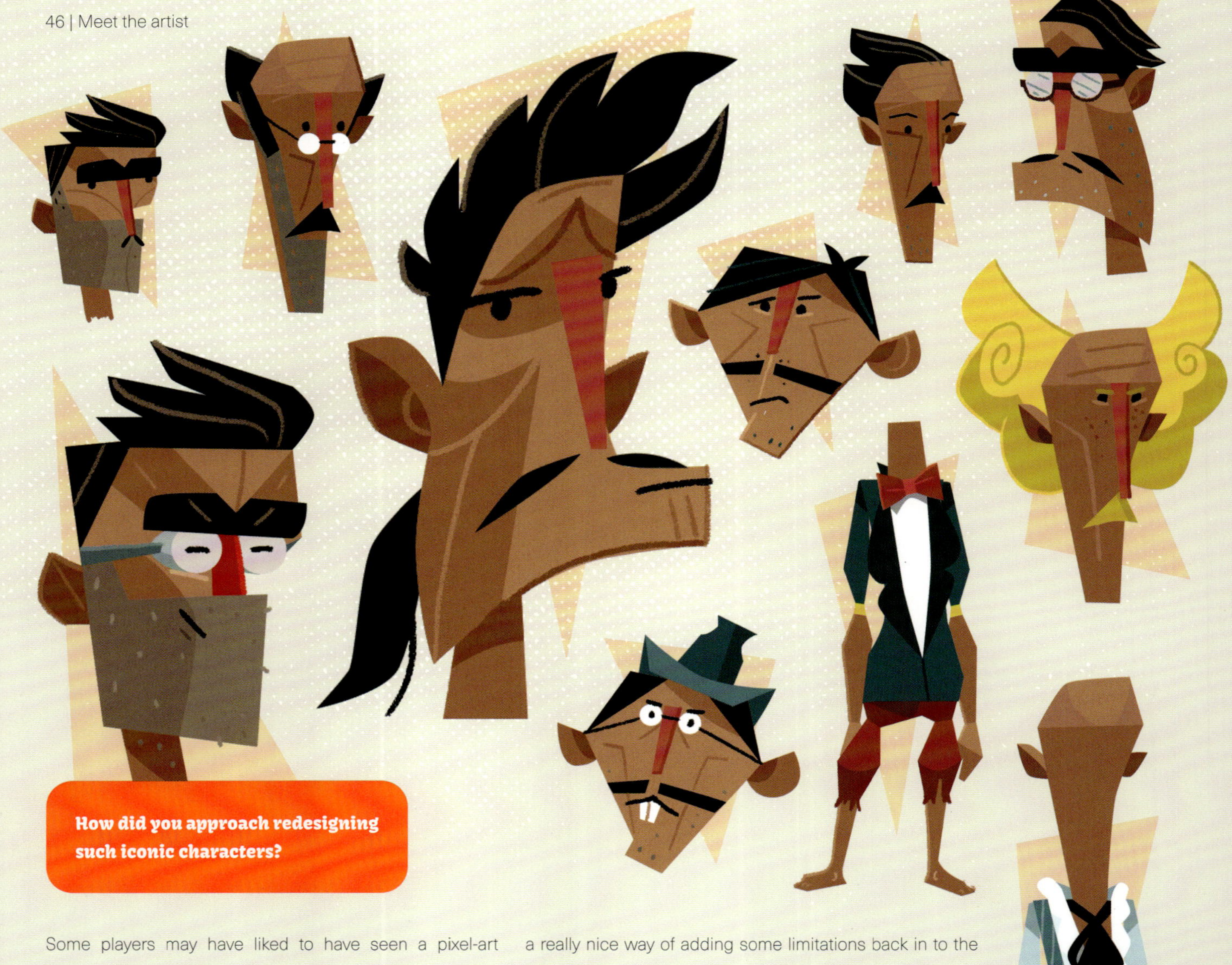

How did you approach redesigning such iconic characters?

Some players may have liked to have seen a pixel-art style and that was initially a concern to me. But ultimately, I was asked to join the project to do 'my thing' and that meant establishing a style that looked forward, while also being very influenced by the past. Every game in the wider *Monkey Island* series has reinvented its look with each new title anyway.

Ultimately, what I wanted to achieve was to create a space between the pixelated characters of the original two games and how they were depicted when painted for the box art. This meant chunky characters with bold, almost boxy silhouettes, that could look like pixel-art characters when small on screen, but with a secondary level of detail, visible brush marks, and a wider variety of shapes and angles, all of which become apparent when seen at a larger scale.

Ron had a nice piece of advice that he mentioned to me while we were working on *RtMI*: "Always consider how someone would cosplay as this character." I think that's a really nice way of adding some limitations back in to the design, so you distil your character down to their most important elements, making sure they are still distinctive and readable, as well as appealing enough for a cosplayer to want to spend all their free weekends building their homemade version of your design.

As I mentioned earlier, the characters had quite strong angles in their designs, which came partially from the boxy pixel-art origins of the series. But more than that, I felt these sharp angles would say something about the pirate world in which the game is set. These characters exist in a rough period of history – everyone was sailing around on ramshackle boats, getting shipwrecked, keelhauled, or thrown out of tavern windows. I wanted the characters to look like they'd had tough lives, that they've literally and metaphorically been bashed about by their experiences. The angular shapes were my way of expressing that.

Early character designs for Ned Filigree, an exiled accountant

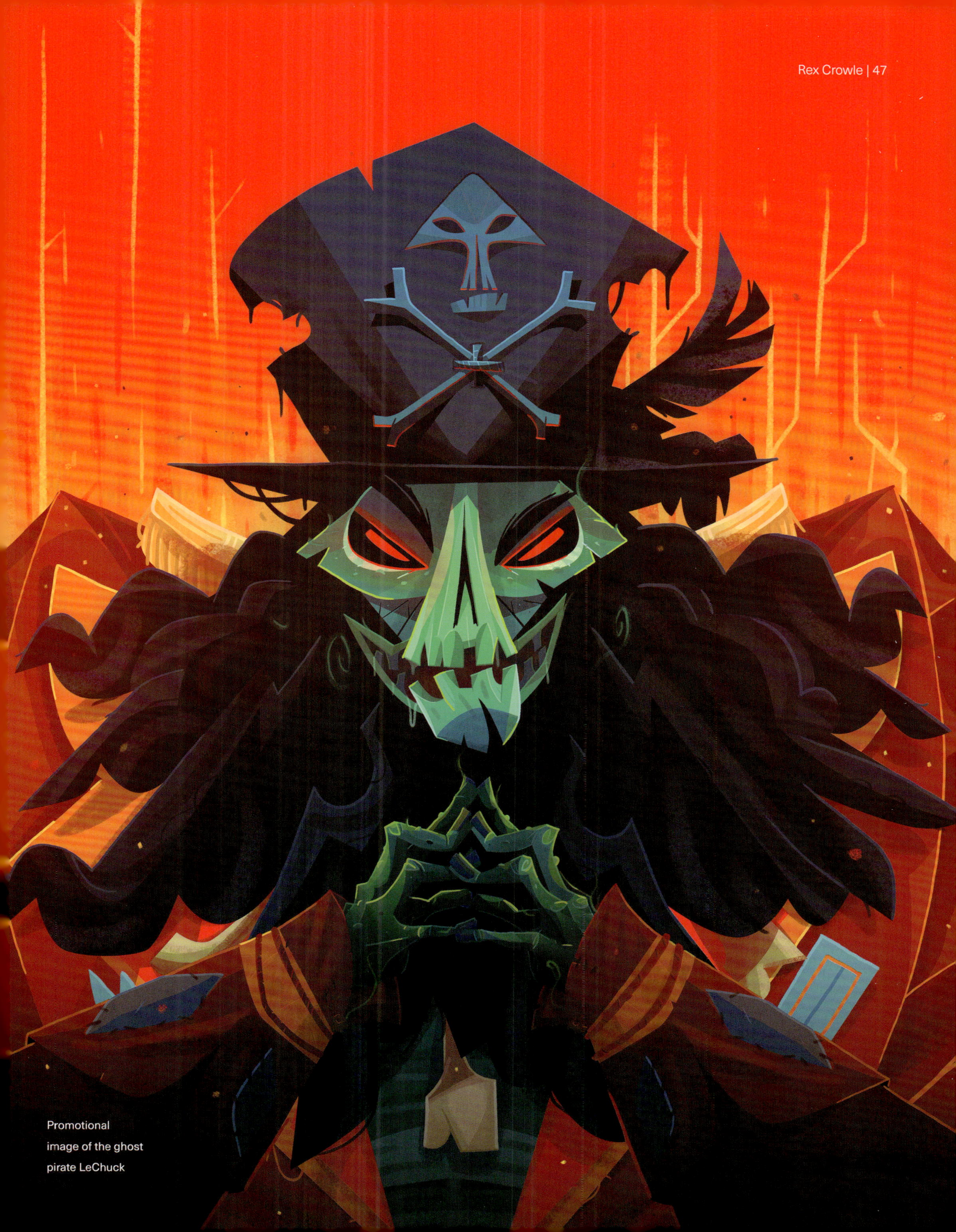

Promotional image of the ghost pirate LeChuck

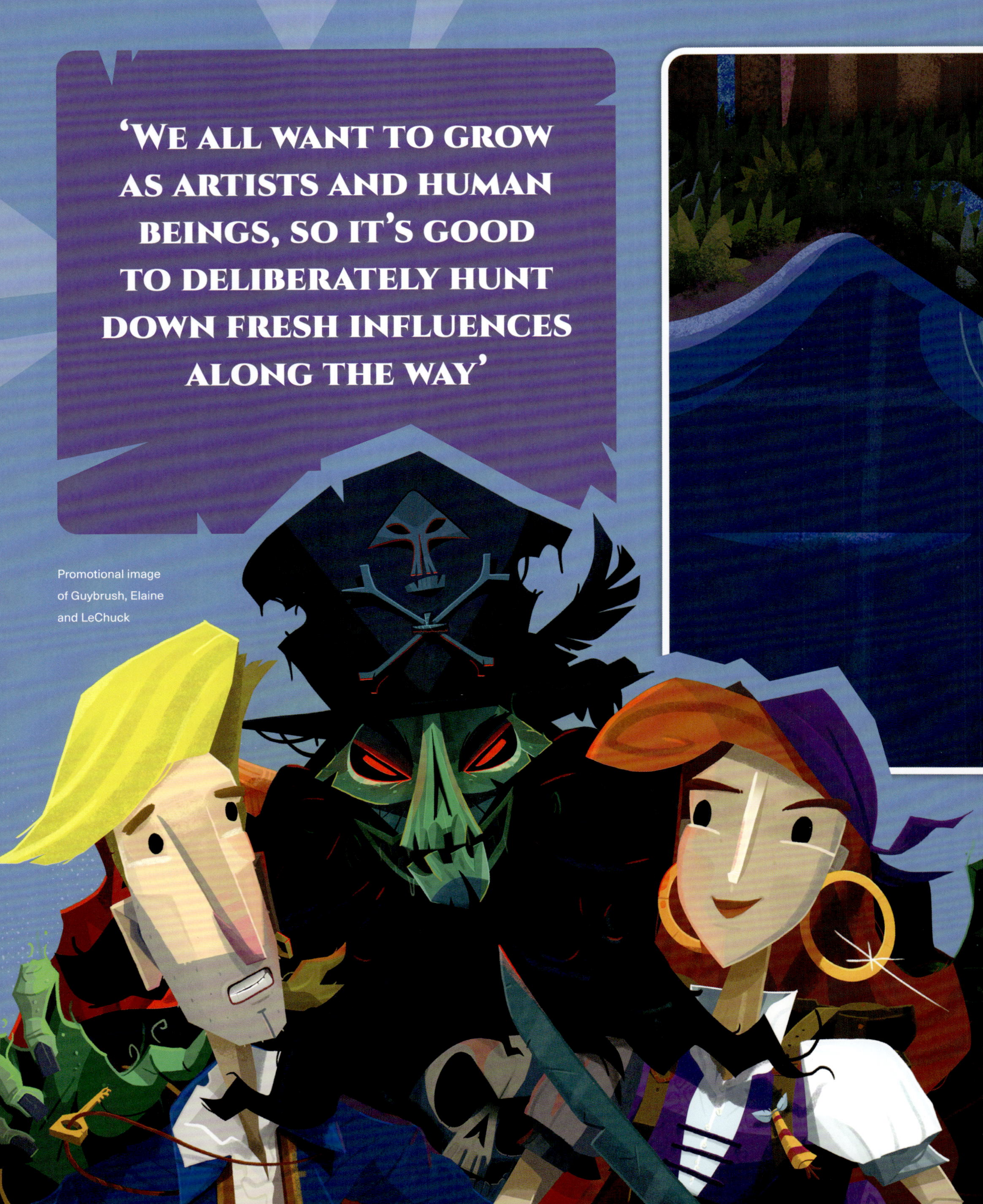

Promotional image
of Guybrush, Elaine
and LeChuck

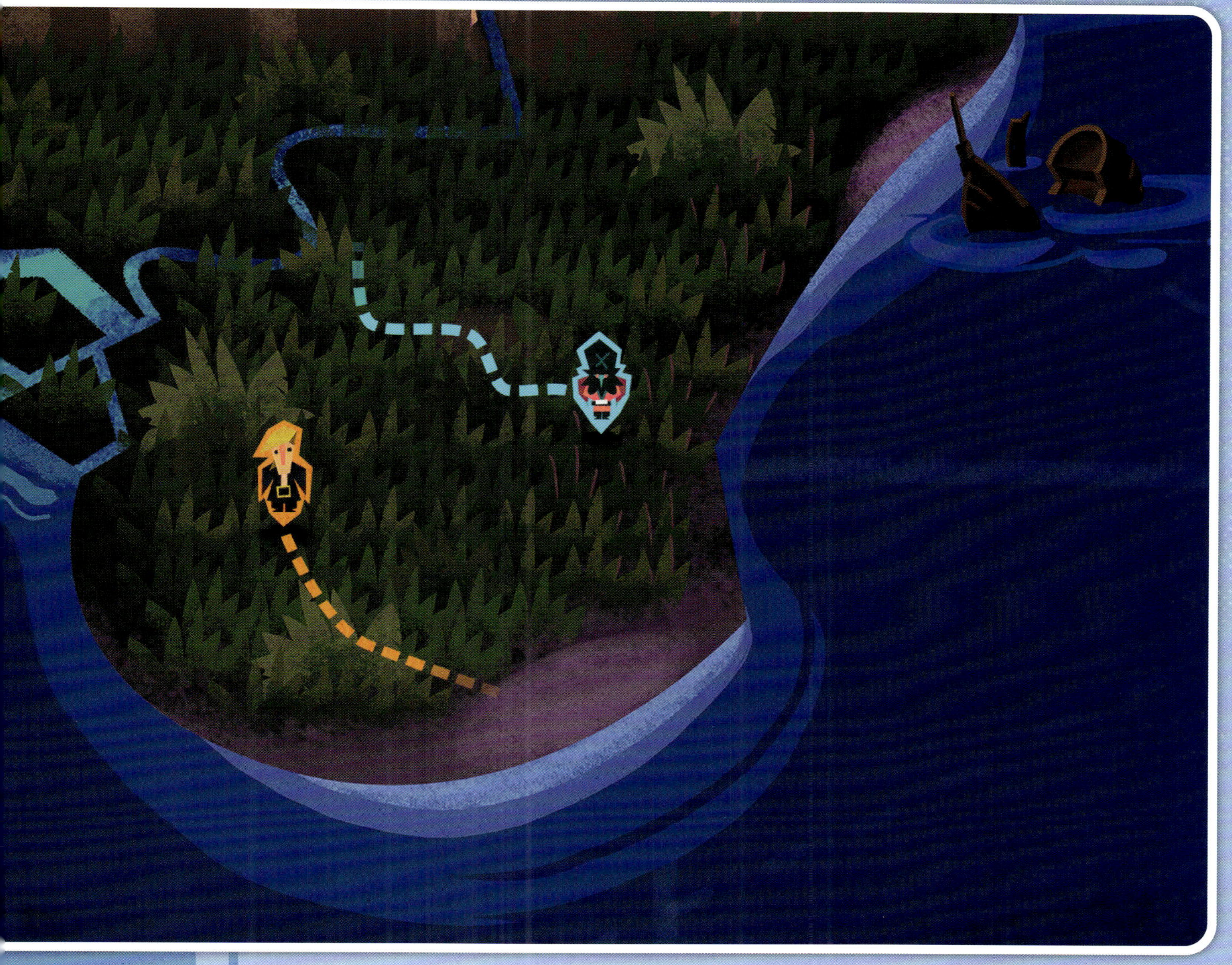

Simplified versions of the main characters, to indicate their positions on a map screen

Finding a truly unique approach to character design and sticking with it is a challenge that a lot of our readers aspire to – do you have any advice for readers looking to find their own unique look?

I think it's better not to think too hard about 'your style' as a special rarefied thing – it's just what comes naturally to you. You subtly develop your style over your whole life by doing what you do, combined with the external influences that interest or excite you. We all want to grow as artists and as human beings, so it's good to deliberately hunt down fresh influences along the way, although I prefer to get these organically, by going for a walk, visiting galleries, or travelling further afield. You're more likely to see, hear, and experience things that surprise you than if you rely on internet algorithms to serve you inspiration.

Also, try not to be overexposed to other artists' work on social media. I'm so glad Instagram didn't exist when I was starting out as I would have been taking on new influences every few seconds! Now I only dip in occasionally so I get a buzz from seeing what everyone else is doing and try not to become overwhelmed by the wealth of talent and styles out there.

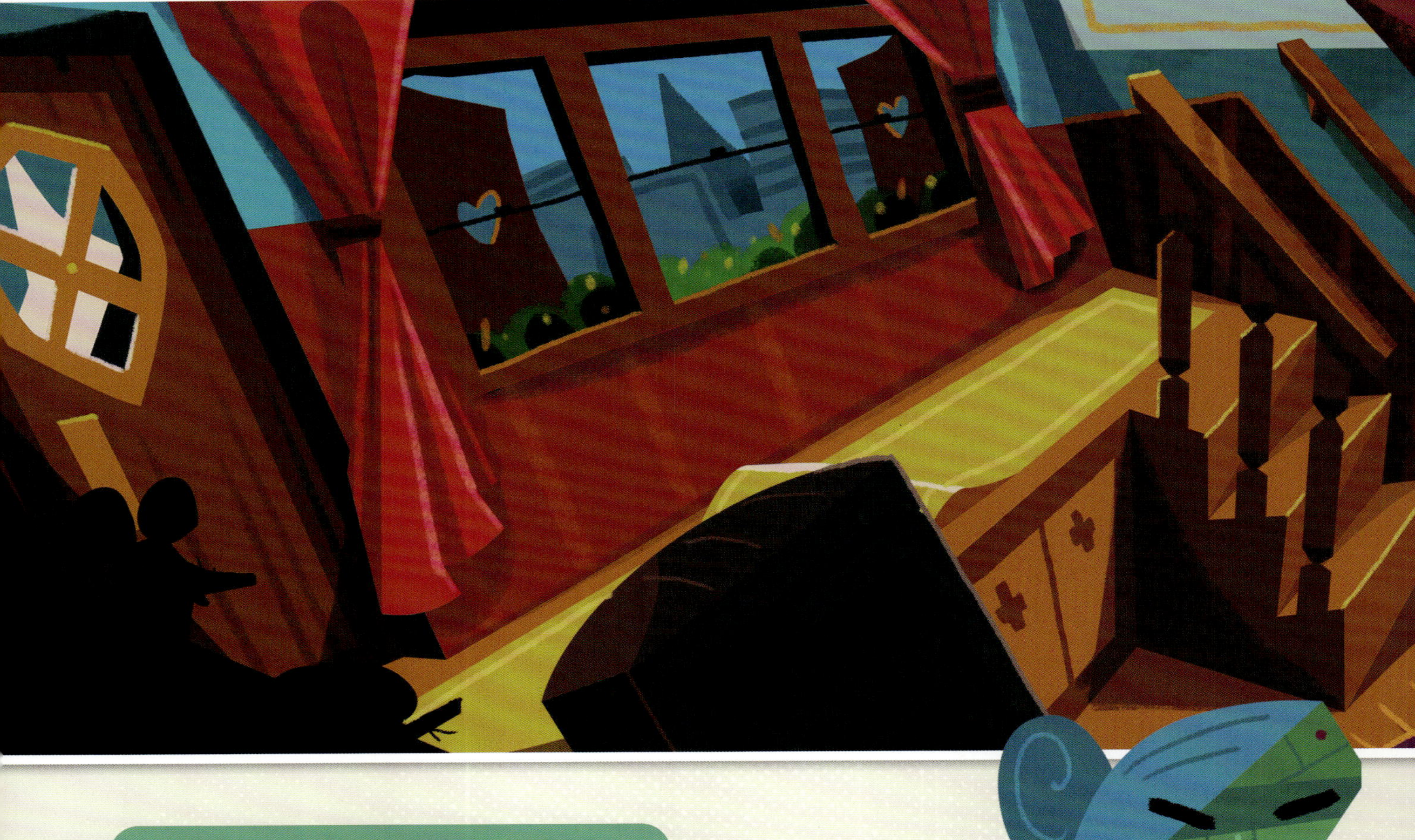

If the character is for one of my own projects, there will be huge amounts of iteration and I'll fill in pages and pages of sketchbooks with little design ideas. I like to draw these designs in cafes and public spaces, so I have lots of random people to be influenced by as they walk past. I also like to create large collections of characters in stream-of-consciousness sessions and then assign them to specific roles later. That's my favourite way of working, as designing a character for a specific job can reinforce unwanted stereotypes. It's more interesting to me to create a range of unusual but well-rounded characters and then decide which one is a librarian or a fishmonger, or whoever.

Only then will I make smaller tweaks to their designs to fully match their roles or requirements.

If the design is for someone else's project, it's usually a much tighter brief. I'll still do a lot of iteration, although I think it's good to not overwhelm your client. I'll usually try to limit the amount of designs I share with them, so they are only seeing my favourites and with the most amount of range between each option. That process will then continue through a few rounds of iteration, honing in on what everyone thinks the character should be.

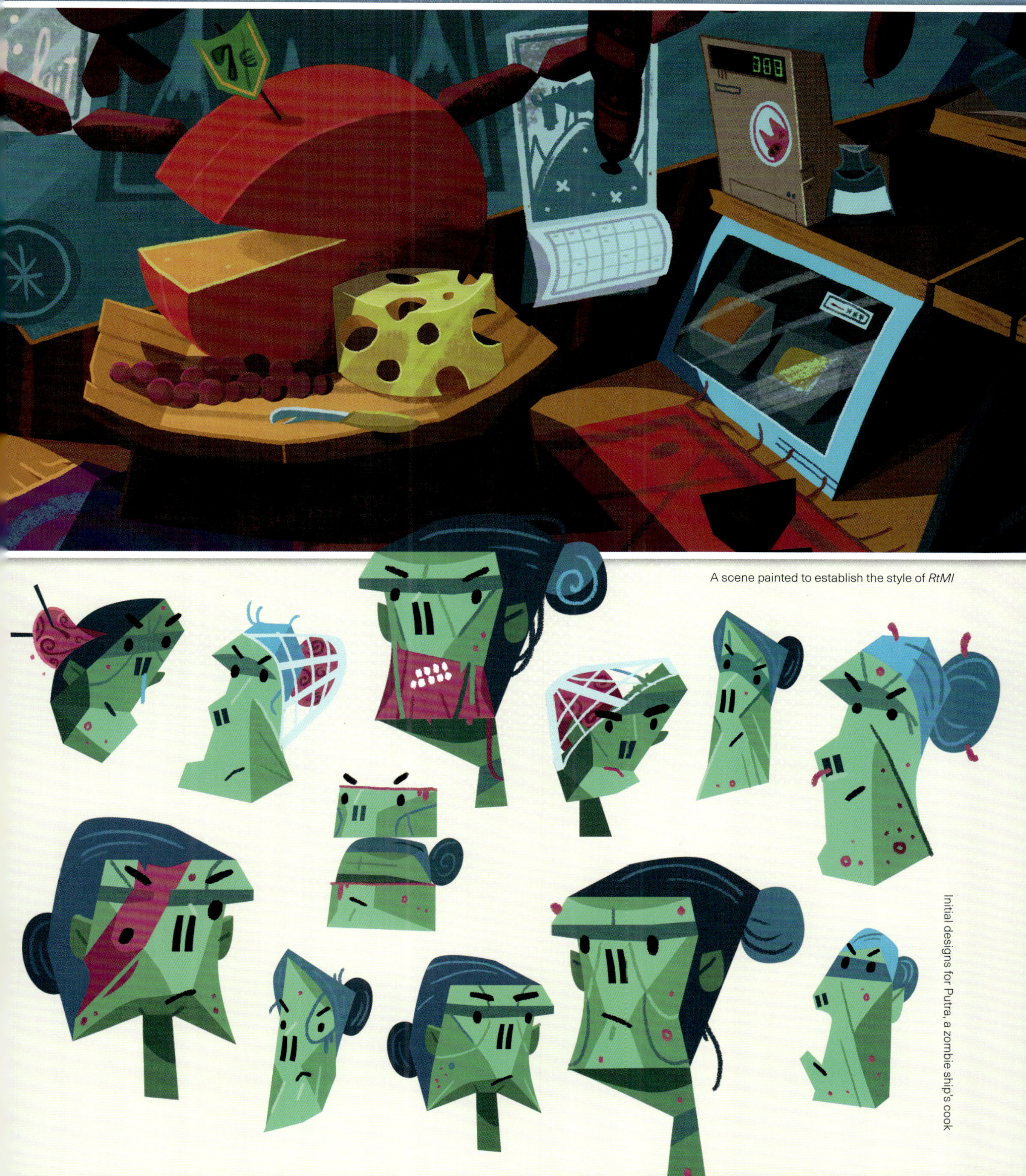

A scene painted to establish the style of *RtMI*

Initial designs for Putra, a zombie ship's cook

The interactivity of games brings unpredictability and potential chaos to everything you make, particularly if it's in 3D. You often don't know exactly where characters will be standing and how they will be framed by the camera, or who they will be interacting with. This is infinitely more complicated when you make games like *LittleBigPlanet* or *Tearaway*, where players can fully customize their characters or make their own scenes out of your art. In those examples, the most important thing was having a very strong and clear idea behind why everything looked the way it did so it will still appear unified, no matter what happens. *LittleBigPlanet* was made to look like a home-made puppet theatre, with everything constructed from craft materials and household items, while *Tearaway* had its papercraft aesthetic to bring everything together.

Because of the tools and workflows used to create games, I think there is always a tendency to design characters and worlds under a microscope. It's easy to get lost in a million tiny decisions, when the most important thing is to design holistically and always consider how everything will look once brought together. An artist might be working on the eyelashes of a less important character and trying to make them the most beautiful eyelashes ever created, but as a result they may be over-detailed for the character's purpose in-game.

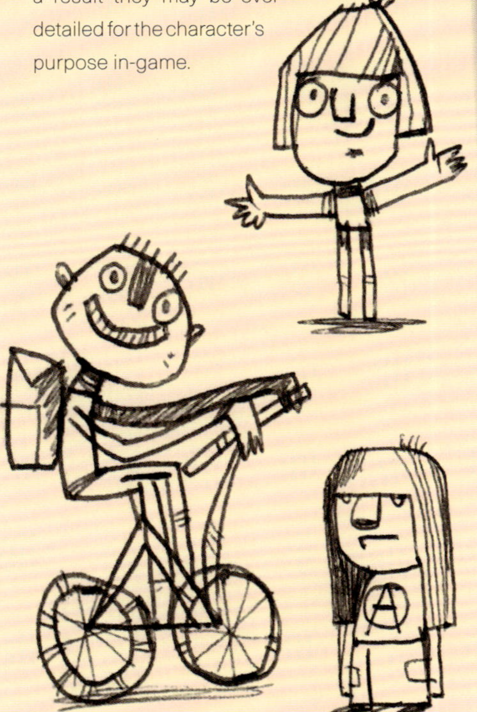

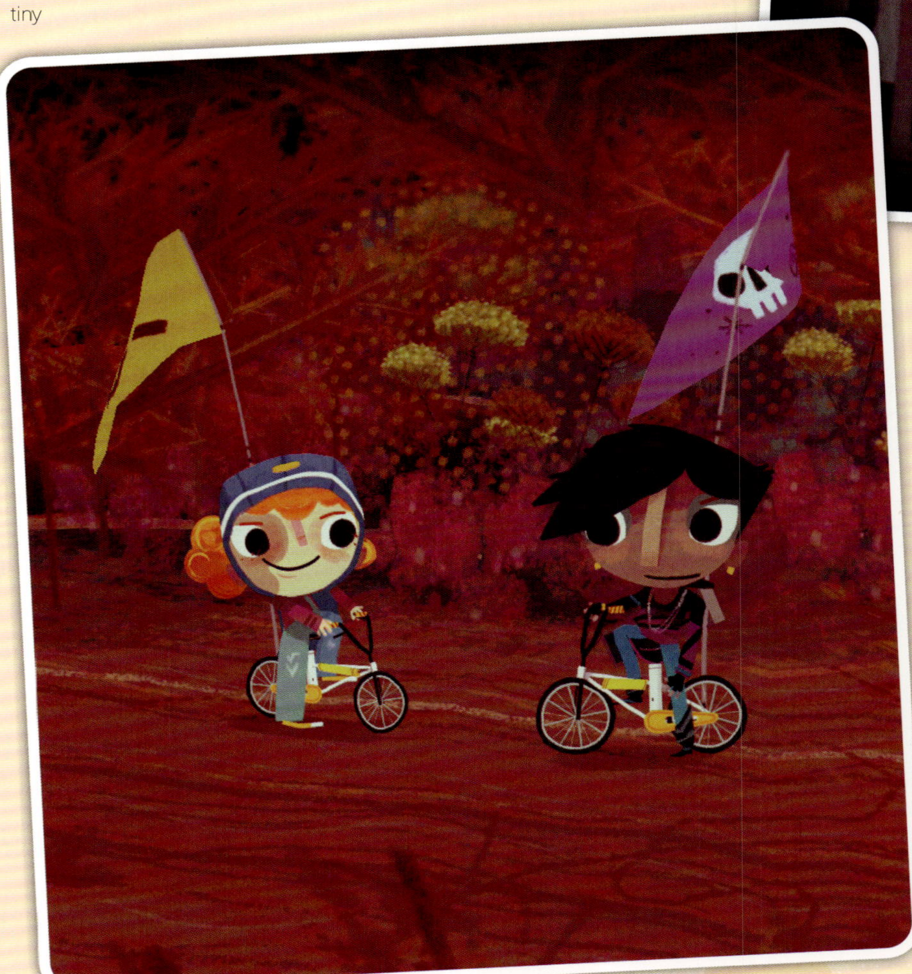

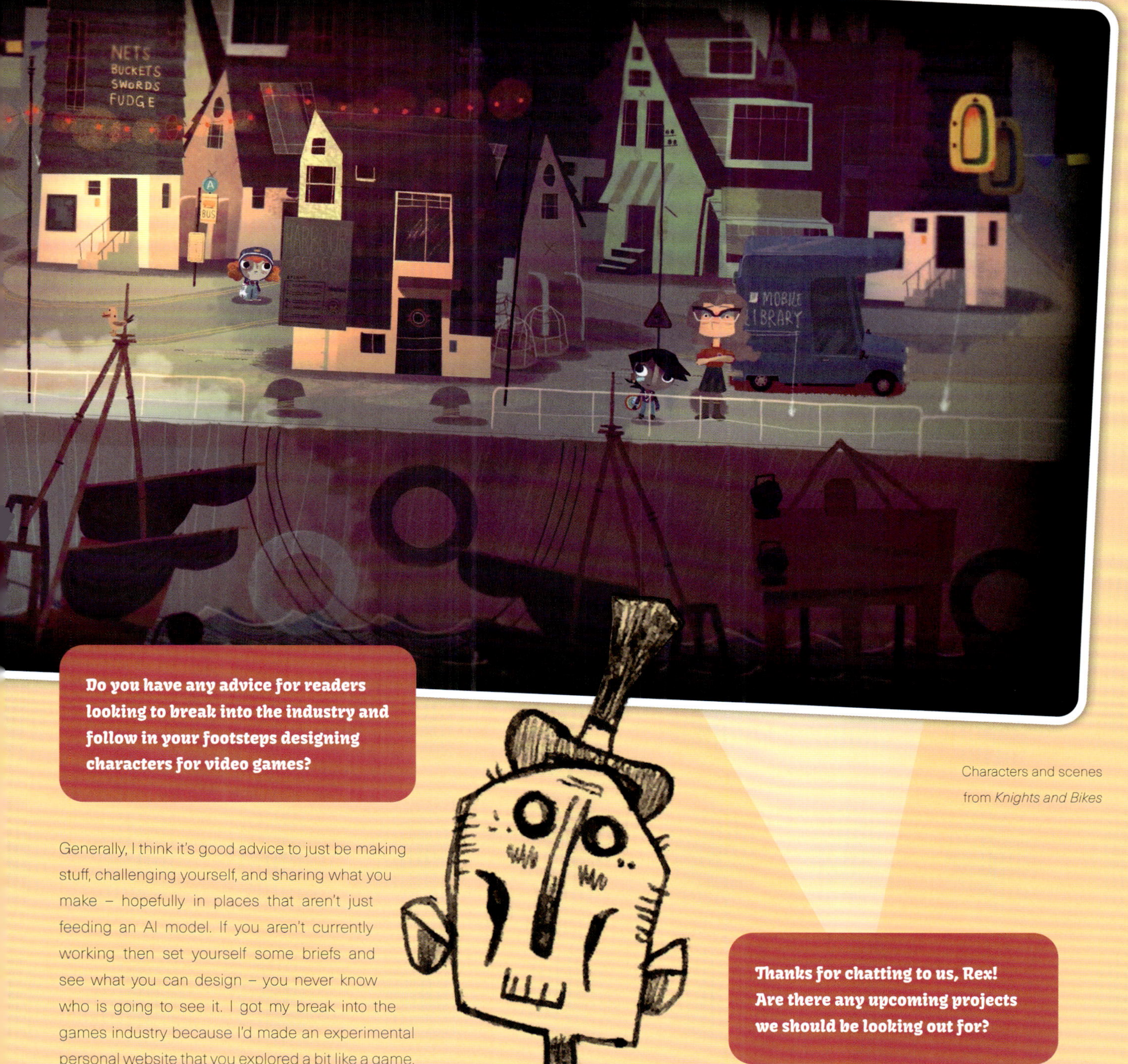

Characters and scenes
from *Knights and Bikes*

Do you have any advice for readers looking to break into the industry and follow in your footsteps designing characters for video games?

Generally, I think it's good advice to just be making stuff, challenging yourself, and sharing what you make – hopefully in places that aren't just feeding an AI model. If you aren't currently working then set yourself some briefs and see what you can design – you never know who is going to see it. I got my break into the games industry because I'd made an experimental personal website that you explored a bit like a game, and someone at a game studio saw it and invited me in.

Game jams can also be a great way to gain some experience, find new collaborators, and quickly create something tangible to show to other developers or employers.

Thanks for chatting to us, Rex! Are there any upcoming projects we should be looking out for?

Thanks for listening! Although I've been able to talk loads about the past, unfortunately I can't talk so much about the future. I'm mostly doing experiments with small projects that are trying to push a bit further away from what games usually are, but I have nothing to show just yet. My lips are sealed!

LAURA PAUSELLI

I started working with line art when I switched from pencil to pen, almost a decade ago. From there I began to explore ink, brush pens, and digital line art. I hope these insights will spark new creativity and exploration in your own artistic journey.

01. Cats' bodies are liquid! Twist them to see how far you can push your design, while keeping the design natural and elegant. I don't worry too much about the lines at this stage and let my ideas flow freely.

02. Line weight is a crucial aspect of line art – vary it to emphasize curves or where elements overlap. Experiment with edgy and curvy lines, open or closed borders. There's a lot to play with that will help add dynamism to the line.

03. One advantage of digital art is the ability to create infinite variations. Before finalizing the piece, I enjoy blocking out layers and experimenting with various line and background colours, such as in this all-white, starry version.

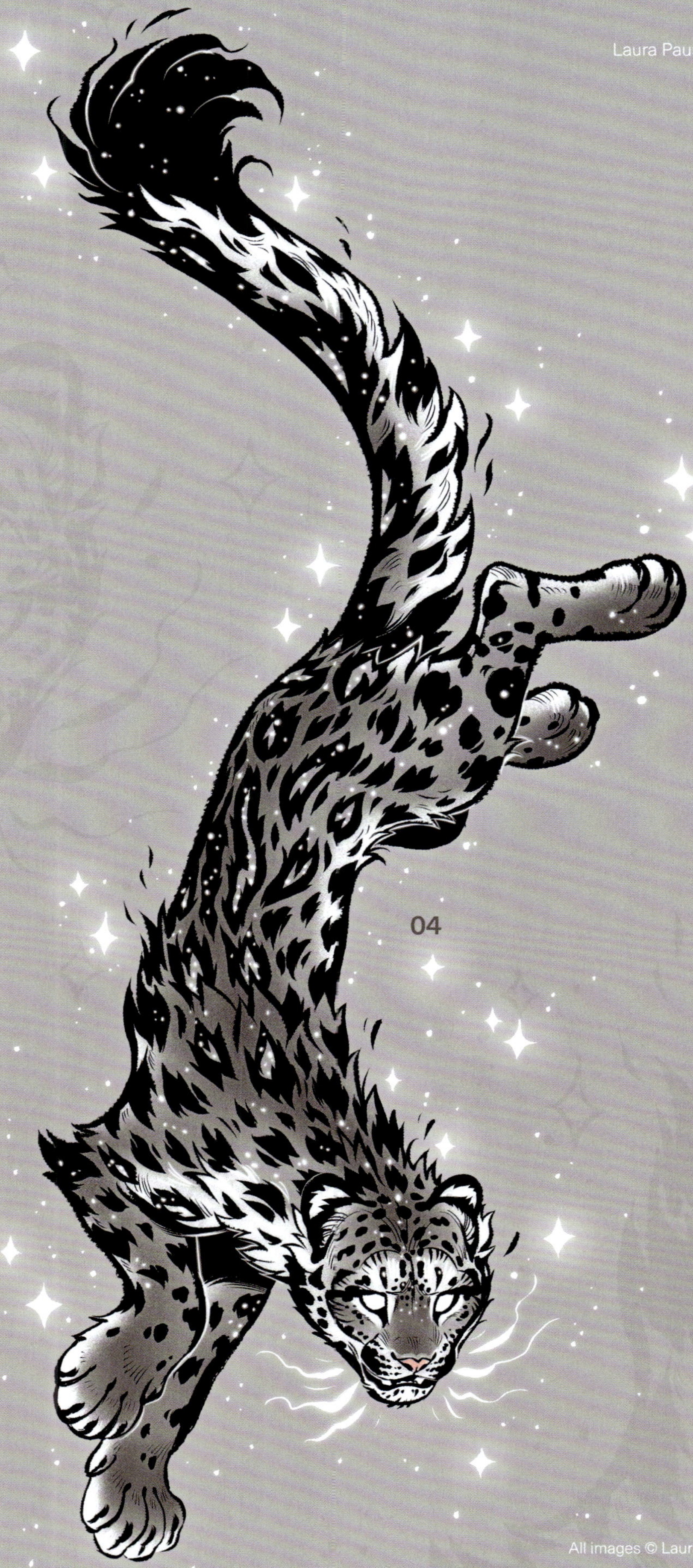

04. When you have captivating line art, simplicity often works better than creating a detailed painting. To close off the piece, I used a slightly grainy brush for flat colours. Even without shadows or light, the image already effectively portrays the look I was going for.

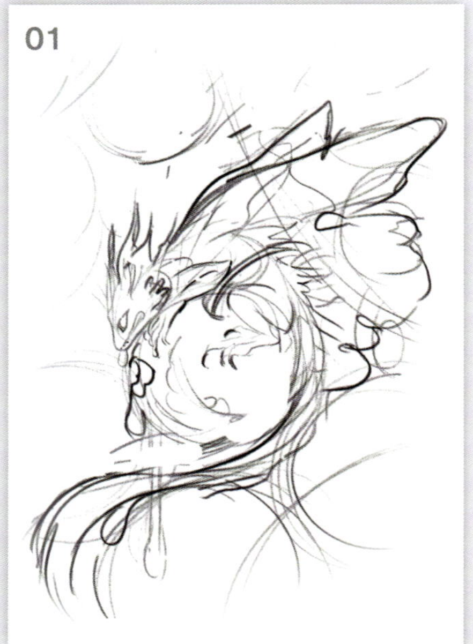

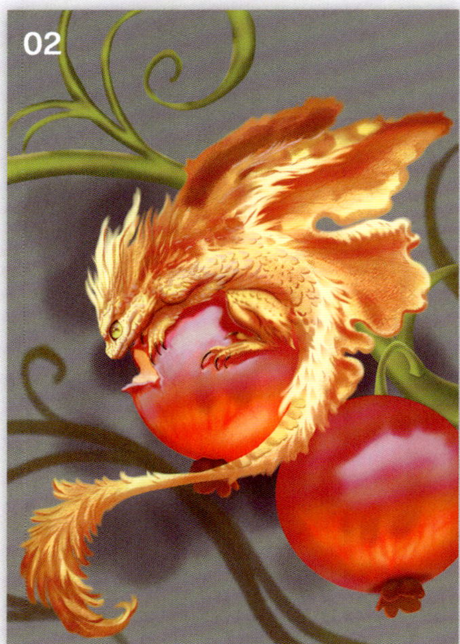

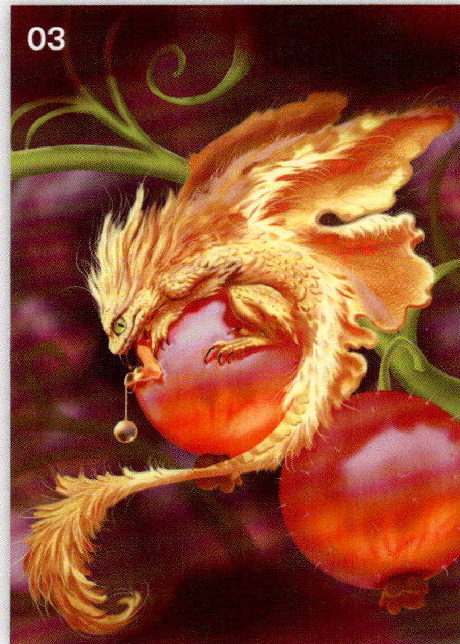

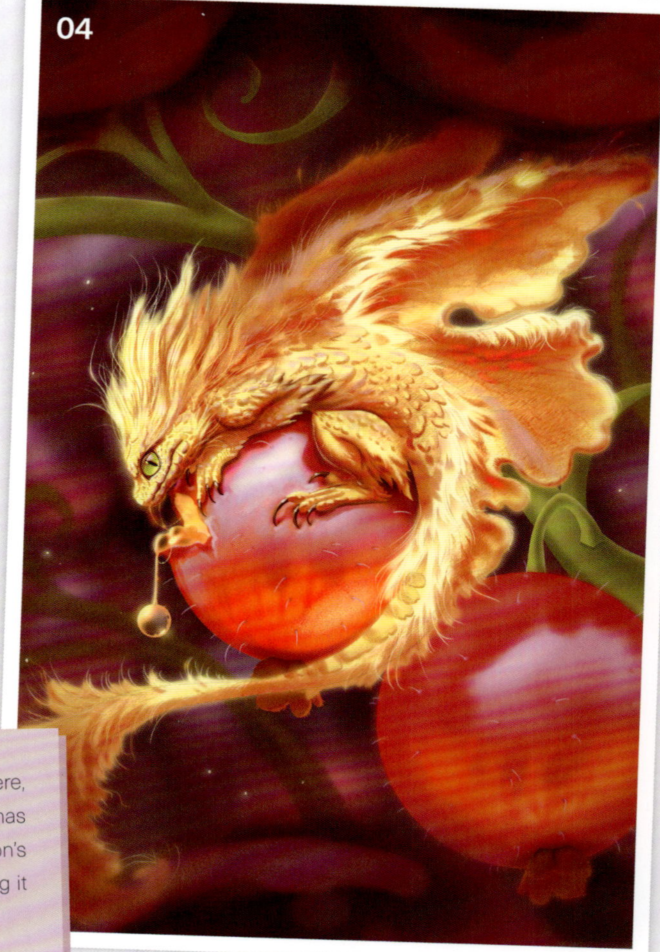

01. In the initial phase of my artistic process I enjoy sketching the first idea that pops into my mind. This helps to preserve the freshness and immediacy of my initial intuitions. I don't want to overthink things too much.

02. Opting for a non-linear workflow, I faced challenges in defining the volumes. I decided to seek help from references, especially checking berries and shadows. I integrated them into the painting and this gave me new motivation to continue.

03. I kept adding details and defining my dragon's body, scales, and fur. After establishing a chunkier base for the fur, I enjoyed drawing intricate individual hairs with a thin brush, adding realism and depth.

04. My favourite step is adding lighting and atmosphere, bringing the drawing to life. While the final piece has a magical fairy-tale feel, I intentionally kept the dragon's eye sharp, hinting at its unfriendly nature, and suggesting it might bite or swiftly flee if you get too close!

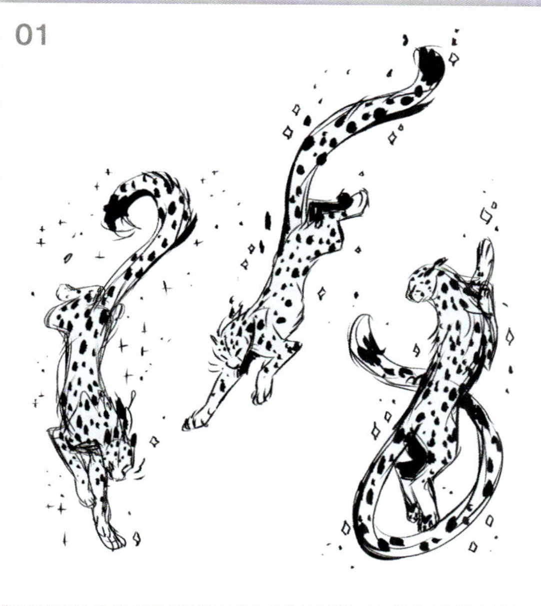

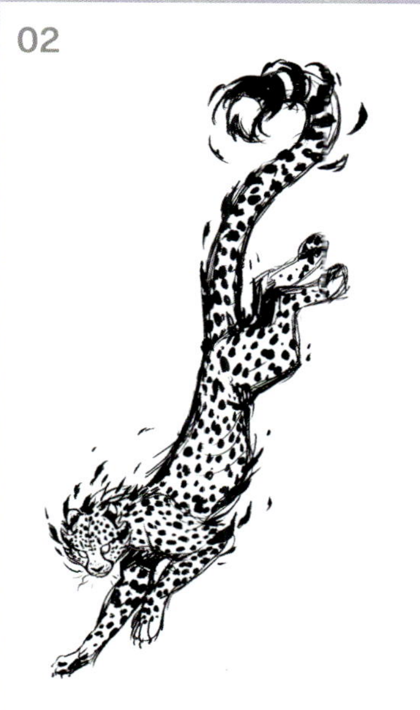

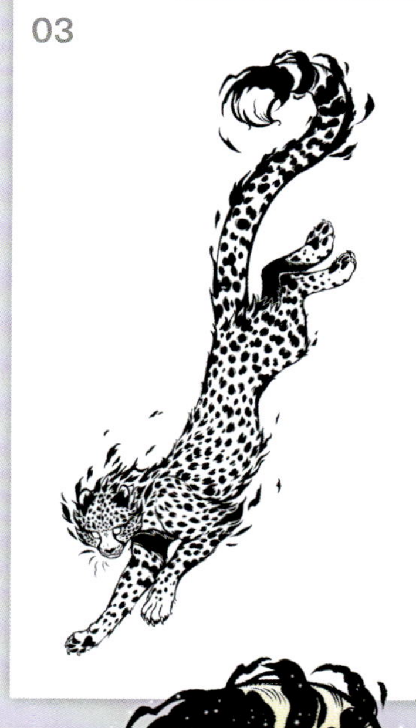

01. I believe many of us have encountered that moment when we present a client with choices and they select the sketch we like the least. Here, my preferred design was the left-most design, but the client wanted the middle option, which has a rather standard pose.

02. Moving forward with someone else's choice of sketch can limit our creativity – creating a polished sketch before diving into the official lines can help you to appreciate the design more. I began to adore this piece when, almost casually, I added spots to the cheetah's tail.

03. After completing all the corrections to the lines, I can relax and apply the definitive strokes, guided by the previous sketch. I love that this pose actually led me to create something I would have never thought of doing.

04. I finish this piece by adding lively colours that harmonize with the pose and mood of the artwork. Your artistic instincts guide this phase – trust your eyes and your client's going to love it!

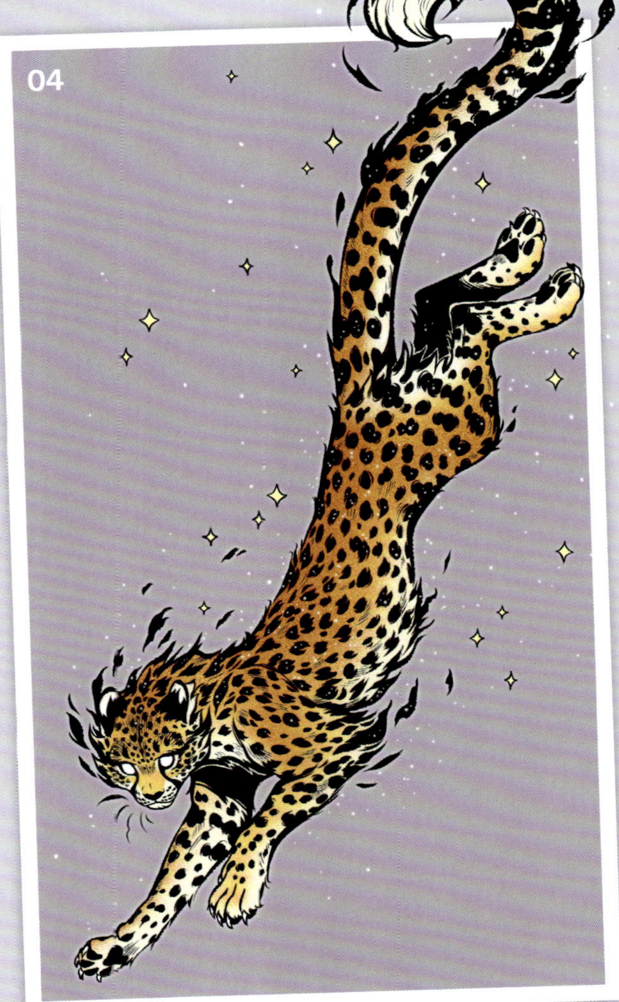

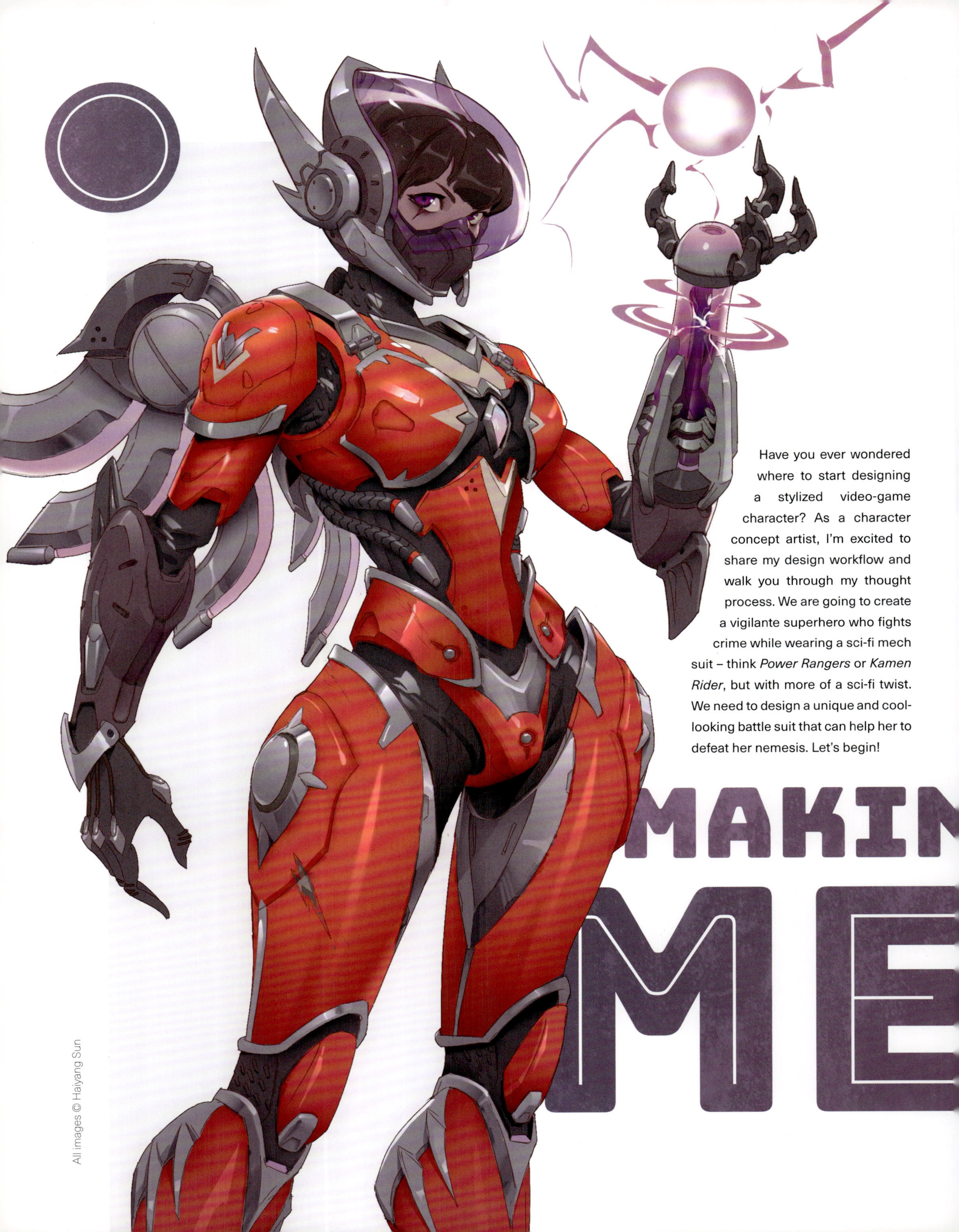

Have you ever wondered where to start designing a stylized video-game character? As a character concept artist, I'm excited to share my design workflow and walk you through my thought process. We are going to create a vigilante superhero who fights crime while wearing a sci-fi mech suit – think *Power Rangers* or *Kamen Rider*, but with more of a sci-fi twist. We need to design a unique and cool-looking battle suit that can help her to defeat her nemesis. Let's begin!

MAKIN
ME

I start by brainstorming various ideas, focusing on balancing the 'mech' and 'sci-fi' parts of the brief. Since mechs are usually quite abstract, I consider adding animalistic elements to the design. It's also important that I specify the type of sci-fi setting I want to create – do we want to go to the future, the past, or a parallel universe? Focusing on atompunk designs of the 50s and 60s would be a cool twist. Expand on your initial ideas as much as possible and look for opportunities to create interesting new designs.

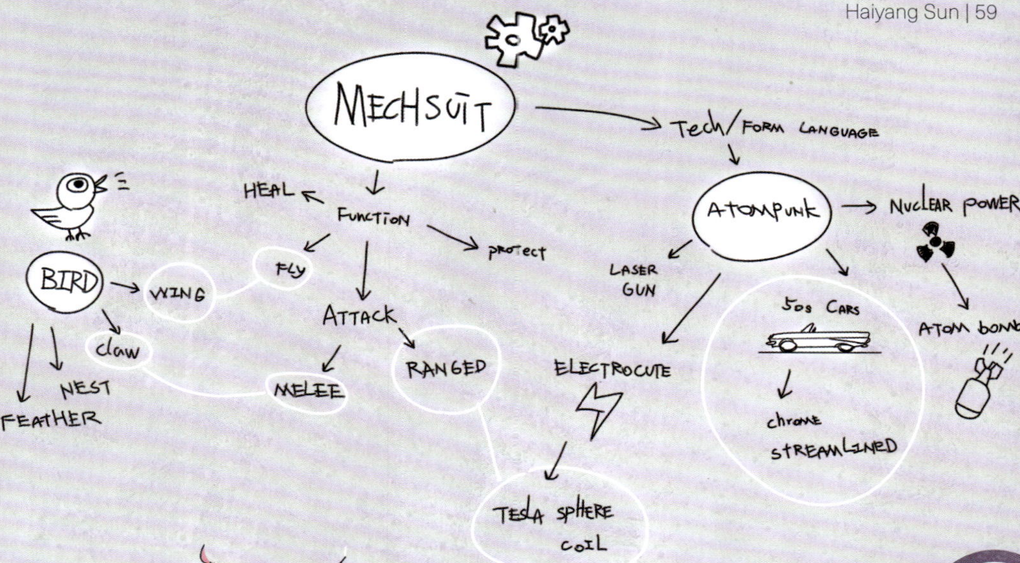

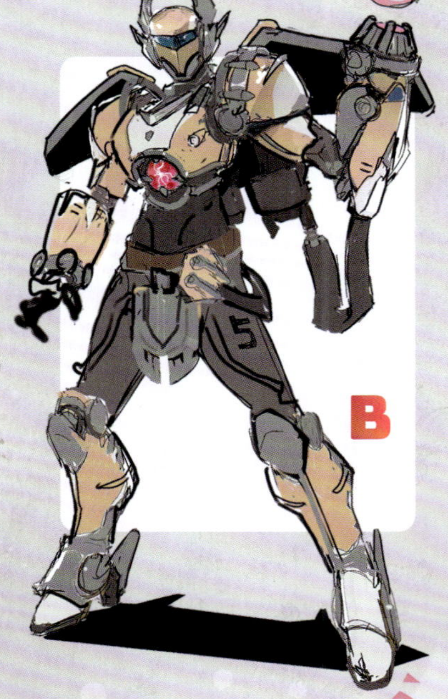

After working through the brainstorming session, I decide on an interesting direction: a vigilante superhero wearing a bird-like mech suit, with atompunk-inspired form language. I make three sketches exploring different body types, shapes, and interpretations of the prompt.

I like different things in my three sketches, particularly the shape of A and the weapon from B. Sketch C is cool but the design is maybe too heavy for a vigilante hero.

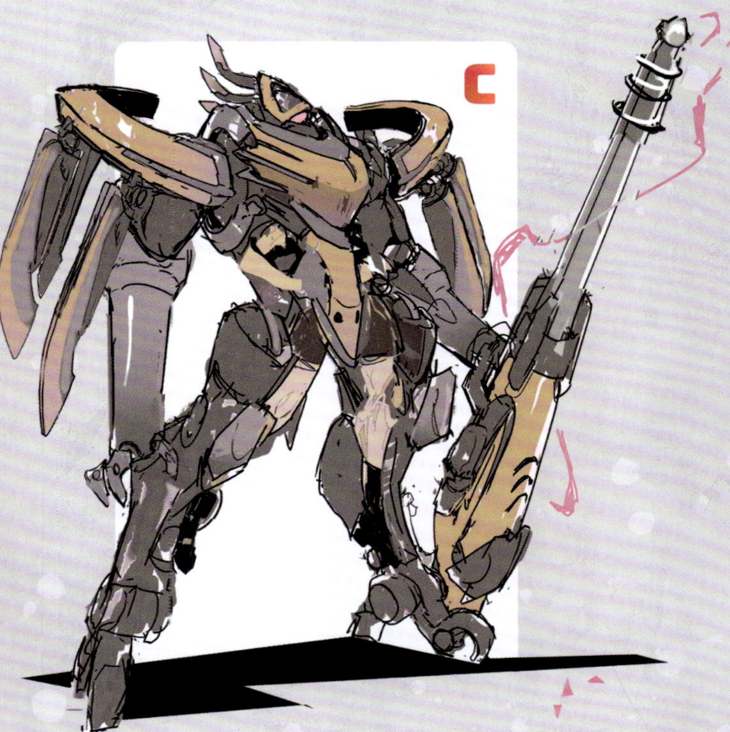

I combine my different ideas for the character and start work on a final drawing. The key is to keep shapes organized and make sure they look functional. Be careful how much detail you add to the character when creating the final line work. Include more information around the focal point of the design and leave empty areas for the viewer's eye to rest elsewhere on the design.

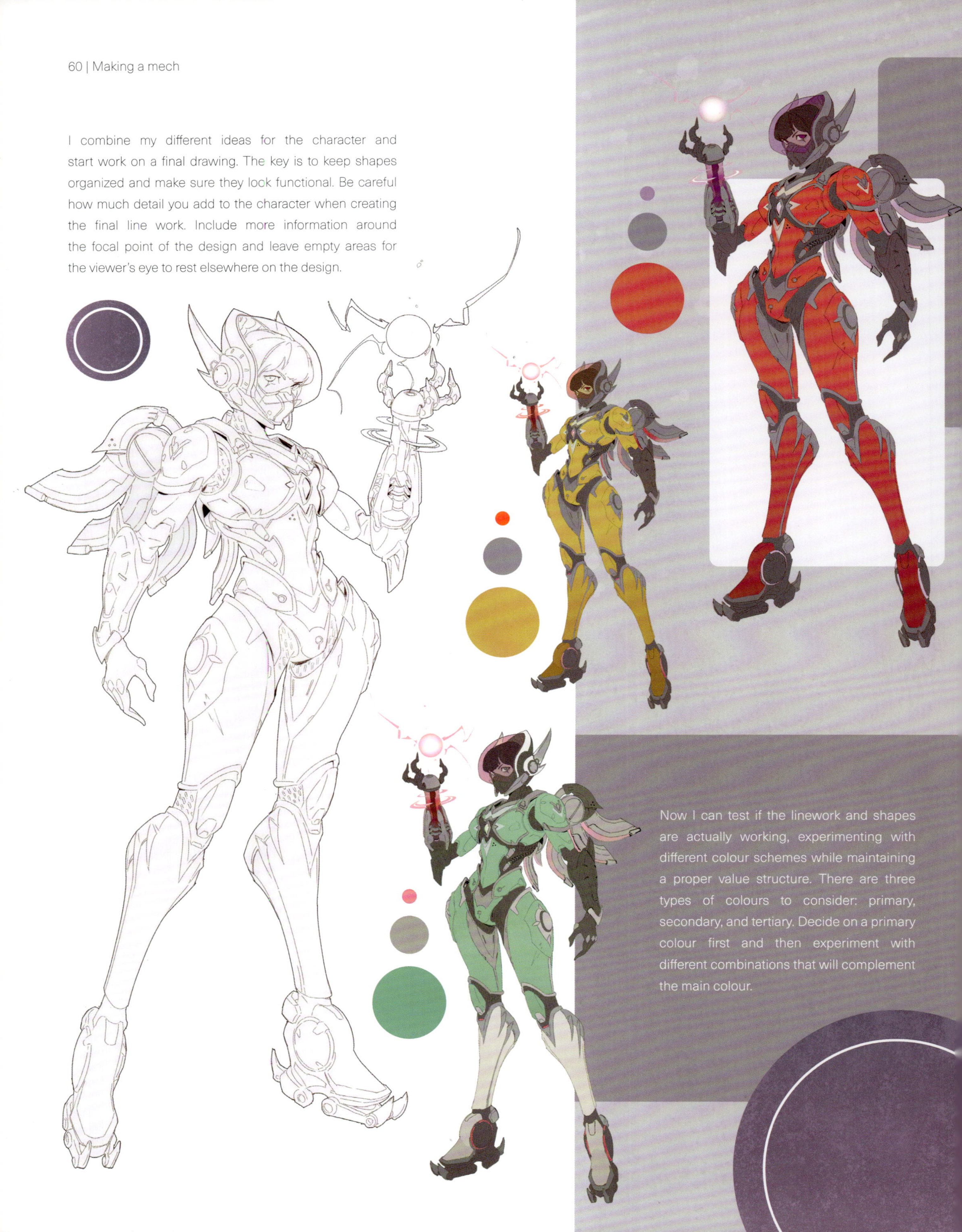

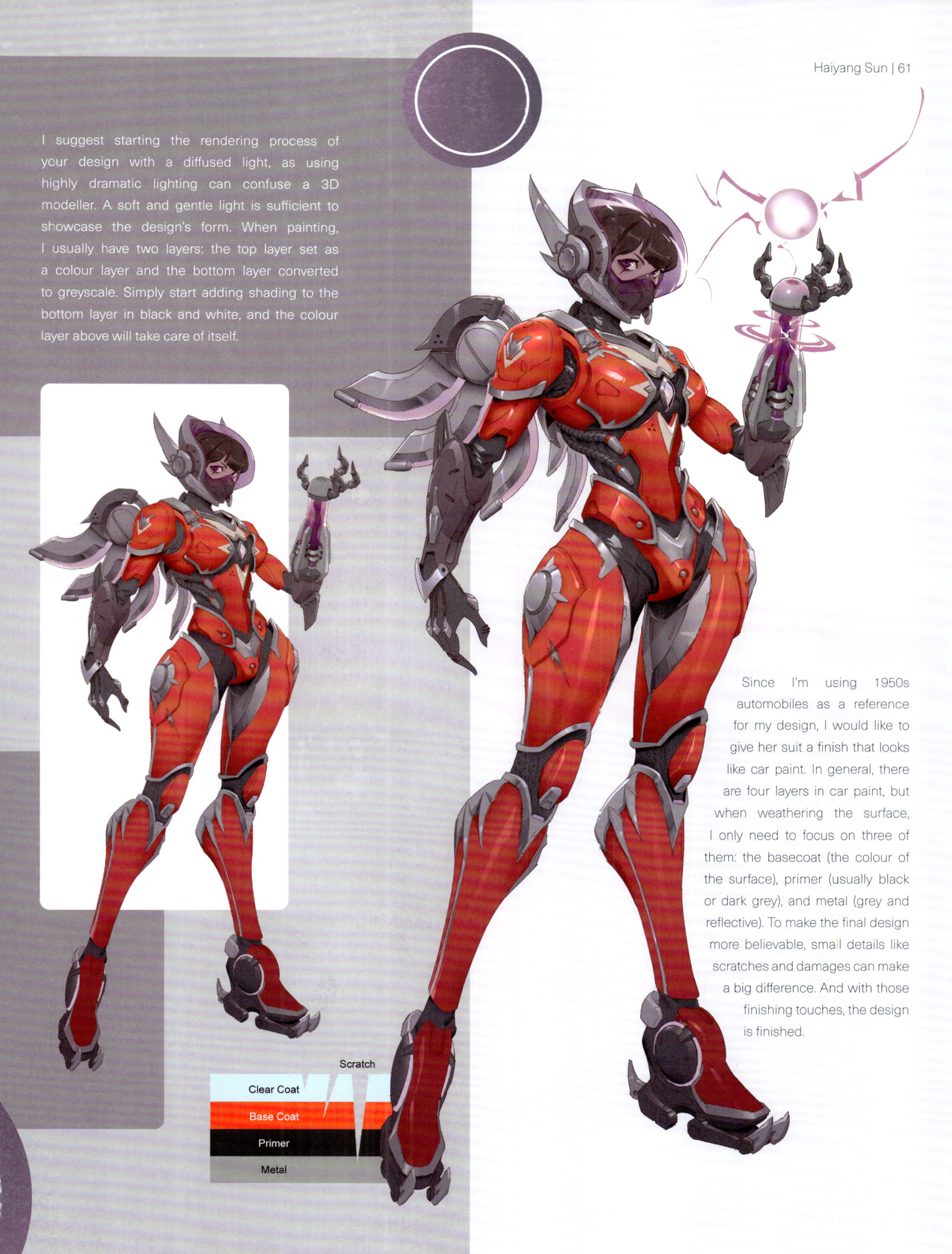

I suggest starting the rendering process of your design with a diffused light, as using highly dramatic lighting can confuse a 3D modeller. A soft and gentle light is sufficient to showcase the design's form. When painting, I usually have two layers: the top layer set as a colour layer and the bottom layer converted to greyscale. Simply start adding shading to the bottom layer in black and white, and the colour layer above will take care of itself.

Since I'm using 1950s automobiles as a reference for my design, I would like to give her suit a finish that looks like car paint. In general, there are four layers in car paint, but when weathering the surface, I only need to focus on three of them: the basecoat (the colour of the surface), primer (usually black or dark grey), and metal (grey and reflective). To make the final design more believable, small details like scratches and damages can make a big difference. And with those finishing touches, the design is finished.

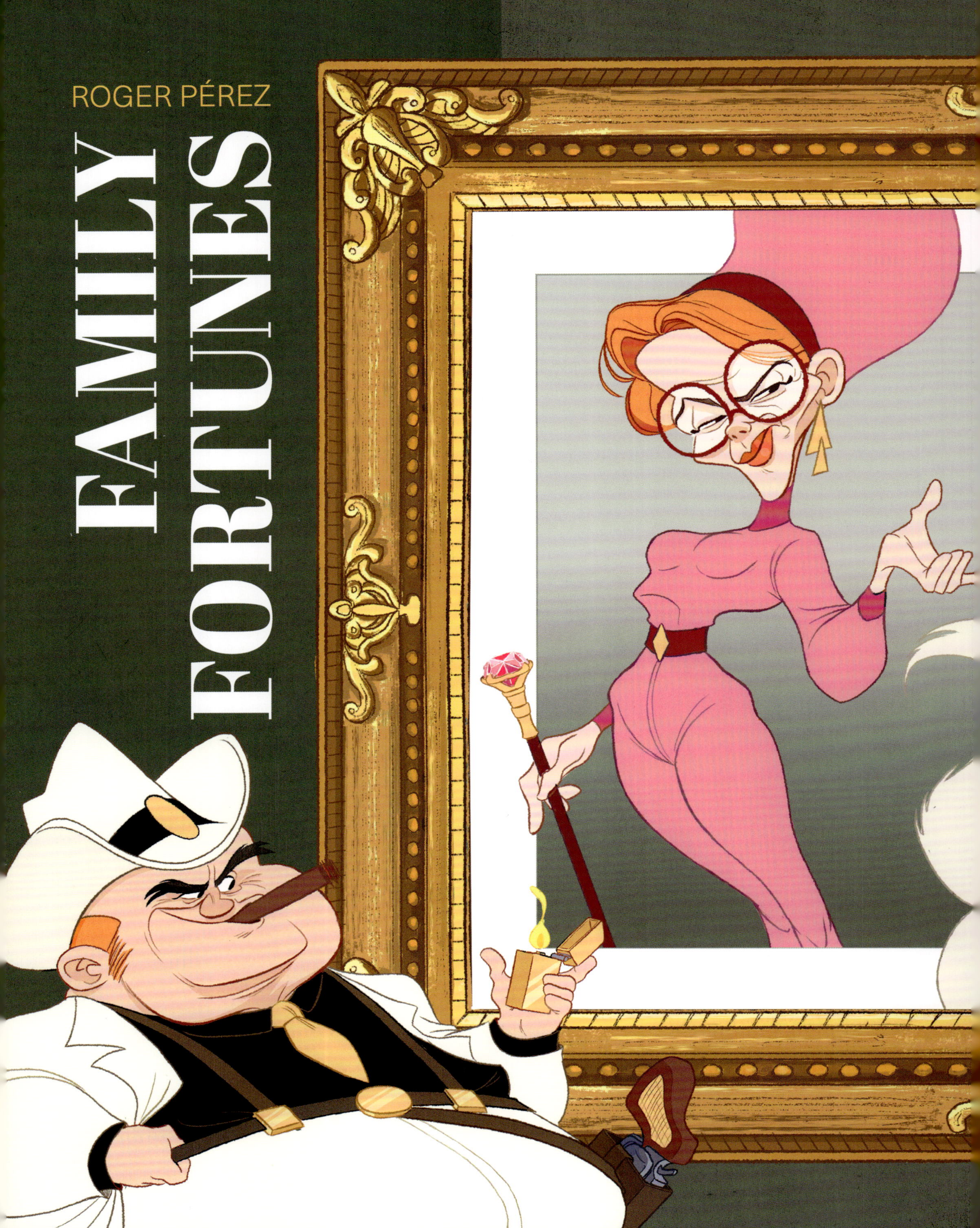

ROGER PÉREZ
FAMILY FORTUNES

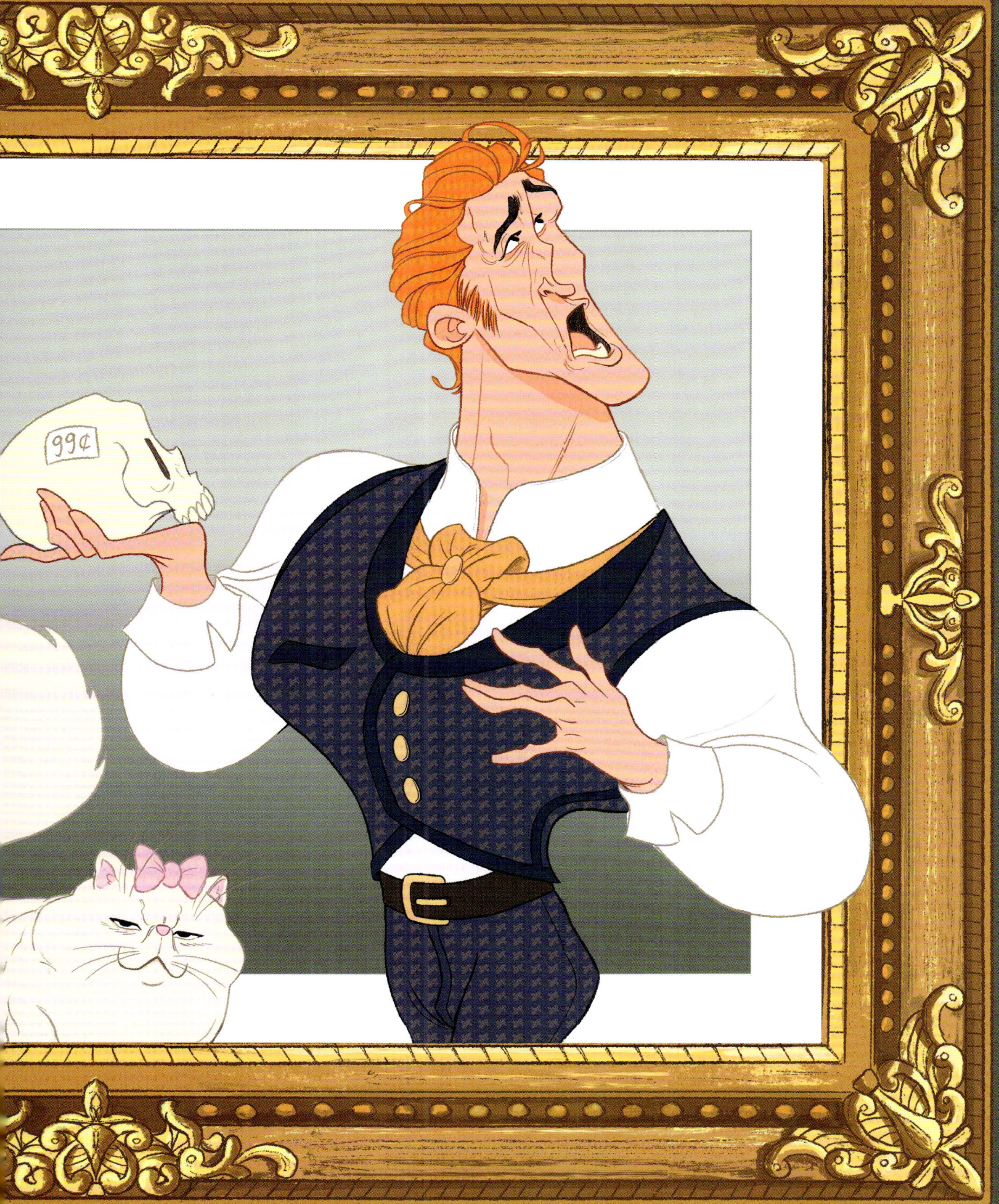
99¢

LADY EUPHEMIA CUNNINGHAM IV

The press went wild last week with news of the death of famed billionaire Lady Euphemia Cunningham IV at the age of 80, leaving an immense fortune to be divided among her heirs. Now her family has gathered to 'talk' about the inheritance – and mourn their loss, of course! Who will end up taking the lion's share? Ready? Fight!

For this tutorial, I was tasked with creating a cast of characters that are unique, but all related in some way. I chose to create the three children of Lady Euphemia, peculiar members of a family of eccentric billionaires. Join me as I work through the steps to create their final designs. I will be using Photoshop throughout.

When creating the three siblings we need to make sure that their personalities and physiques are distinct, while still clearly related to one another. I start by looking for references for each of them.

GERTRUDE
THE SOCIALITE

Gertrude is the eldest of the three, sophisticated, and posh. She says she works, but no one really knows what she does. I use Glenn Close, Iris Apfel, and Katherine Hepburn as references for her model.

TRISTAN
THE ACTOR

The youngest of the family, Tristan is cocky and conceited. He supposedly receives thousands of offers to perform on the best stages in the world, but he turns them down, waiting for a role that is up to his high standards. Bruce Campbell, Rupert Everett, and Hugh Jackman are my references for this character.

FRANCIS
THE BUSINESSMAN

The middle of the three children, Francis is a greedy, swindling businessman. He owns a thriving business selling second-hand appliances that he claims almost never fail. I look at images of Danny De Vito, Zero Mostel, and John Candy for inspiration.

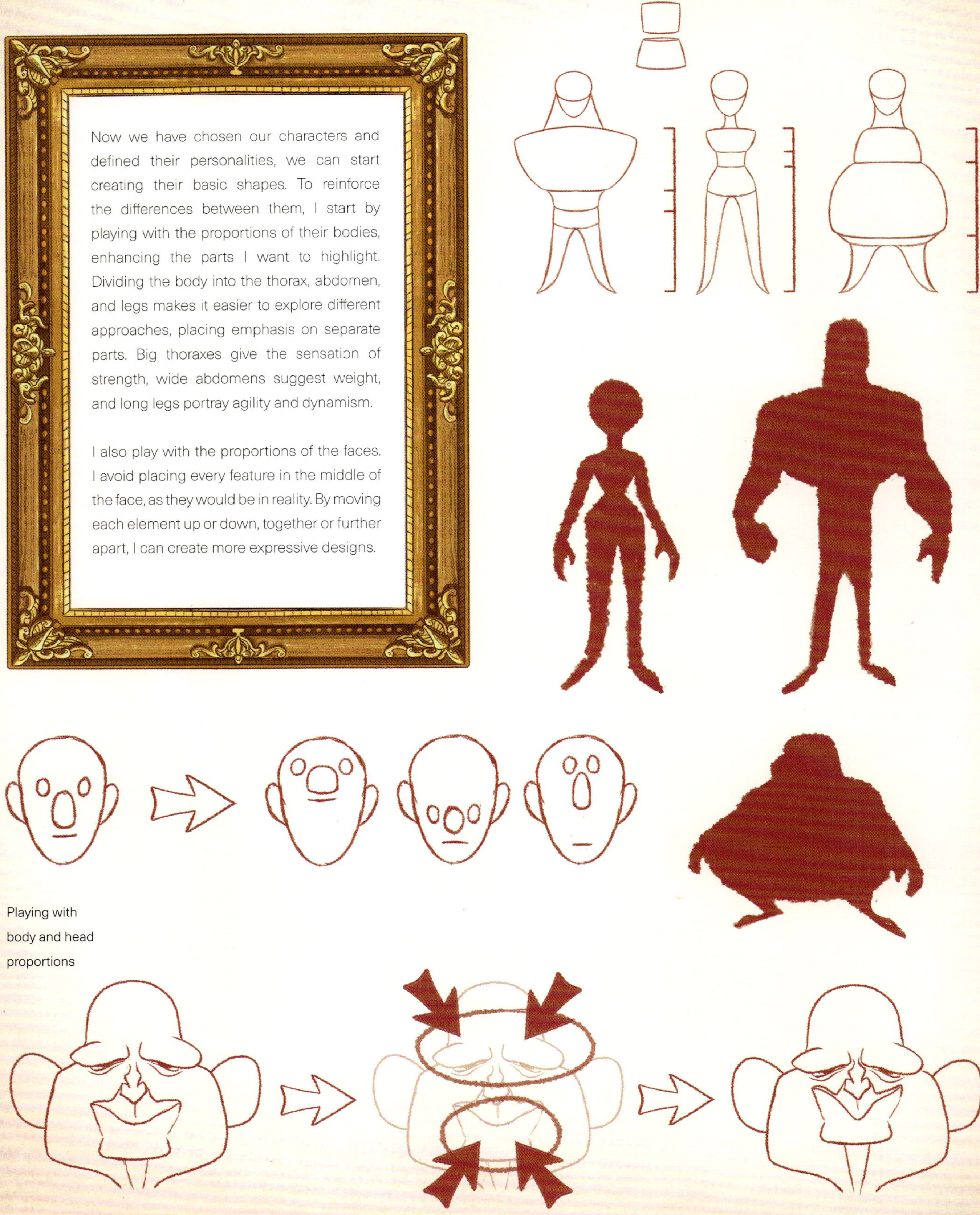

Now we have chosen our characters and defined their personalities, we can start creating their basic shapes. To reinforce the differences between them, I start by playing with the proportions of their bodies, enhancing the parts I want to highlight. Dividing the body into the thorax, abdomen, and legs makes it easier to explore different approaches, placing emphasis on separate parts. Big thoraxes give the sensation of strength, wide abdomens suggest weight, and long legs portray agility and dynamism.

I also play with the proportions of the faces. I avoid placing every feature in the middle of the face, as they would be in reality. By moving each element up or down, together or further apart, I can create more expressive designs.

Playing with
body and head
proportions

Basing the design of each character on simple geometric shapes helps us to create faces and bodies that look unique at first glance. I sketch a series of faces based on square, triangular, or round shapes, which helps me get an idea of what we're looking for.

Round shapes give us a sense of softness and are good for gentle or physically harmless characters. Triangular shapes convey aggression and danger, ideal for edgy characters. Square shapes bring stability to the design, ideal for portraying stoicism or characters with a strong physique.

Picking the shape that matches the character's personality is key

I ensure the key elements of each design are still obvious in silhouette

When drawing the characters, we need to ensure their silhouettes are clear and we can still recognize the key parts of their design. If we can't tell from the outline of a character who it is or what they are doing, then we should look for a more legible pose. I make sure to leave empty space between the different parts of the body that I want to be recognizable, so that they still stand out even if they are integrated within the silhouette of others.

We must also make sure that the attitude and pose of our characters is exaggerated, so that we can tell what their role in the story is from just a single drawing. The lines of action can help to give more dynamism, even in static poses.

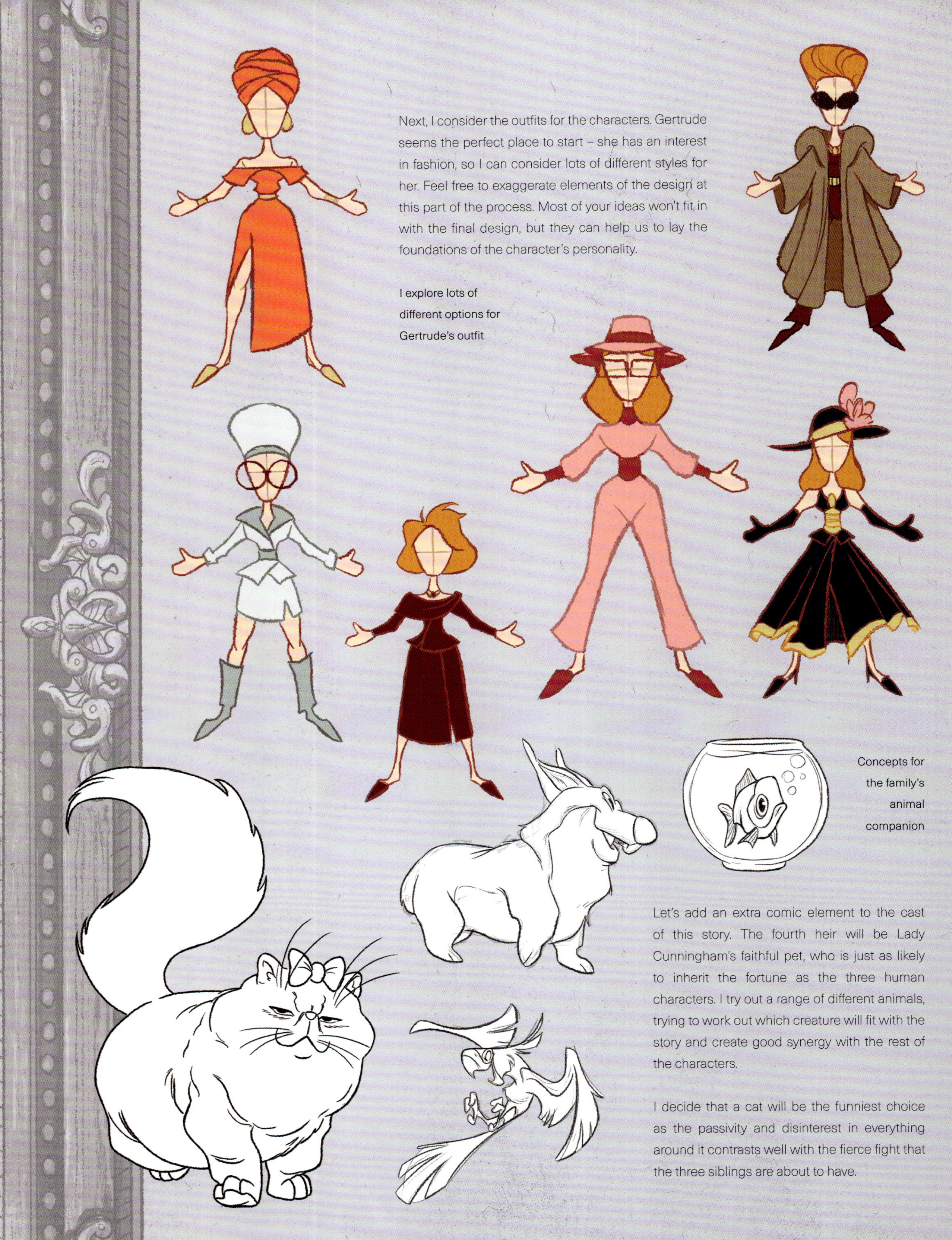

Next, I consider the outfits for the characters. Gertrude seems the perfect place to start – she has an interest in fashion, so I can consider lots of different styles for her. Feel free to exaggerate elements of the design at this part of the process. Most of your ideas won't fit in with the final design, but they can help us to lay the foundations of the character's personality.

I explore lots of different options for Gertrude's outfit

Concepts for the family's animal companion

Let's add an extra comic element to the cast of this story. The fourth heir will be Lady Cunningham's faithful pet, who is just as likely to inherit the fortune as the three human characters. I try out a range of different animals, trying to work out which creature will fit with the story and create good synergy with the rest of the characters.

I decide that a cat will be the funniest choice as the passivity and disinterest in everything around it contrasts well with the fierce fight that the three siblings are about to have.

We now have enough elements in place to start designing the final characters, starting with the line work. It's very important to make sure that we're respecting the volumes of the characters so that they don't look flat, and on the other hand focus the details in those areas that we want to highlight (usually the face or hands). I leave the less important parts of each body looking much cleaner, so that the eye is not directed towards them.

I select everything I have workshopped so far, take what works and discard what doesn't, until the final design starts to emerge. Once I'm happy that every part of the design is adding to the story I'm trying to tell, I'm ready to move on to painting.

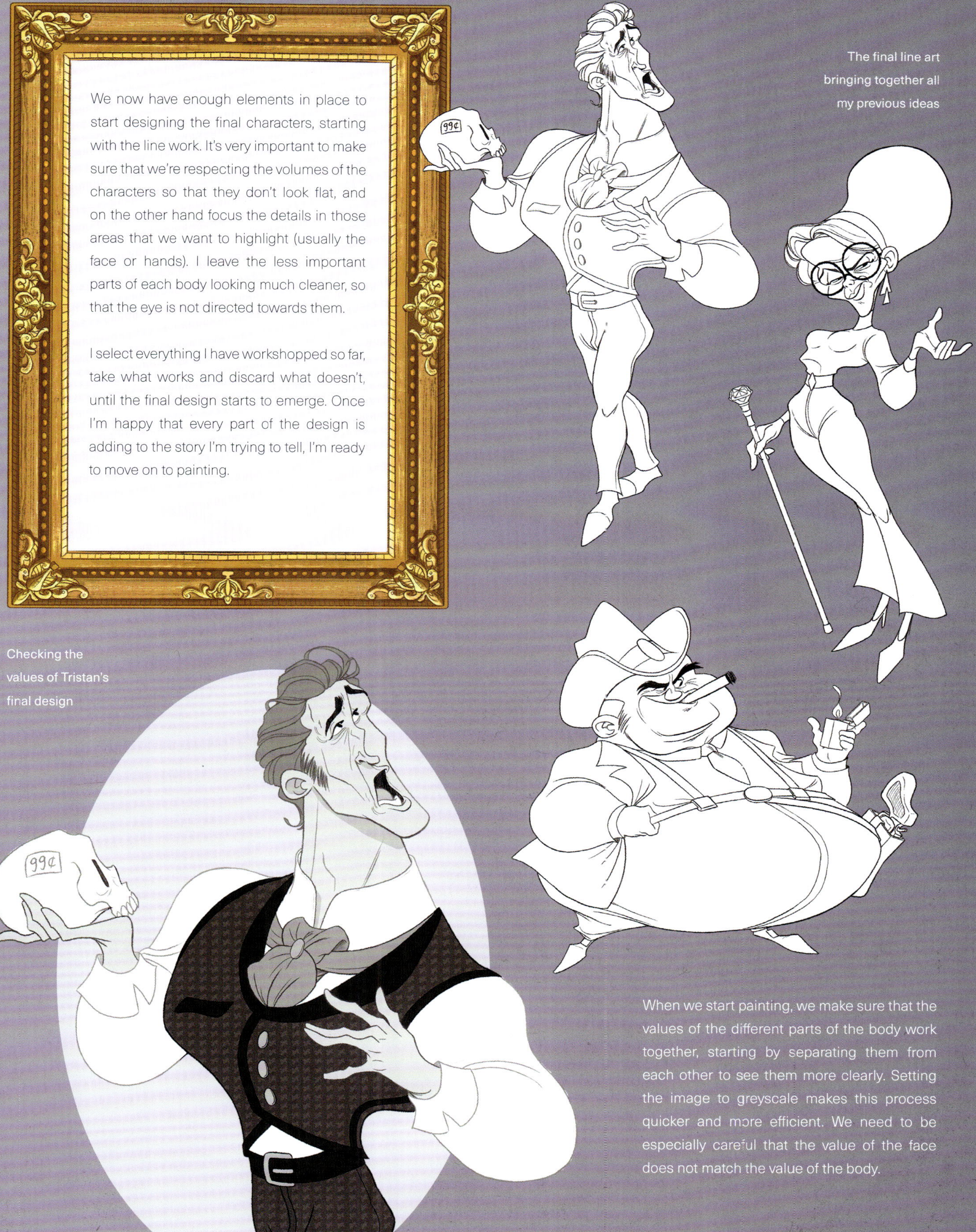

The final line art bringing together all my previous ideas

Checking the values of Tristan's final design

When we start painting, we make sure that the values of the different parts of the body work together, starting by separating them from each other to see them more clearly. Setting the image to greyscale makes this process quicker and more efficient. We need to be especially careful that the value of the face does not match the value of the body.

Try not to use extensive colour palettes, unless it fits the character's personality and context. In general, characters that are part of the same story and that are going to share scenes should have colours that aren't too dissonant.

Ideally, characters should look good with simple, flat colours. Shadows and lighting will improve any design, but if the flat colours don't work well, it's better to fix them as soon as possible.

Characters that are too saturated can look bad, or attract too much attention to unwanted places, while desaturated colours will give a design a sad, drab look.

We use colour to further the narrative wherever we can. In this case, the final touch for the three characters is to give them the same colour hair, to show they are siblings.

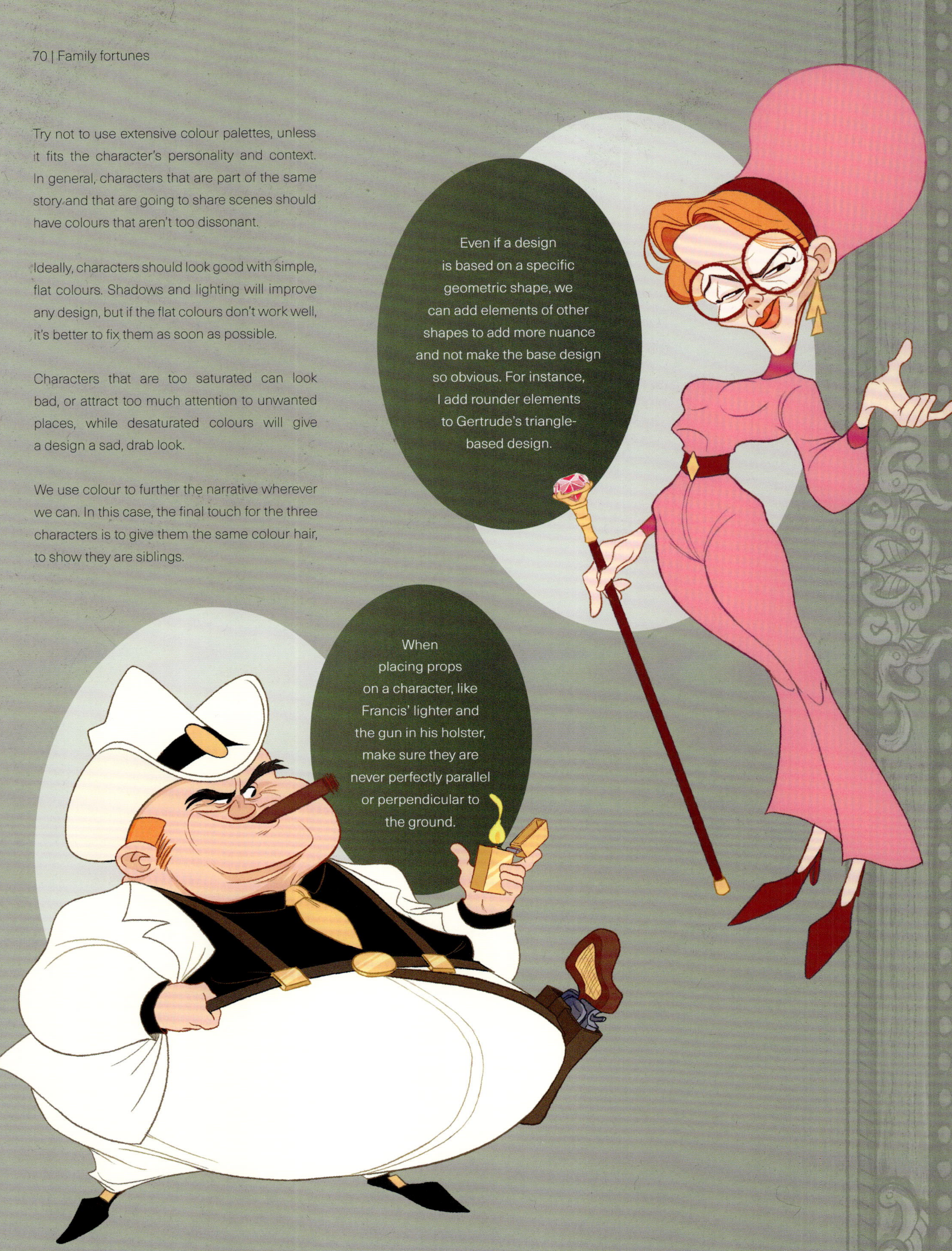

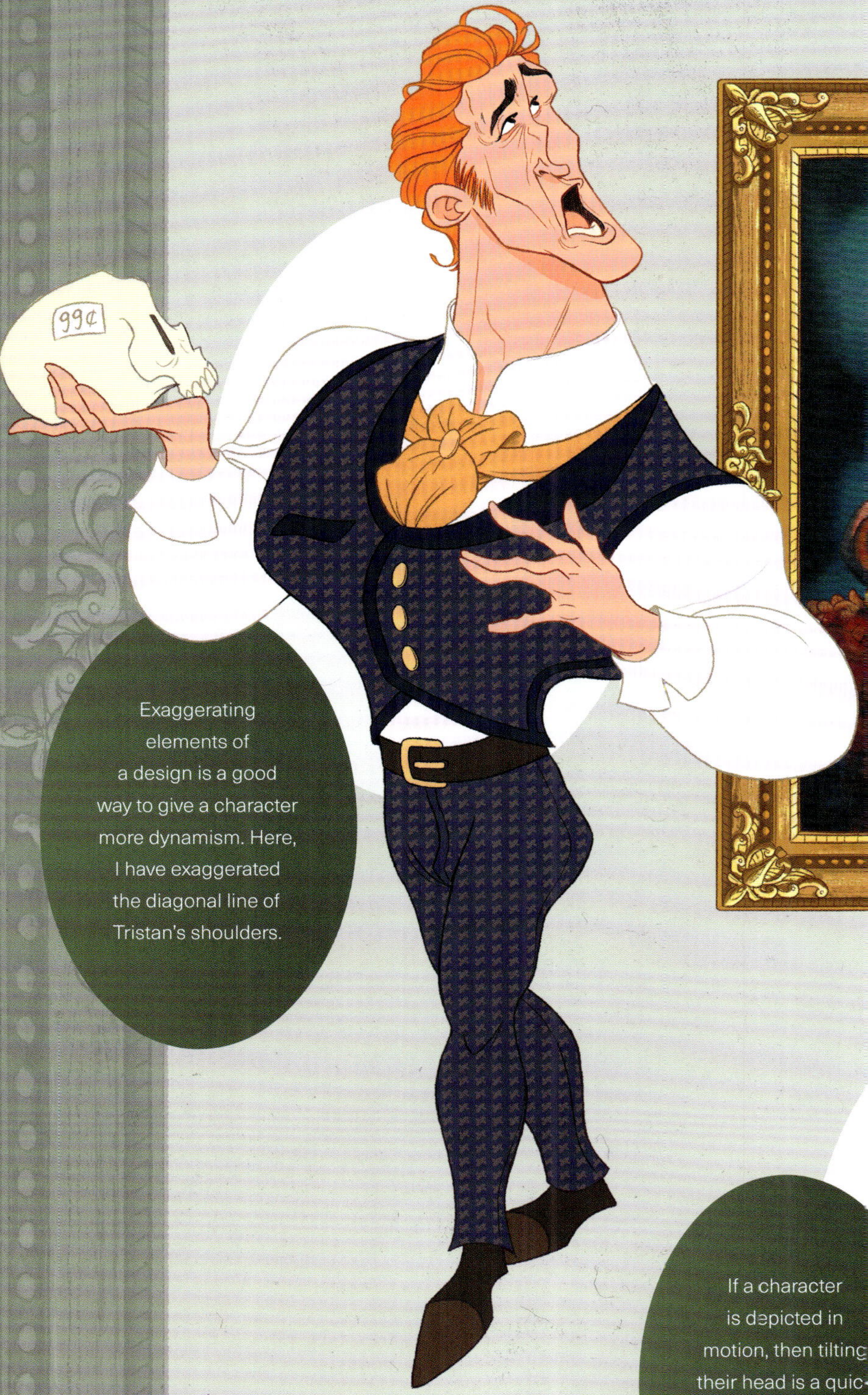

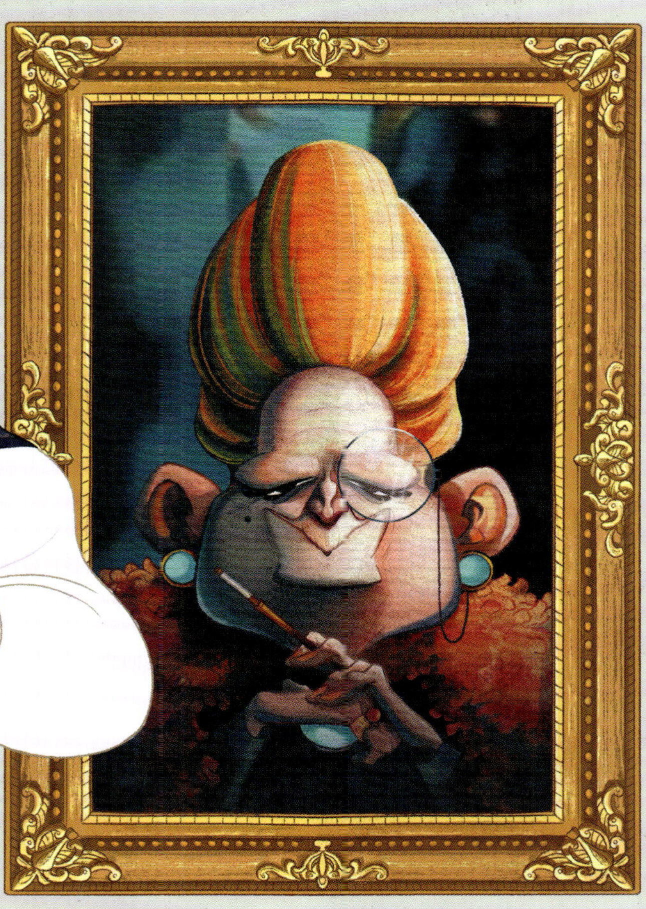

Exaggerating elements of a design is a good way to give a character more dynamism. Here, I have exaggerated the diagonal line of Tristan's shoulders.

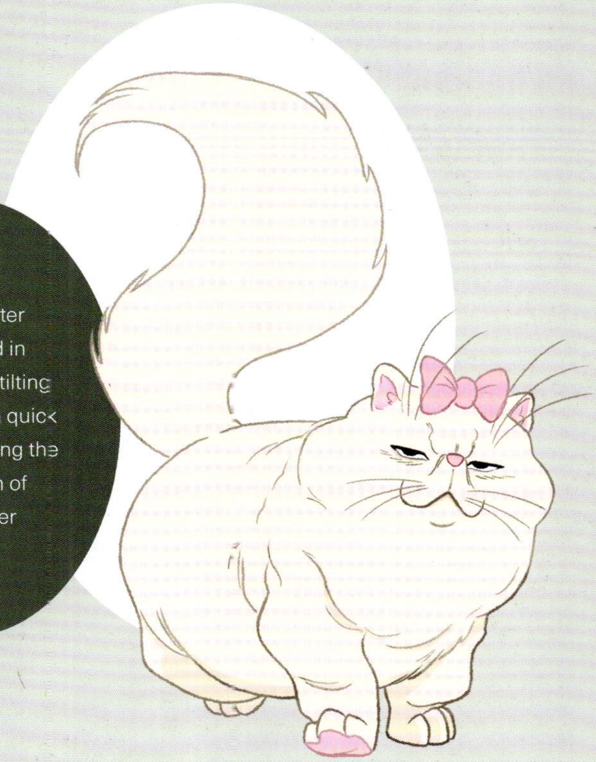

If a character is depicted in motion, then tilting their head is a quick trick for creating the impression of a character moving.

Taking time to make sure the base colours work will make adding lighting and shadow easier

MARCO FERRARIS

I'm a cartoonist and I mainly draw adventure comics for kids in France and the USA. When I create a character, I know that I will have to draw them many times throughout the book. To make sure this isn't too much of a chore, I try to limit the number of asymmetries in my designs, things like a watch on one arm, a sword scabbard on a belt, or pins and medals on their clothing. Instead, I make my characters recognizable by focusing on their shape.

01. For me, the initial draft is the most important part of the whole process. At this stage I focus on the composition and shapes of the character. It's pointless trying to have clean lines and add all the necessary details this early in the process – instead, I focus on making sure the design is visually balanced and pleasing to look at.

01

02. Next, I focus on drawing a more refined version of the design. I look for brushes that simulate the softness of a real pencil as much as possible, mixing them together to create texture. While this is my final drawing, I'm not bothered if it still looks sketchy – I want it to appear as soft and analogue as possible.

02

03

03. Colour is fundamental to my light line drawings. I start by adding a base of the dominant colour, which in this case was green. I then apply successive layers of the other colours on top, so that they are affected by the base green.

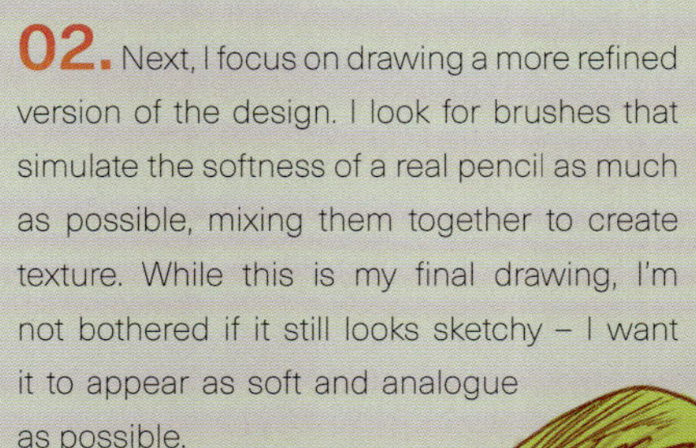

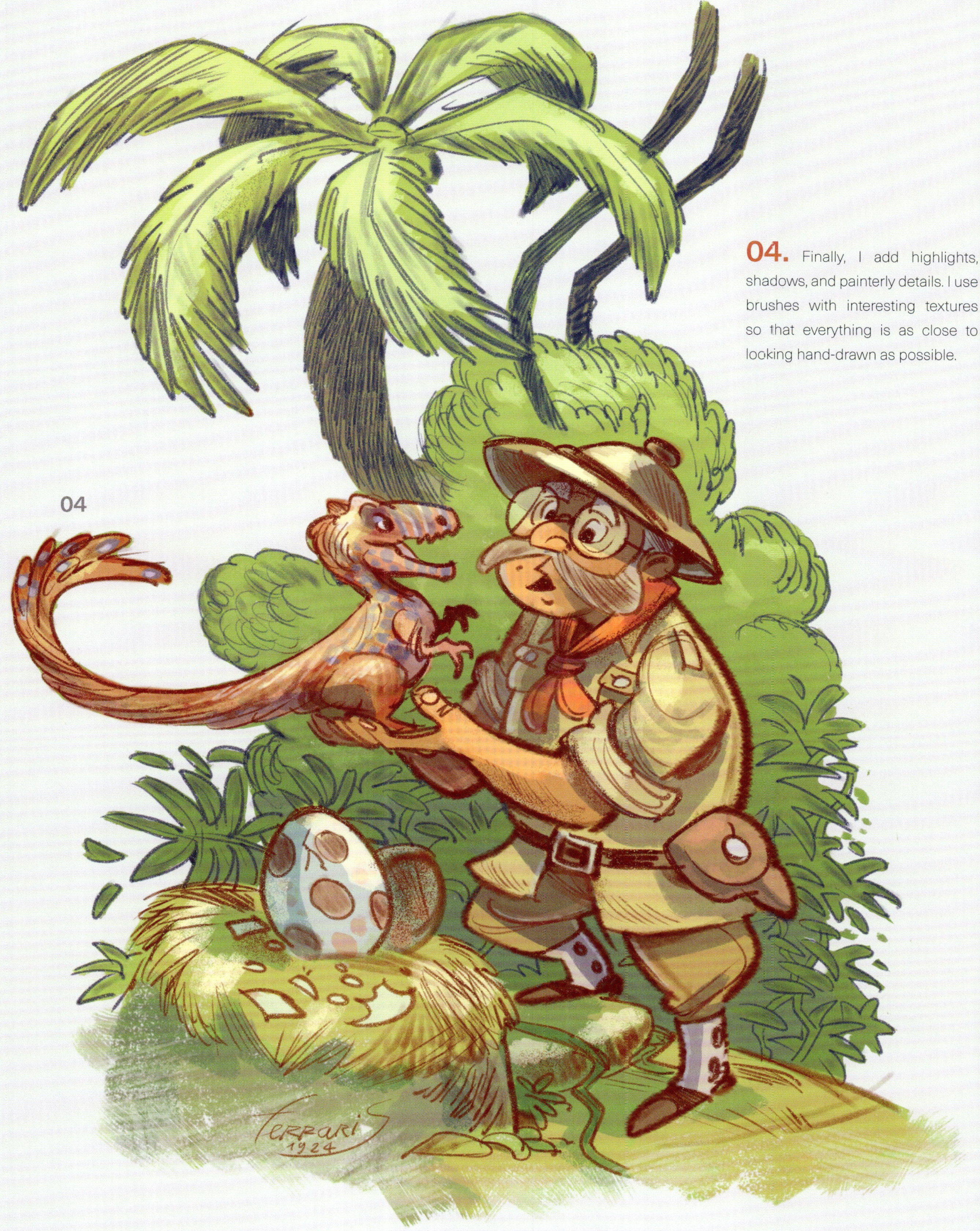

04. Finally, I add highlights, shadows, and painterly details. I use brushes with interesting textures so that everything is as close to looking hand-drawn as possible.

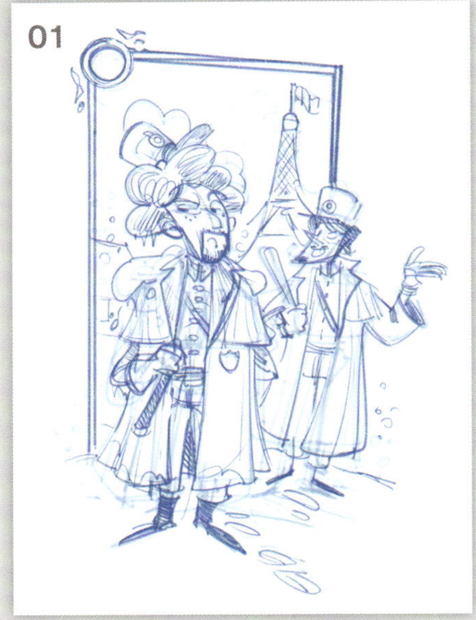

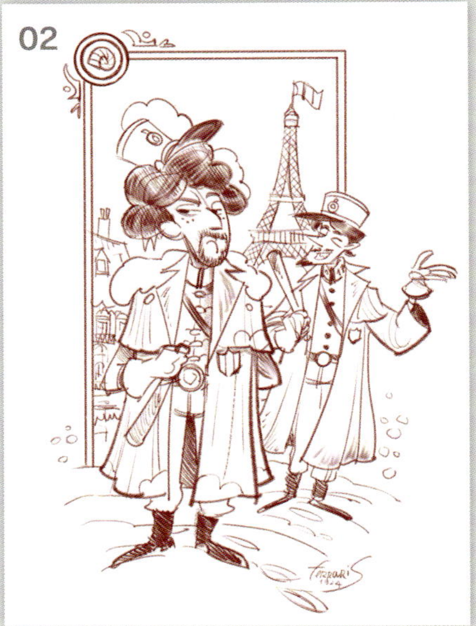

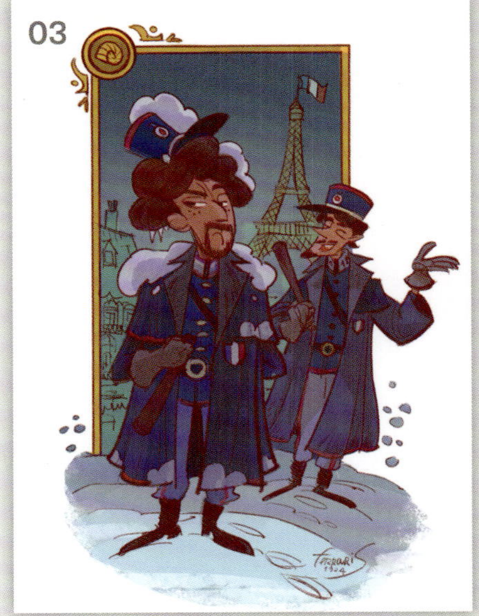

01. I find the best way to create effective characters is to draw them in skits or in small scenes. The advantages are many: the characters appear less rigid, interact with each other or the environment, and convey their personalities quickly.

02. For this drawing, I have two different characters with identical uniforms. Instead of playing with body shapes to differentiate between the two, I decided to use two characters with similar physicality, but very different faces. At this stage, I focused on the shapes of the faces and hair to make sure both characters are instantly recognizable.

03. This scene is set at night, in winter, with two characters wearing the same dark uniform, so it was essential to clearly separate the planes to detach the characters from each other and the background. Blue is a difficult colour to use, because it is often not suitable for printing.

04. I used a different colour light to completely separate the characters from the dark background. The points with greater light-dark contrast will draw the attention of the audience. For this reason, it's best to focus the greatest contrasts on the faces of the characters.

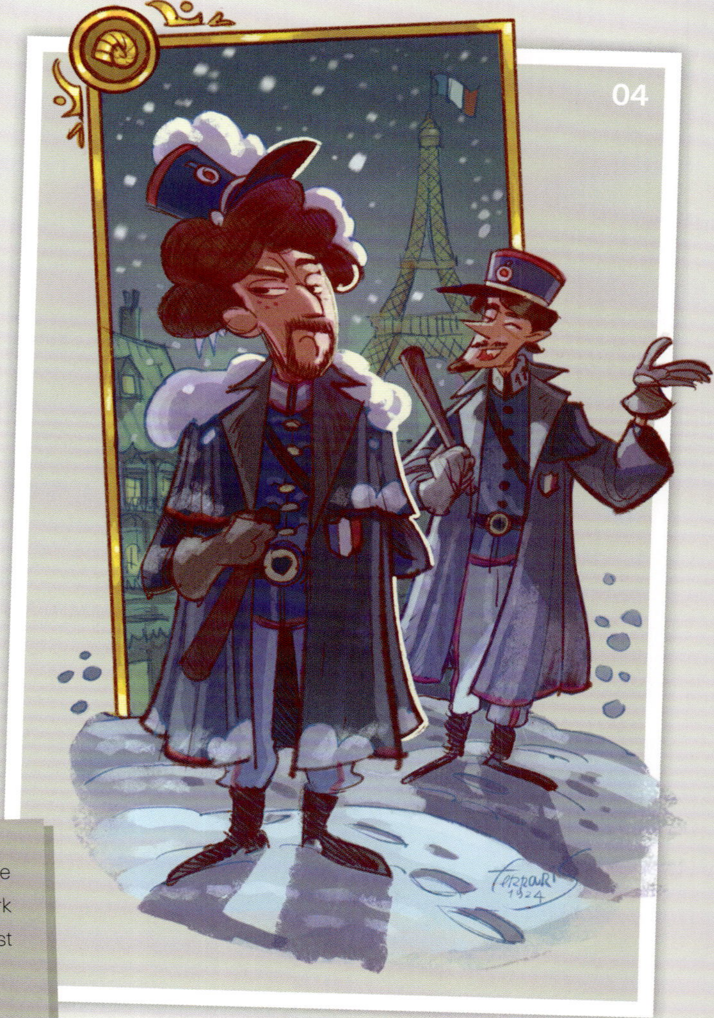

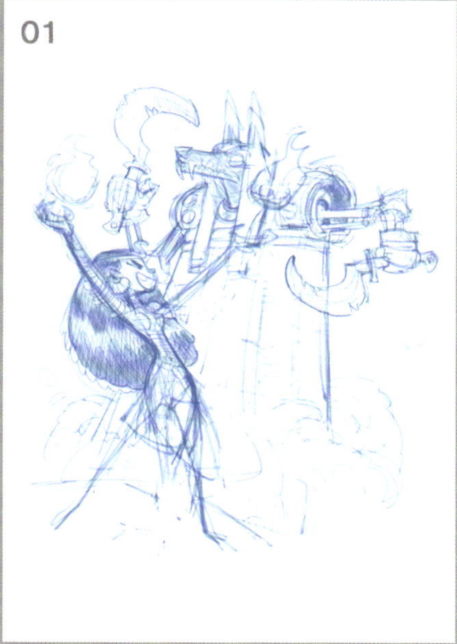

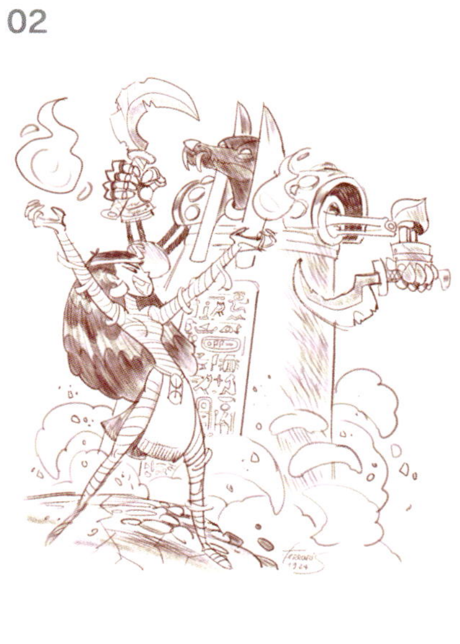

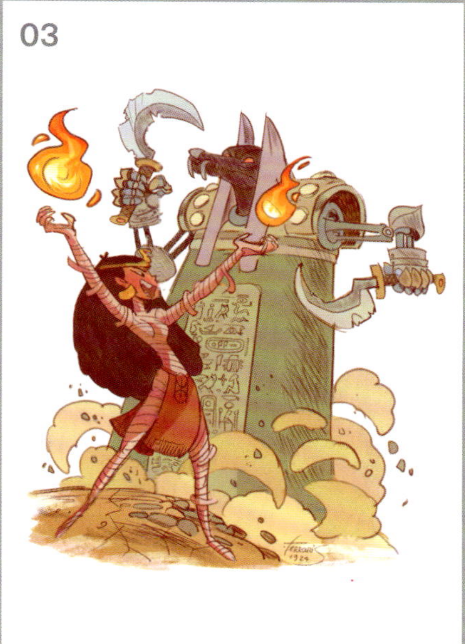

01. Simplicity is a fundamental building block of any well-drawn character. Often when working in comics or animation you will need to redraw the same character hundreds of times in different poses and in complex settings.

02. This character is curvy and slender, contrasting well with the mechanical golem, which is massive and square, inspired by an obelisk. The girl's dynamism is due to the fact that the whole design follows a single line, from her right hand to her left foot.

03. The colour palette is dictated by the context. We are in the Egyptian desert, so we expect to see a very warm palette of yellows and oranges. The girl is using fire magic, so I use a dark-red palette for her design.

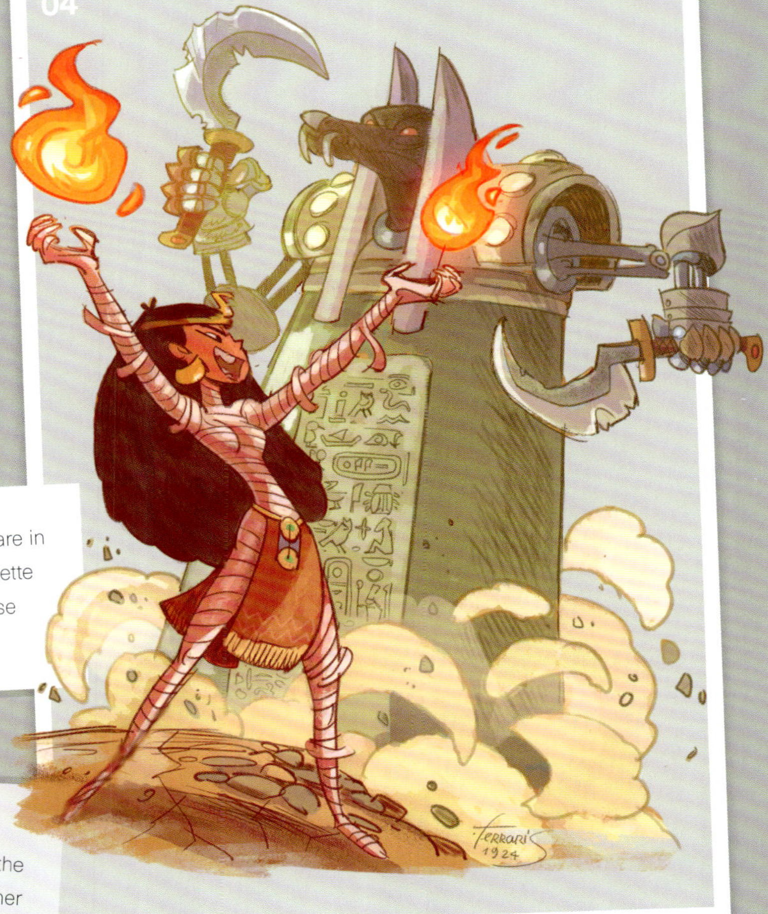

04. Colouring the strokes is a useful trick to detach distant background objects, adding depth to a drawing. Now the golem clearly appears further away than the mummy girl. I add other details and filters to further separate the planes.

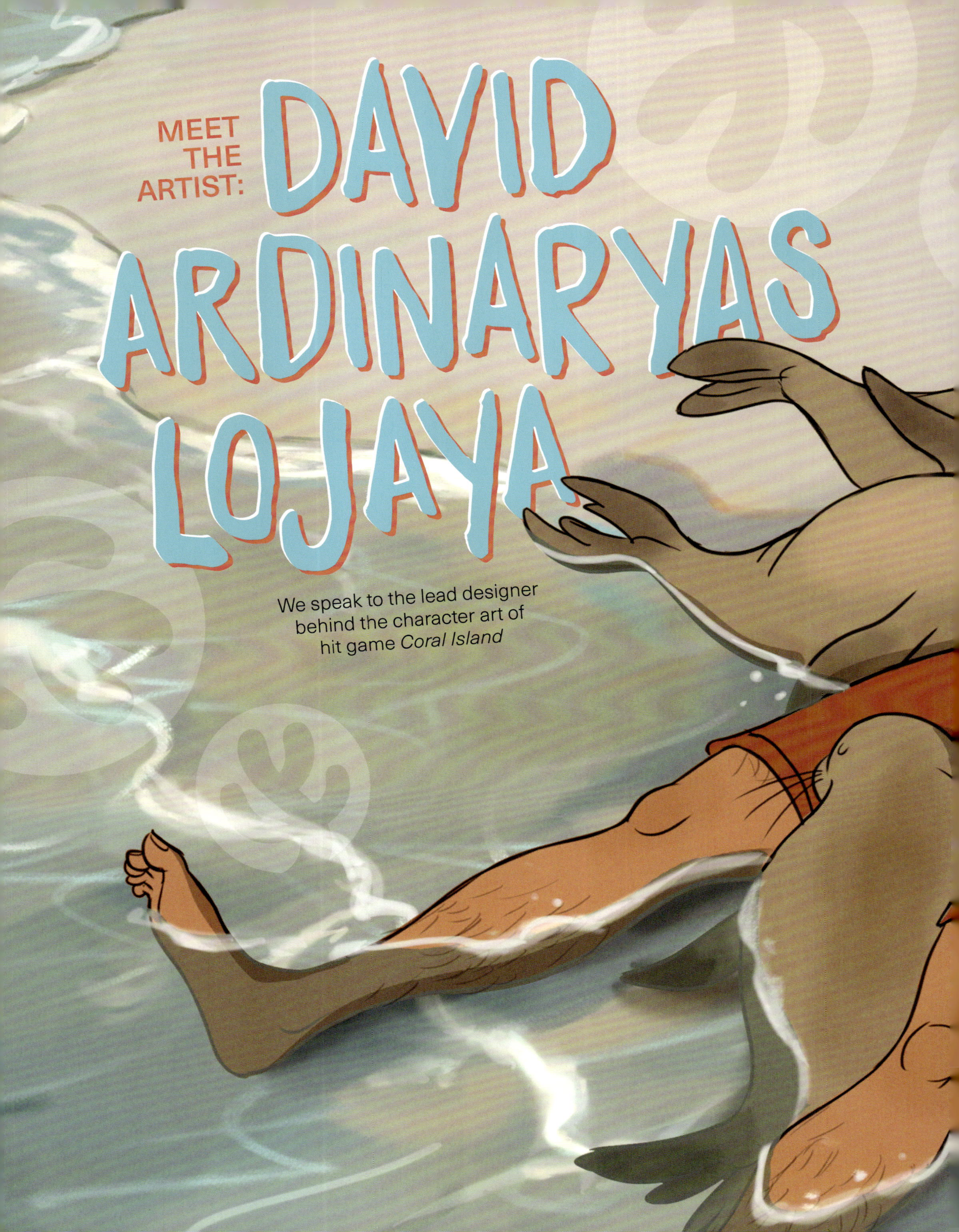

MEET THE ARTIST:
DAVID ARDINARYAS LOJAYA
We speak to the lead designer behind the character art of hit game *Coral Island*

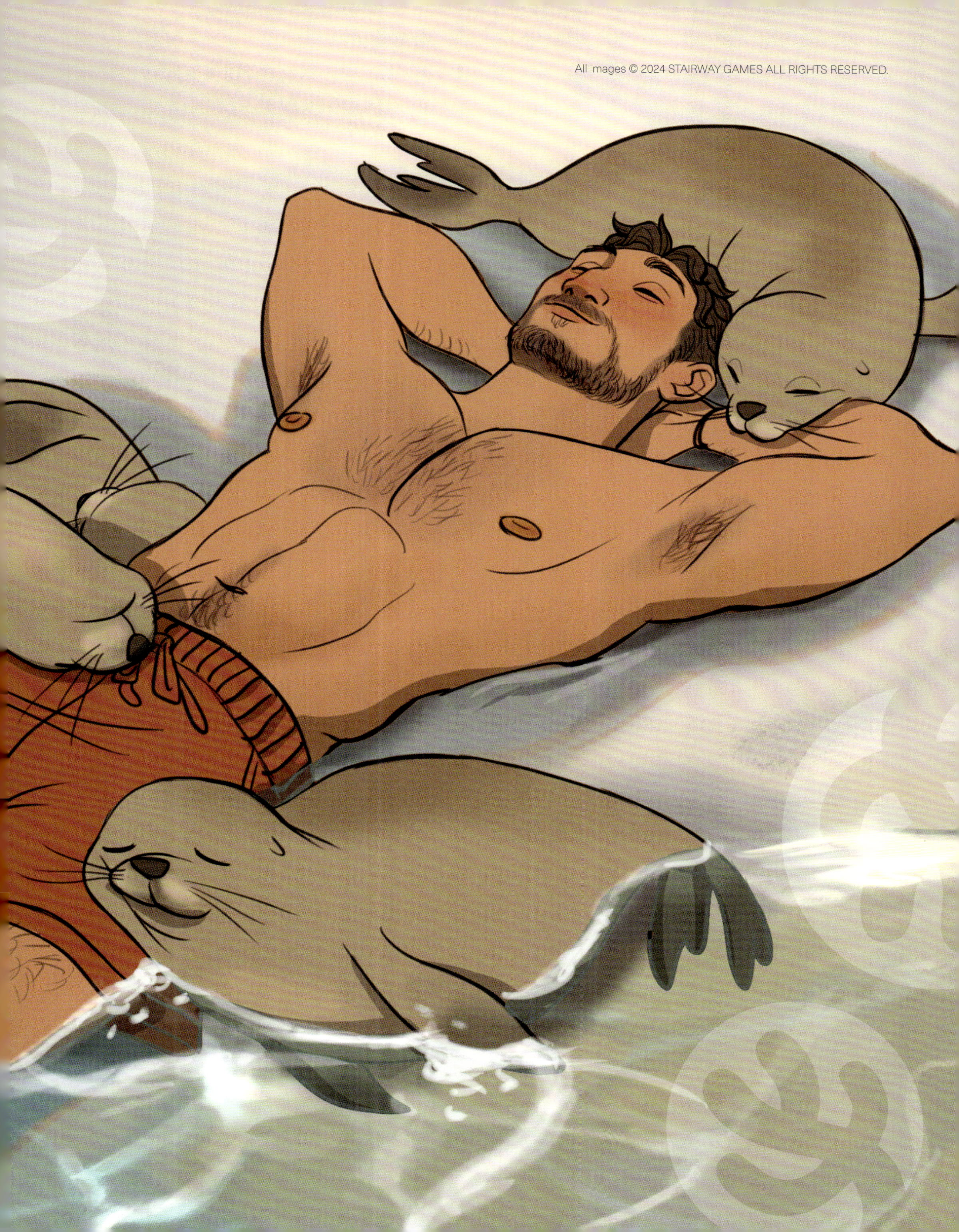

Hi David, thanks for chatting to *CDQ*! Could you start by telling our readers a little about your career so far?

Hi guys! I'm currently an art director at a game studio called Stairway Games, working on *Coral Island*, and I'm also a character designer and visual development artist for animation. I've been working professionally for twelve years, originally in the animation industry. My first job was adding 3D lighting to animated scenes. While I realized early on this wasn't my passion, it was an important step on my art journey, teaching me the fundamentals of how light and shadow work. After working for a year in this role, I took another path and became a freelance character designer and illustrator. If I'm honest, the early days of freelancing were hard, and I was grateful for the internet for finding work back then. Eventually, I was given the opportunity to become an art director on *Coral Island*.

Who and what are the inspirations behind your art style?

I grew up watching anime and Disney. My favourite show was *Doraemon*, an anime for kids about a giant blue robot cat. The first Disney film I saw was *The Little Mermaid*. I loved the underwater scenes – I drew a lot of fish back when I was a kid. So, my first drawings were in an anime-ish style, but with that Disney influence present as well. After years of watching animation, I was introduced to Ghibli films, which I love so much, and they became a great influence on my art journey as well.

I took Animation as my major at college where I was taught the Disney approach to 2D animation. My art style gradually shifted from there to the more cartoony style that I have today.

Besides animation, I also love classical painters, like Bouguereau, Waterhouse, Rembrandt, Van Gogh, and more. I find their work very sophisticated and have always strived to combine their approach with a cartoon style.

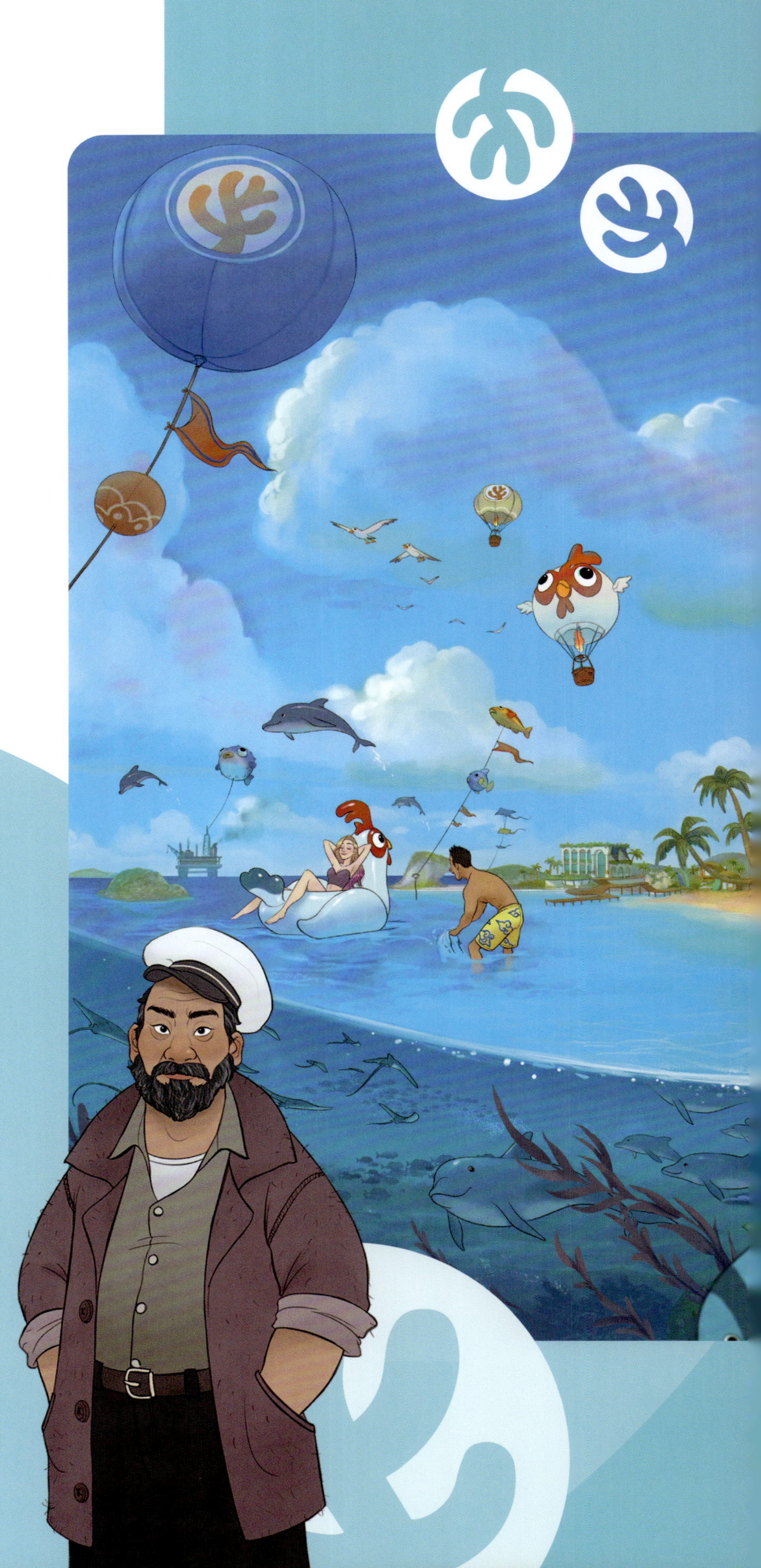

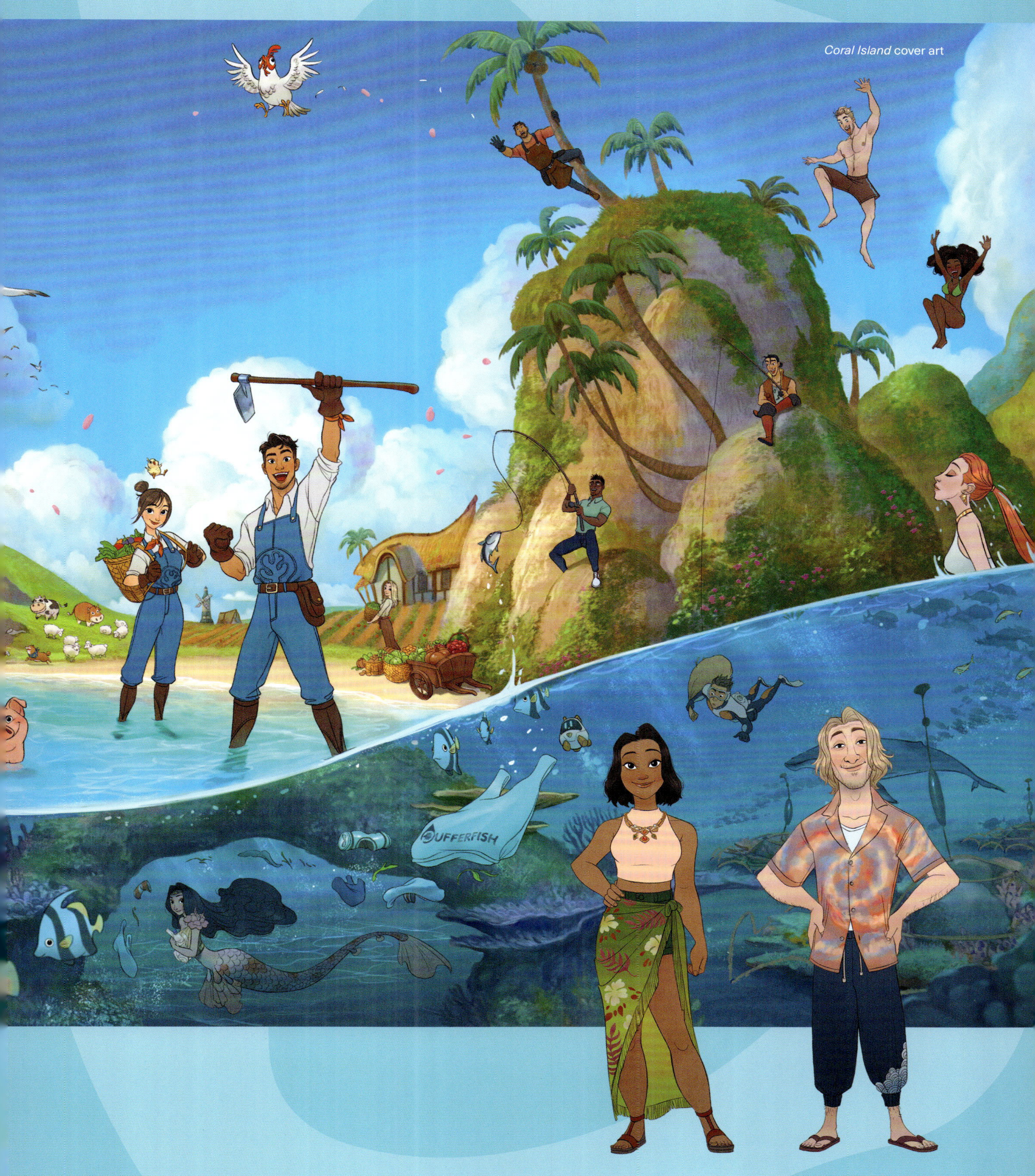

Coral Island cover art
PUFFERFISH

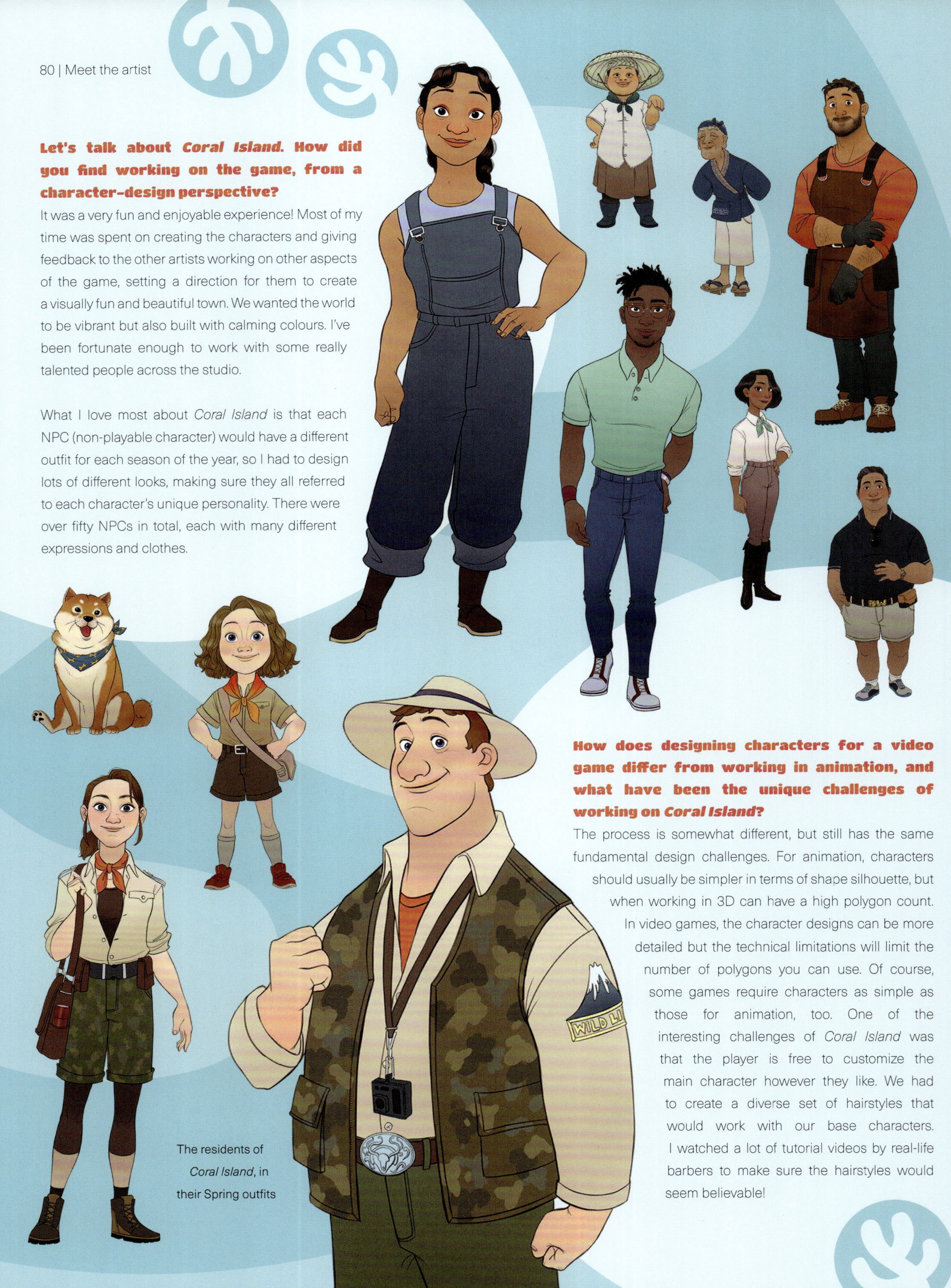

Let's talk about *Coral Island*. How did you find working on the game, from a character-design perspective?

It was a very fun and enjoyable experience! Most of my time was spent on creating the characters and giving feedback to the other artists working on other aspects of the game, setting a direction for them to create a visually fun and beautiful town. We wanted the world to be vibrant but also built with calming colours. I've been fortunate enough to work with some really talented people across the studio.

What I love most about *Coral Island* is that each NPC (non-playable character) would have a different outfit for each season of the year, so I had to design lots of different looks, making sure they all referred to each character's unique personality. There were over fifty NPCs in total, each with many different expressions and clothes.

The residents of *Coral Island*, in their Spring outfits

How does designing characters for a video game differ from working in animation, and what have been the unique challenges of working on *Coral Island*?

The process is somewhat different, but still has the same fundamental design challenges. For animation, characters should usually be simpler in terms of shape silhouette, but when working in 3D can have a high polygon count. In video games, the character designs can be more detailed but the technical limitations will limit the number of polygons you can use. Of course, some games require characters as simple as those for animation, too. One of the interesting challenges of *Coral Island* was that the player is free to customize the main character however they like. We had to create a diverse set of hairstyles that would work with our base characters. I watched a lot of tutorial videos by real-life barbers to make sure the hairstyles would seem believable!

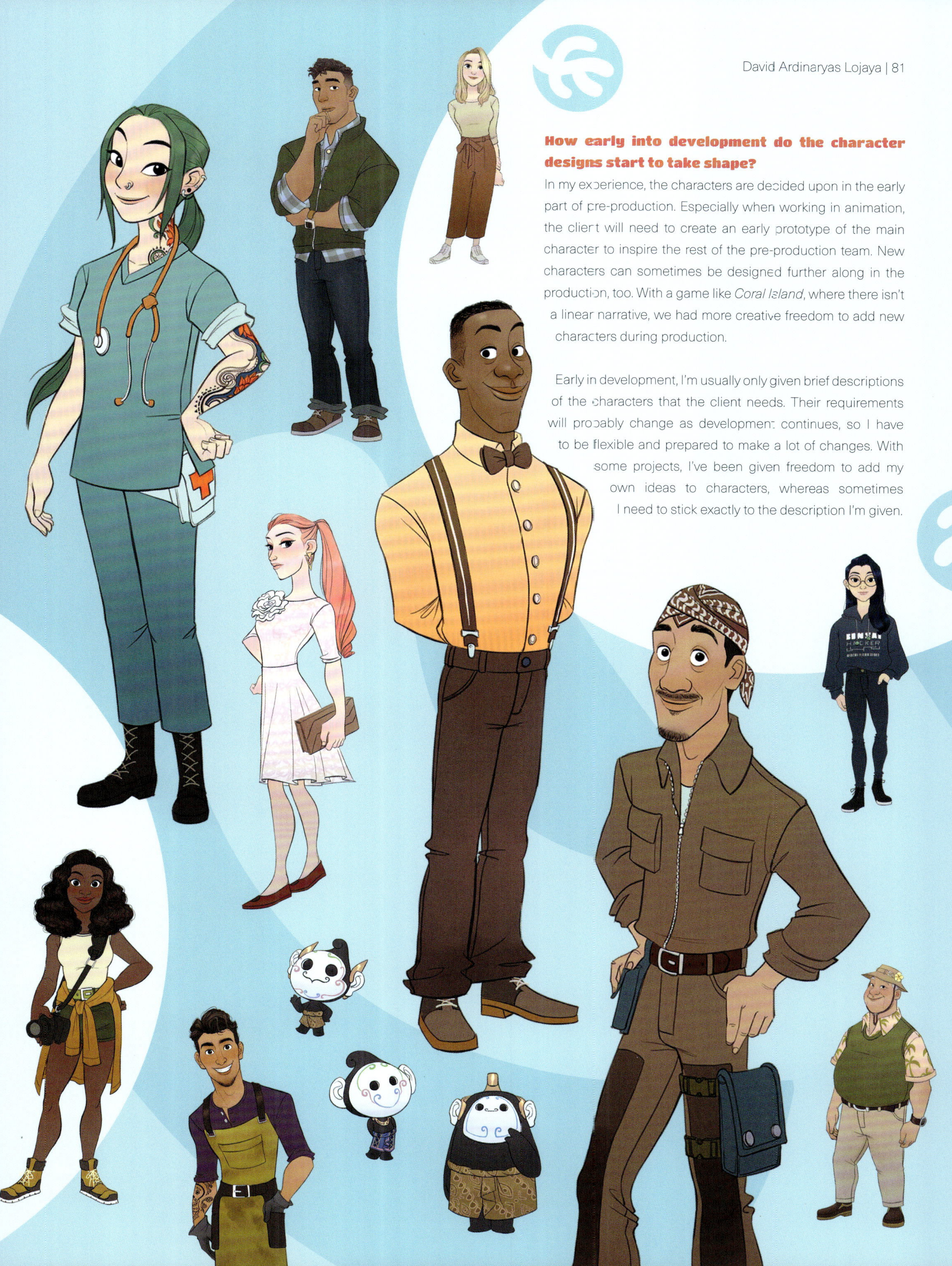

How early into development do the character designs start to take shape?

In my experience, the characters are decided upon in the early part of pre-production. Especially when working in animation, the client will need to create an early prototype of the main character to inspire the rest of the pre-production team. New characters can sometimes be designed further along in the production, too. With a game like *Coral Island*, where there isn't a linear narrative, we had more creative freedom to add new characters during production.

Early in development, I'm usually only given brief descriptions of the characters that the client needs. Their requirements will probably change as development continues, so I have to be flexible and prepared to make a lot of changes. With some projects, I've been given freedom to add my own ideas to characters, whereas sometimes I need to stick exactly to the description I'm given.

Do you have a favourite character you worked on in the game, and why?

For *Coral Island*, I can't pinpoint one single character, because every character is fun and unique in their own way. But perhaps my favourite process was creating the merfolk. As I mentioned earlier, the first Disney film I loved was *The Little Mermaid*, so I had lots of fun creating my own take on people living under the sea – it was really a dream job to design them! I drew many different options for fish tails so there would be lots of variety for the merfolk in the game. There are more than fifteen merfolk being added in a future update to the game – look out for it!

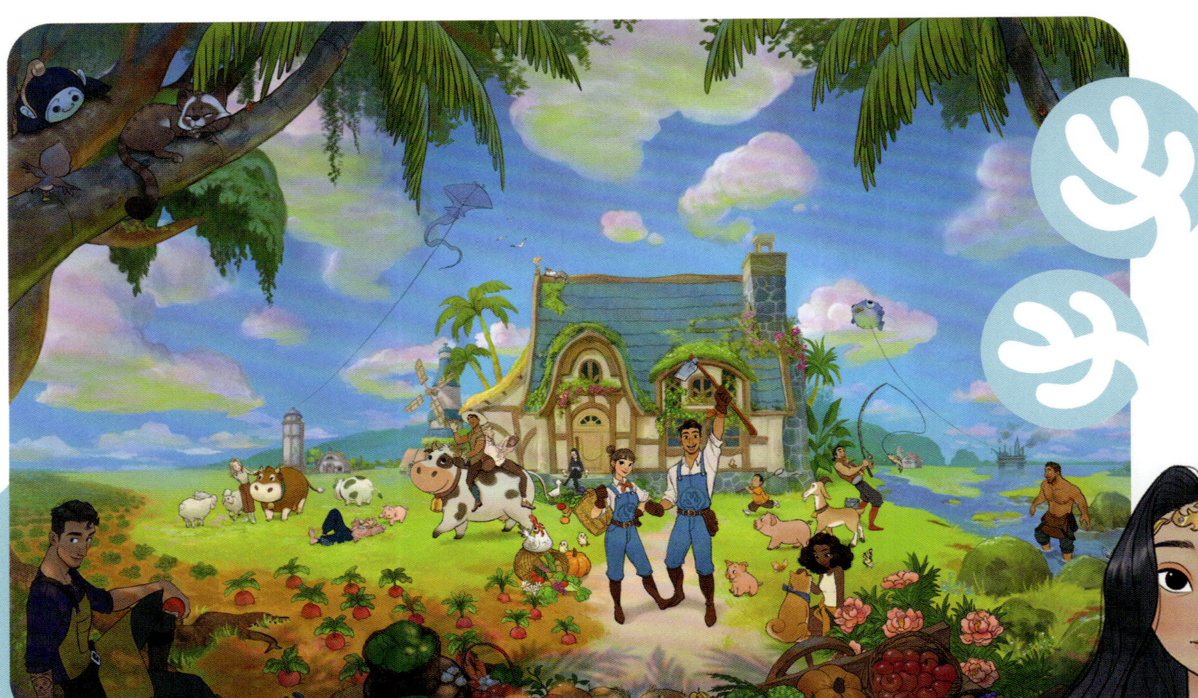
Showing off life on *Coral Island*

How many iterations of each character did you generally make, and did any character in particular pose a significant challenge to get right?

I would usually start by creating four options for any given character, based on the description I was given. We would then narrow these designs to two, and then choose a final version. While in the iteration process, it's very helpful to add a pose that captures the character's personality. Adding some expressions also helps me to better visualize what the client has in mind.

The merfolk designs I previously mentioned were a bit of a challenge. We wanted to create something fresh and unique, but still visually enjoyable, and relatable to the current audience. The problem was how to design the merfolk's scales that cover their fish tails. The *Coral Island* drawing style relies a lot on 2D lines – adding a lot of lines in one area could easily look over-complicated and draw the focus of the viewer's eye away from the character's face. To stop their tails from being too distracting, I had to make the scales bigger, reducing the lines and creating a harmonious, balanced design overall.

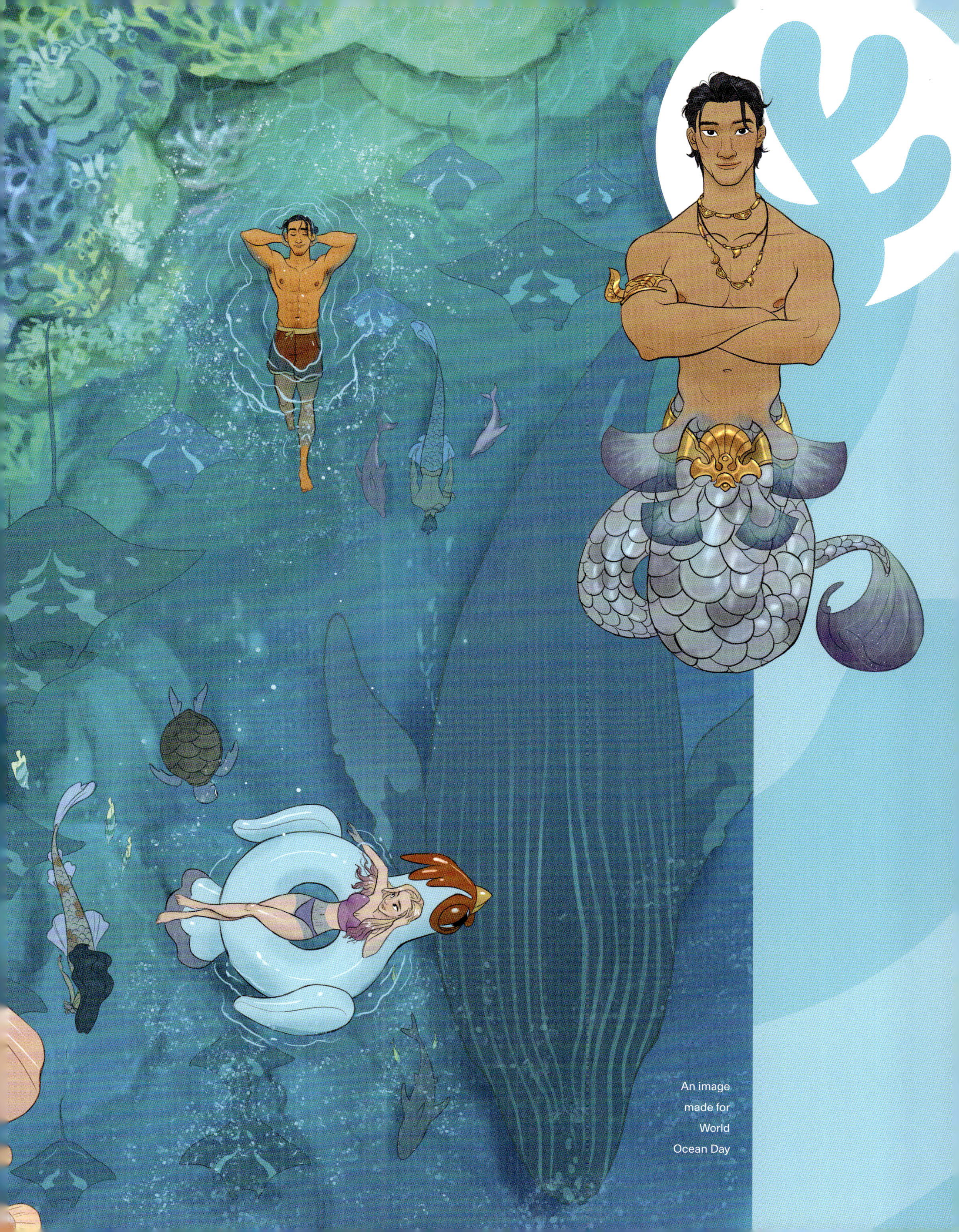
An image
made for
World
Ocean Day

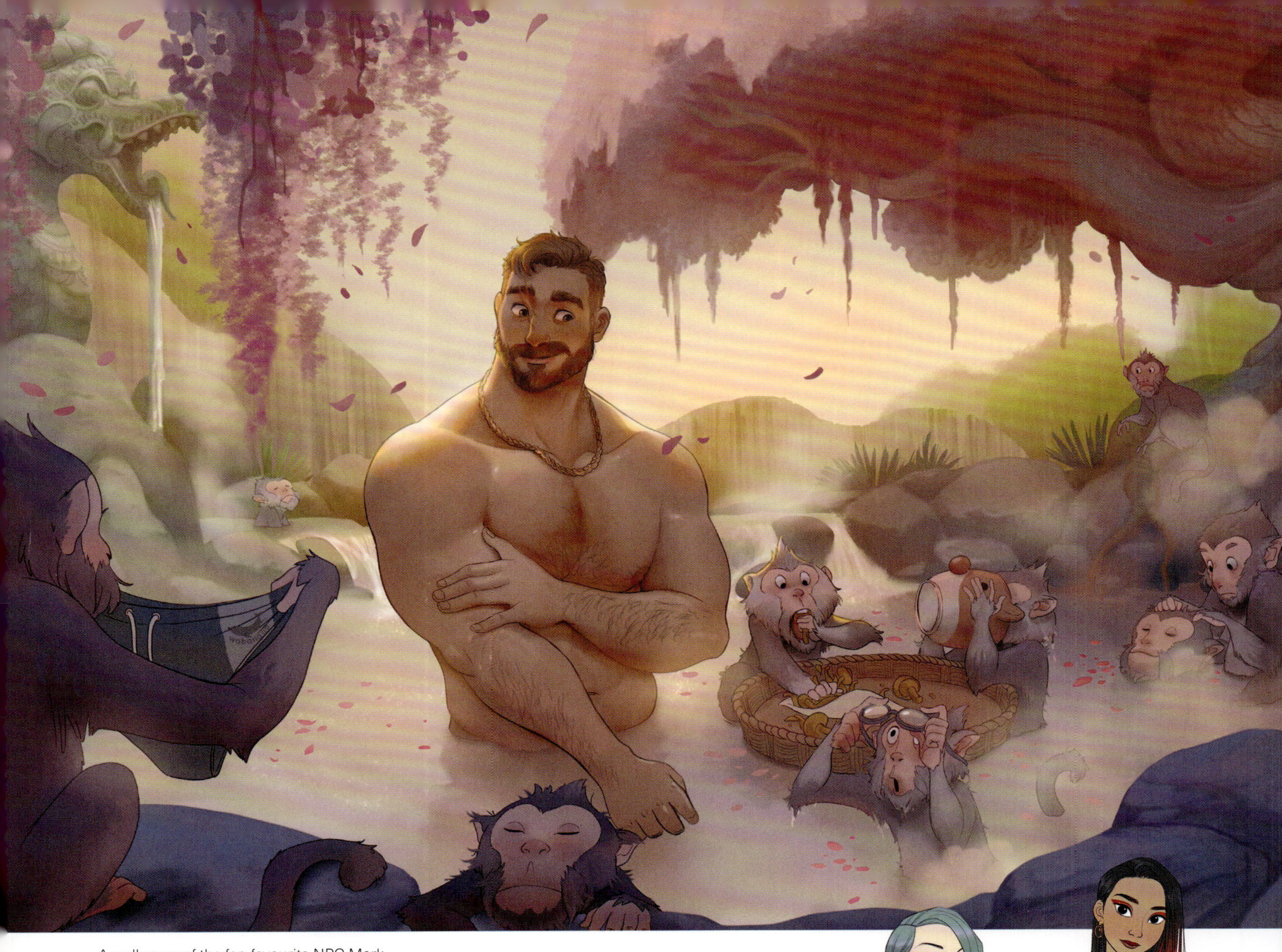

A wallpaper of the fan-favourite NPC Mark

Do you have any advice for young character artists who would like to work in video game development?

First and foremost, always learn the fundamentals! I know it's boring advice, but having a good grasp of the basics of design will be useful for your future career. Never compare yourself to other artists. I believe that every person has their own speed at which they learn – we're all on our own timeline. Your friend might have a cool job now, but don't let it bother you. Keep practising and always try new things – believe in yourself and you'll be successful one day. You need to keep your passion burning.

Even as you become more established, keep studying new styles and techniques. If you are a 2D artist, learn to work in 3D, and vice versa. The more diverse your range of styles and skills, the better. Finally, be sure to rest when you start to feel burnt out. Keep that passion for character design alive and you'll never truly get tired in the long run.

Thanks for talking to us David! What's coming up next for you?

Thank you for having me, it was fun. We are continuing to develop and add more content to *Coral Island*. Stay tuned to our socials for more information!

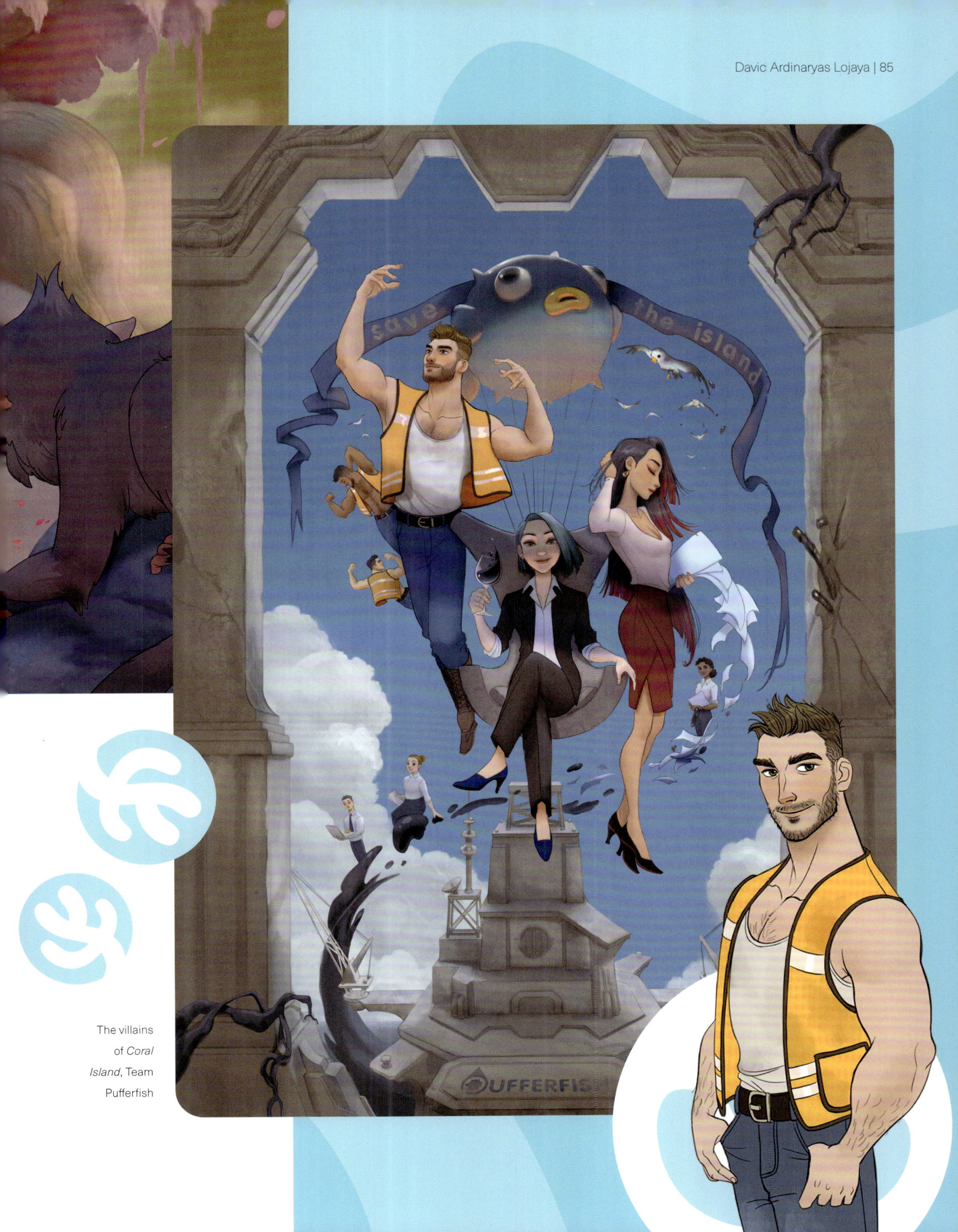

The villains of *Coral Island*, Team Pufferfish

HOW I STYLIZE

Yaroslava Apollonova shares a collection of tips for creating stylized character designs in Procreate

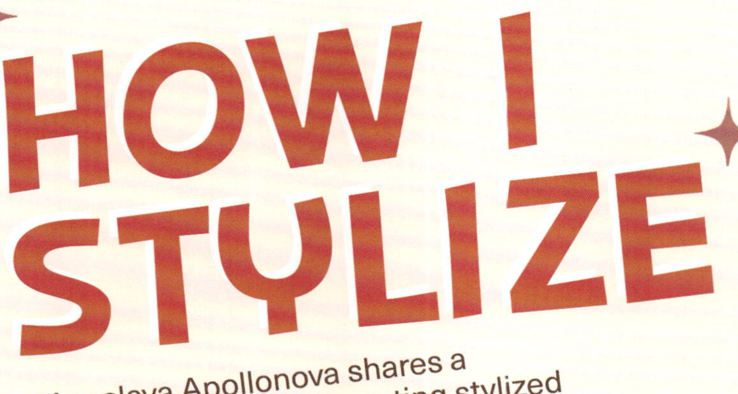

THE ARTIST'S SECRETS

Being self-taught, I've always been curious about an artist's process and any special tricks they use when drawing. As my experience grows, I want to share some of the tips I use in my own creative process. Not everything may work for you, but hopefully some of these ideas will help to make your next character design a more fun and interesting process. I'll be using Procreate for iPad throughout.

DRAWING WITHOUT A BRIEF

If you don't have a certain brief, just sketch for an hour exploring different personalities until you find something that you like. Use references of real people and objects when needed.

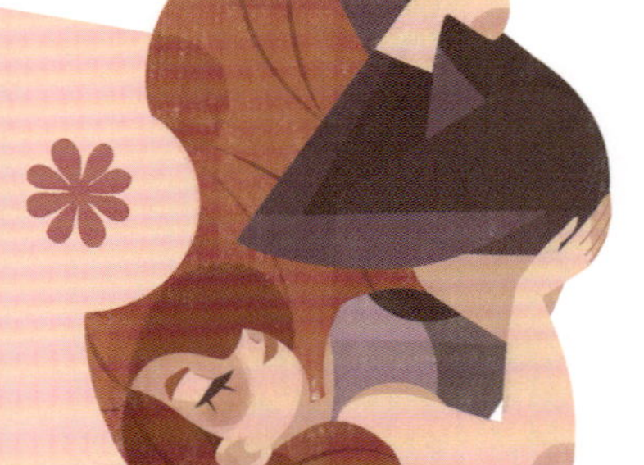

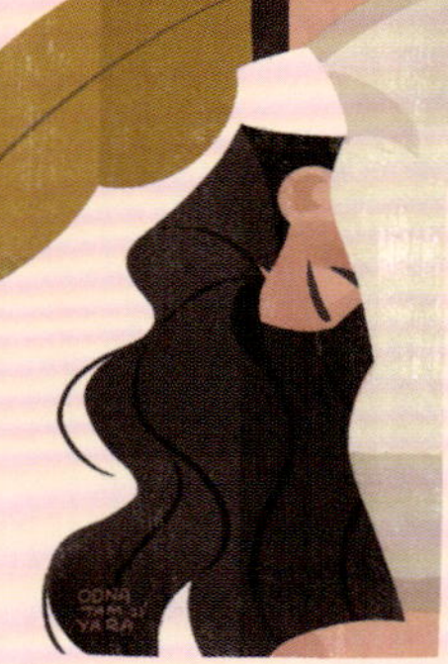

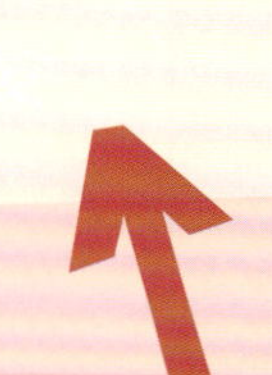

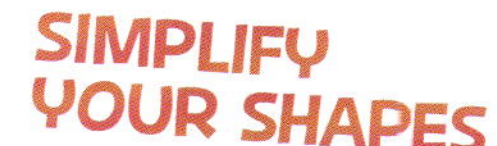

SIMPLIFY YOUR SHAPES

Don't be afraid to simplify shapes. Take a look at this witch character and the way her arms and shoulders are one straight line. I don't add any extra curves that might overcomplicate the silhouette. Her sweater is formed with simple straight lines that contrast nicely with the curvy lines on her sleeves.

'DON'T BE AFRAID TO SIMPLIFY SHAPES'

PERFECT SHAPES FOREVER

If you're using Procreate, the QuickShape tool can help you to quickly draw clean lines. Draw a square line and hold your pencil on the canvas until the tool appears. Drag the points to get a perfectly straight line. I use this trick all the time to draw my shapes in a cleaner way.

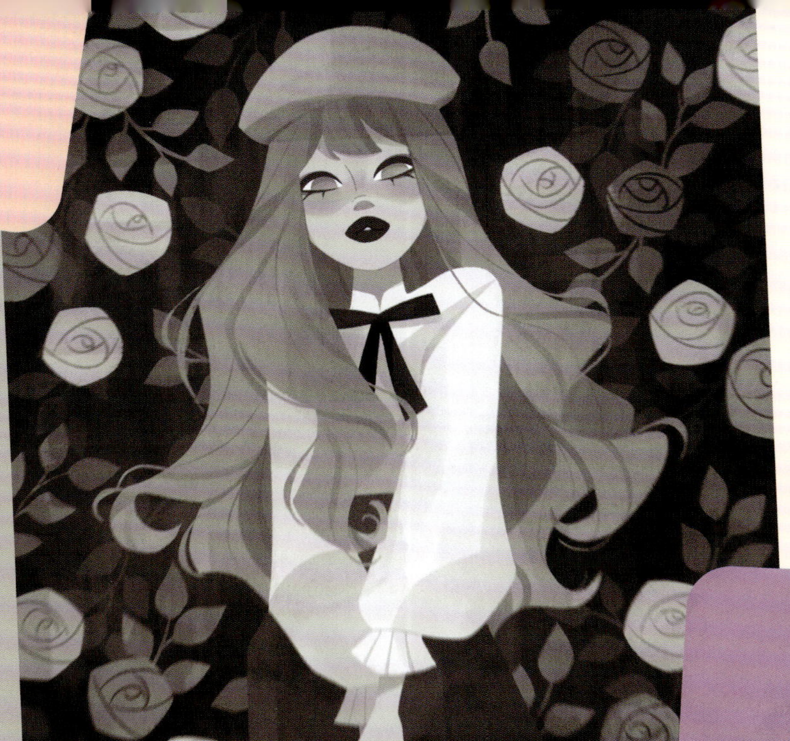

CHECK YOUR CONTRAST

Always check the black-and-white contrast by lowering the saturation. For example, with this image we can see that the lips and bowtie are darker than everything else, leading the viewer's attention to the character's face.

DRAWING ASSIST IS YOUR FRIEND

Another handy Procreate feature is Drawing Assist, which is useful for cutting shapes. For this drawing, I use it to cut the character's hair, so the tips are running completely parallel to the ground.

SAVE YOUR LAYERS

If you're struggling with too many layers in Procreate and running out of memory, you could place objects that are far away from each other on the same layer. For instance, in this image I place all five characters' hair on one layer, and all their clothes on another.

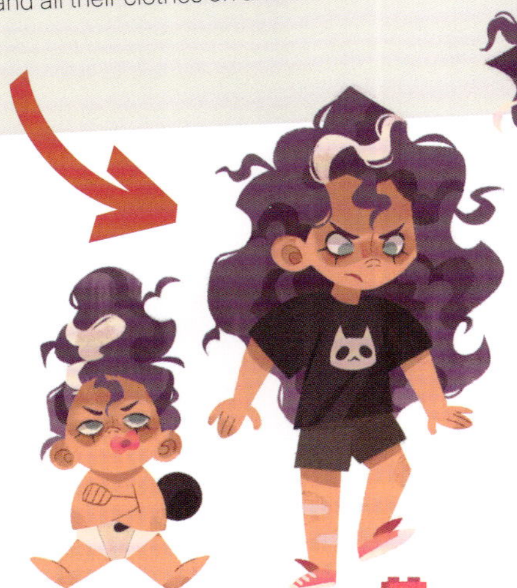

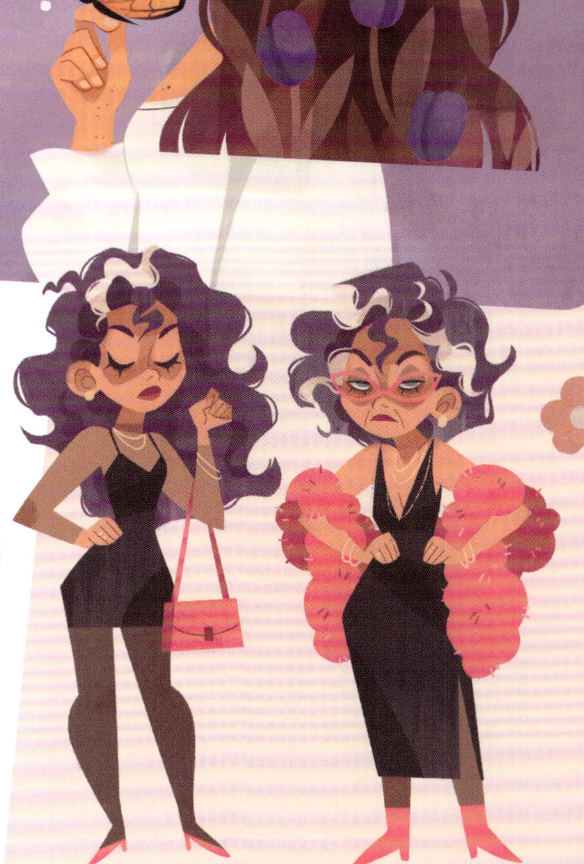

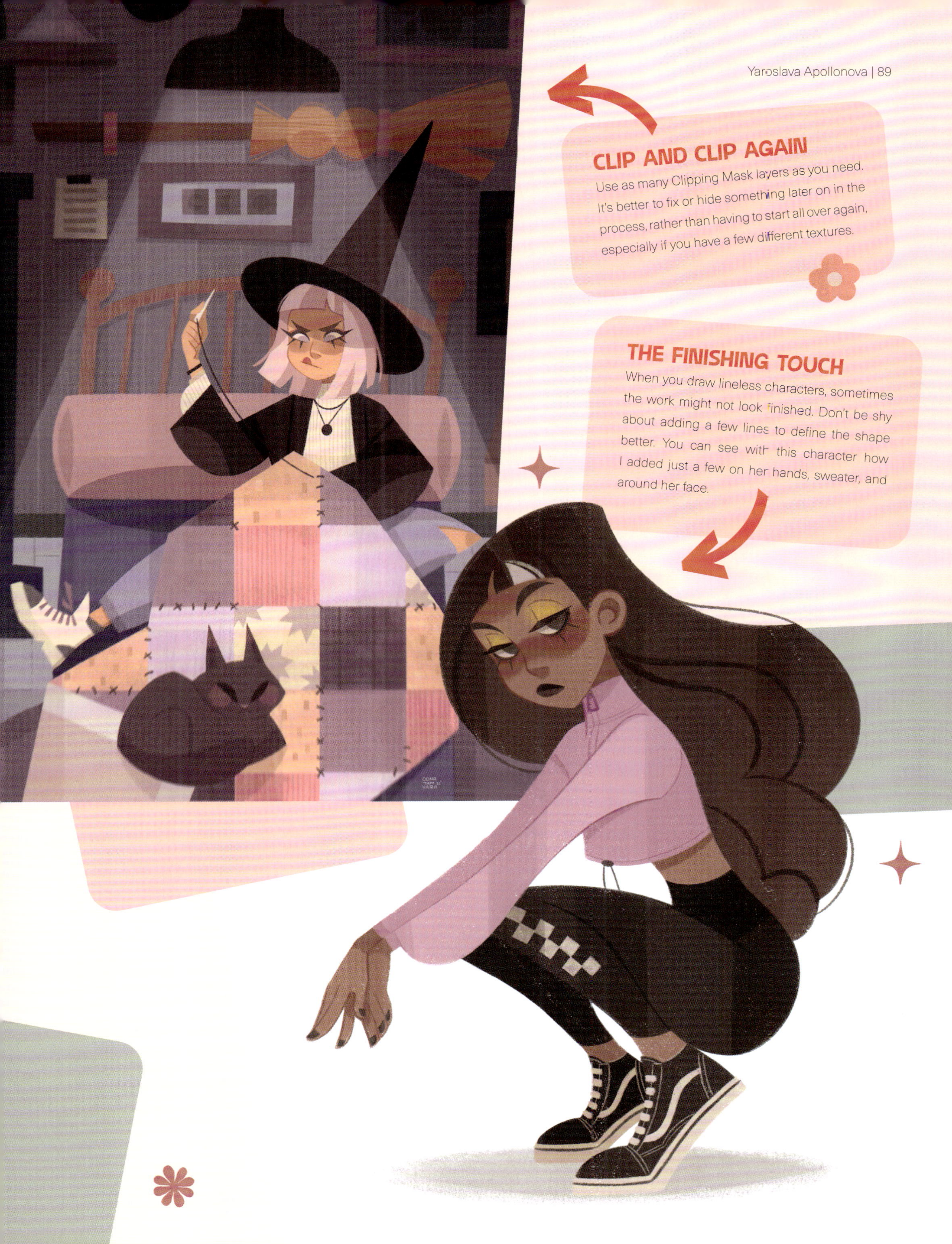

CLIP AND CLIP AGAIN
Use as many Clipping Mask layers as you need. It's better to fix or hide something later on in the process, rather than having to start all over again, especially if you have a few different textures.

THE FINISHING TOUCH
When you draw lineless characters, sometimes the work might not look finished. Don't be shy about adding a few lines to define the shape better. You can see with this character how I added just a few on her hands, sweater, and around her face.

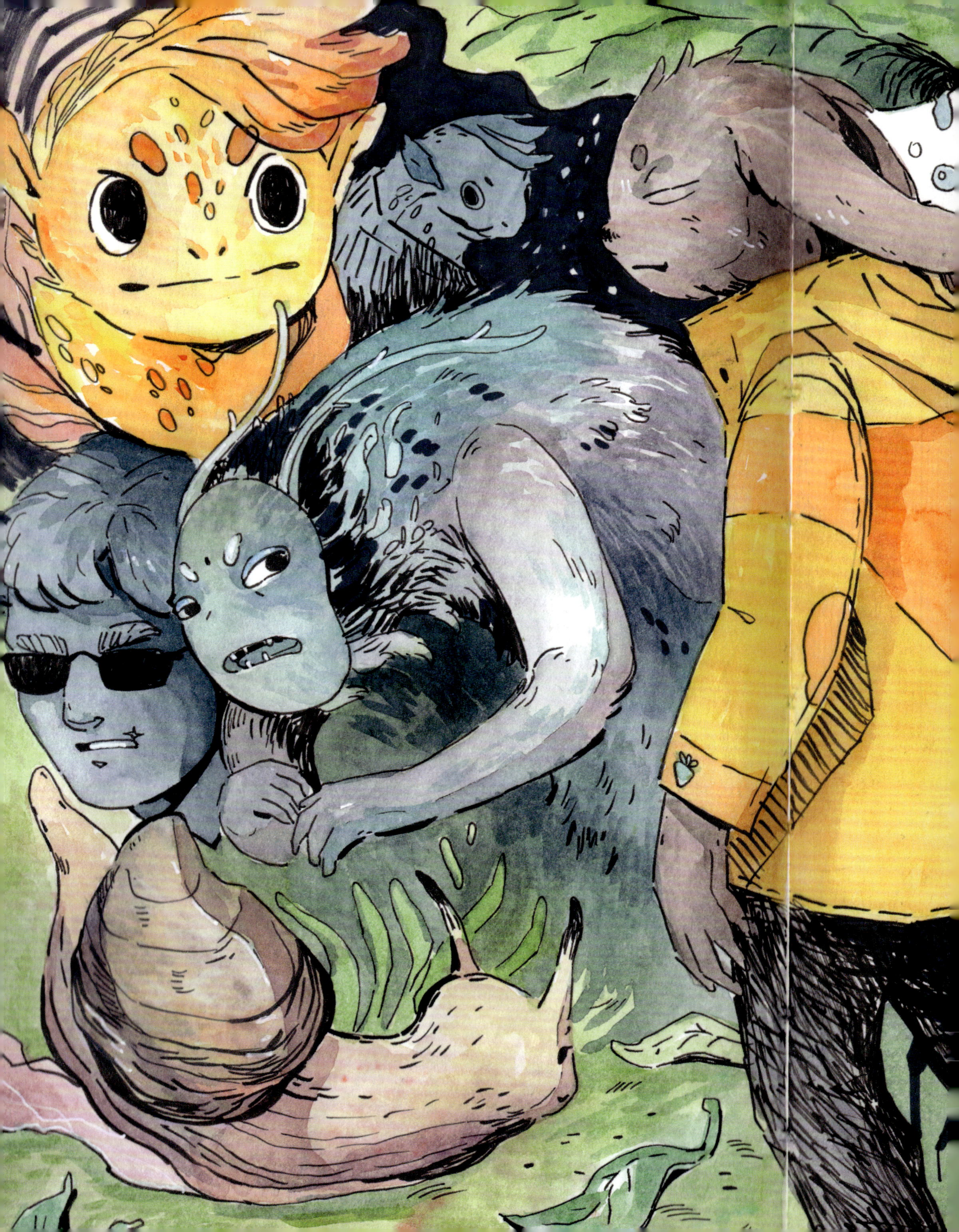

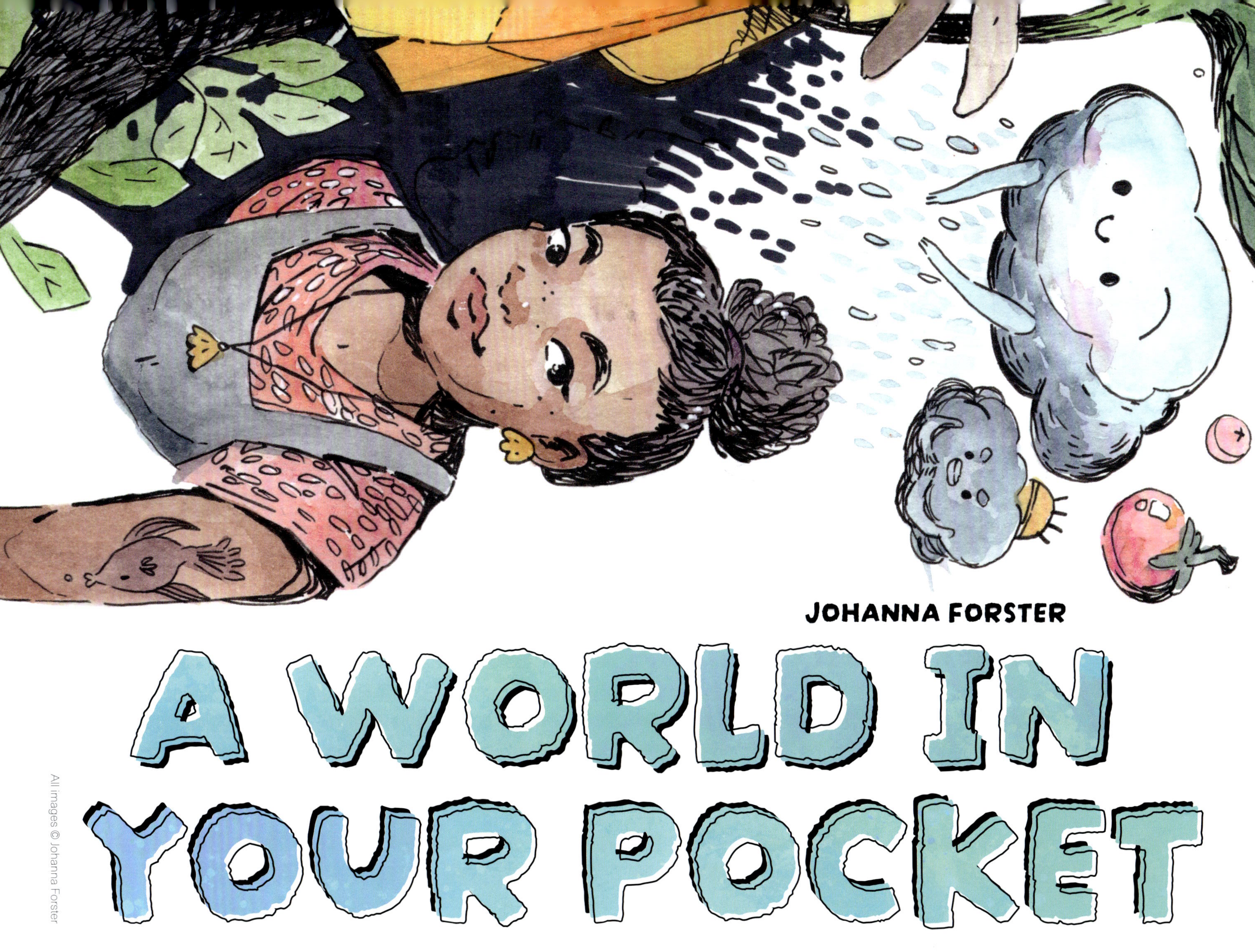

JOHANNA FORSTER
A WORLD IN YOUR POCKET

Capture your worldview

Between all the beautiful drawings that already exist and the pretty pictures AI can come up with in seconds nowadays, how can we, as artists, still create something unique? I think what makes our drawings meaningful is how only humans can experience the beauty of this world through our own eyes and capture it on paper.

Whether you create art for others or just for yourself, keeping a sketchbook (and using it regularly) will help you to find and define a creative voice. Let me take you inside my sketchbook and show you how it enriches my work as an artist.

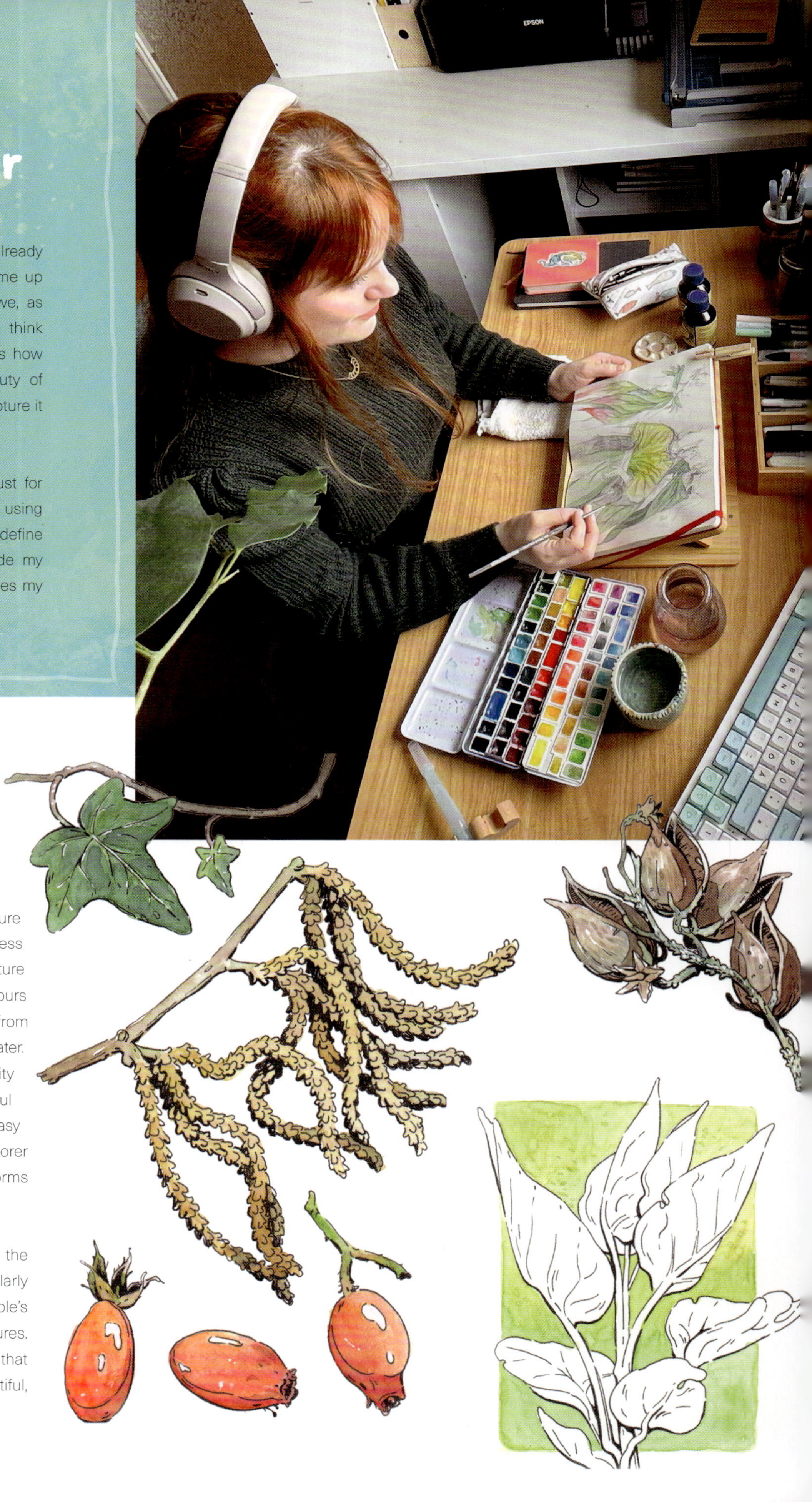

Capture the beauty of life

Most of my sketchbook drawings are nature studies. The natural world offers an endless source of inspiration and I love to capture the beautiful organic shapes and colours of plants. Often, I collect little treasures from nature on my daily errands to draw them later. This part of my art has a meditative quality for me and opens my eyes to beautiful details in the world that are normally easy to overlook. It makes me feel like an explorer from the 18th century, discovering lifeforms for the first time.

To fuel your inspiration, find and draw the things in the world around you that particularly interest you, whether it be plants, people's faces, or maybe even technical structures. Use your sketchbook to collect everything that makes you think how interesting, beautiful, grandiose, or grotesque is that?!

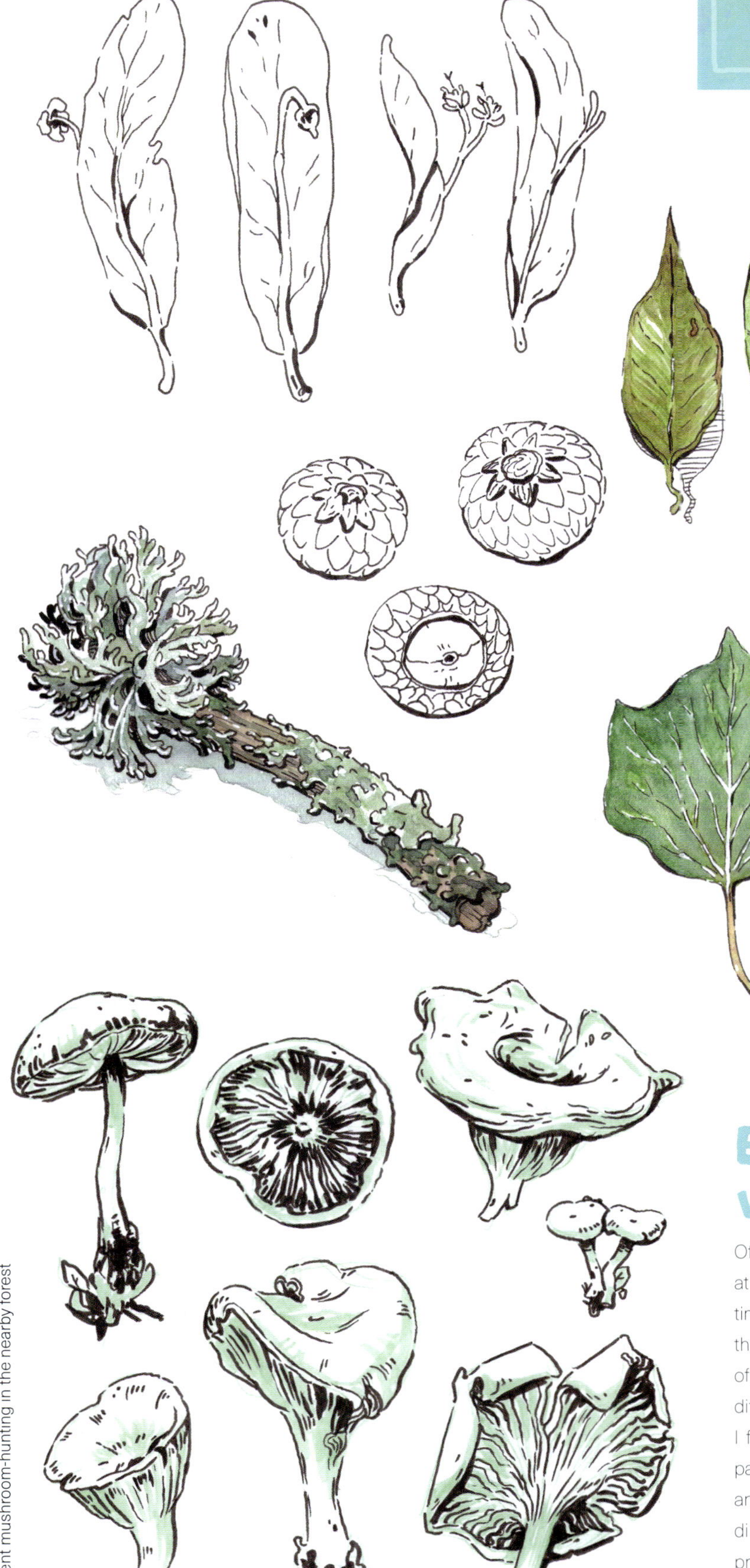

I collect these
study objects
in a box on
my desk

We went mushroom-hunting in the nearby forest

Expand your visual library

Of course, you will become increasingly skilled at depicting the things you have drawn many times before. The things you love, the recurring themes of your drawings, are an important part of your style as an artist. For instance, by studying different mushrooms from several perspectives, I feel I've improved at drawing mushrooms, in particular. If you sketch the same subject again and again, you'll eventually be able to draw them directly from your imagination and change their proportions to design something more creative.

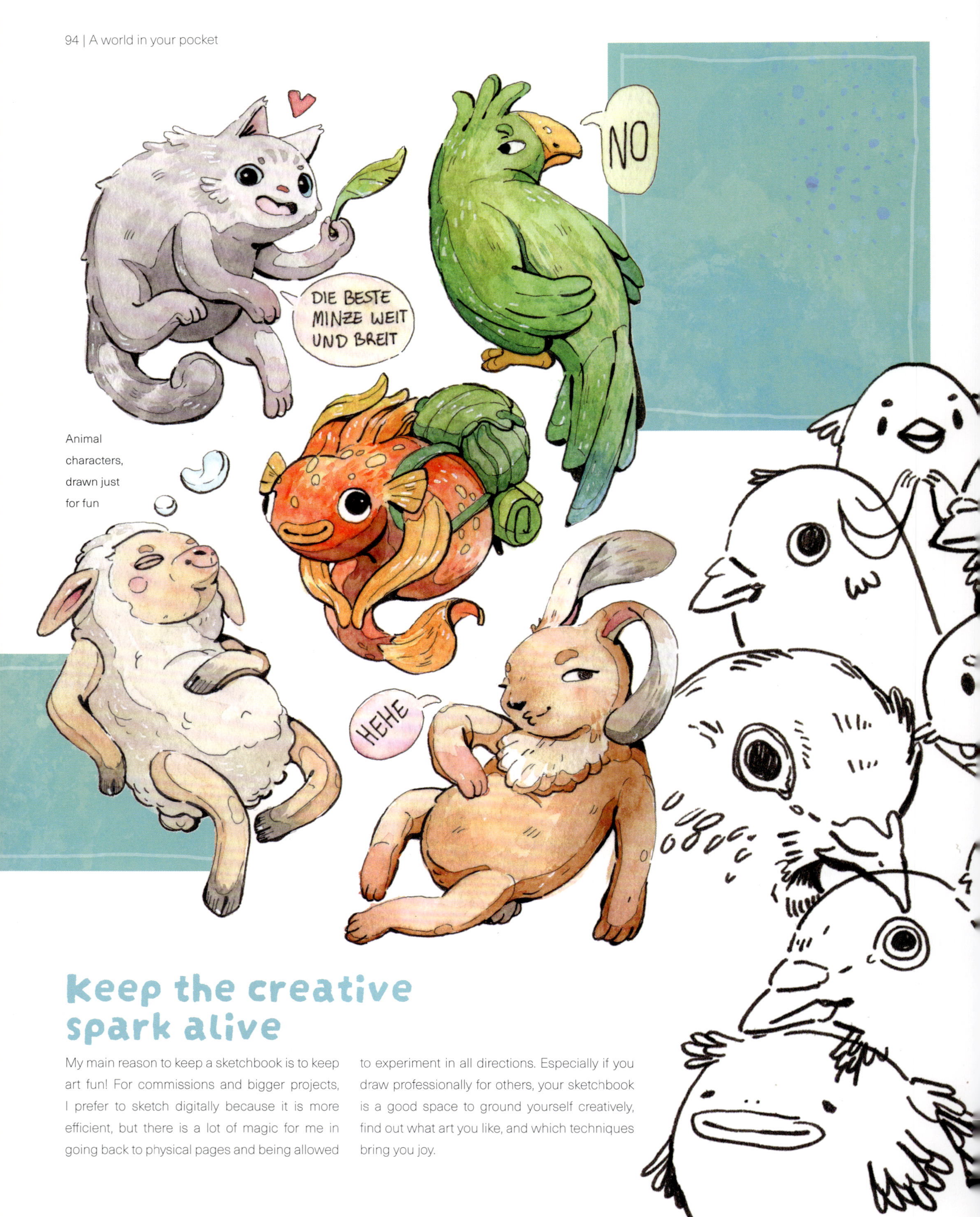

Animal characters, drawn just for fun

keep the creative spark alive

My main reason to keep a sketchbook is to keep art fun! For commissions and bigger projects, I prefer to sketch digitally because it is more efficient, but there is a lot of magic for me in going back to physical pages and being allowed to experiment in all directions. Especially if you draw professionally for others, your sketchbook is a good space to ground yourself creatively, find out what art you like, and which techniques bring you joy.

Let your imagination run wild

In contrast to my nature studies, on other pages I try to draw only from imagination or memory. I think, as an artist, it's important to create from within yourself sometimes and go beyond what you can see with the naked eye. Your weird, unique, and creative view on the world will make your drawings more valuable and worthwhile than any AI-generated picture could ever be. A good exercise is to draw the first thing that comes to your mind – no idea is too weird for your sketchbook.

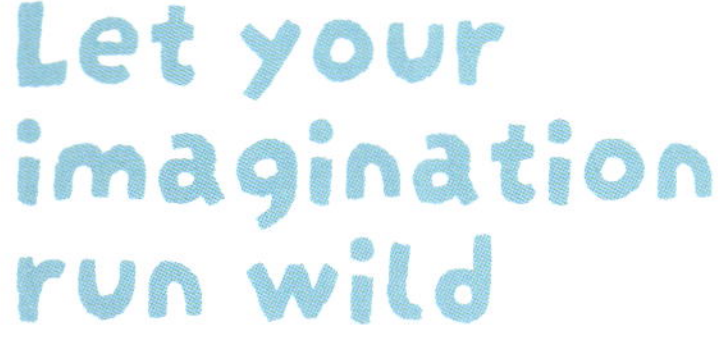

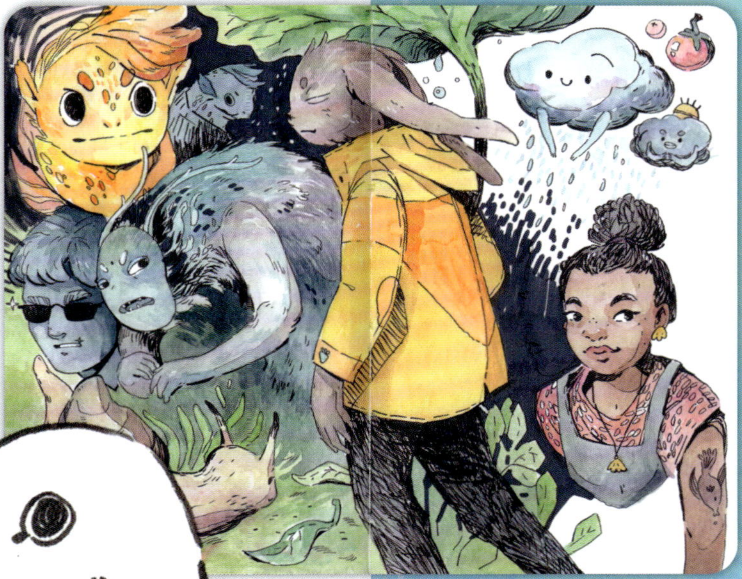

The random first thoughts that came to my mind one day

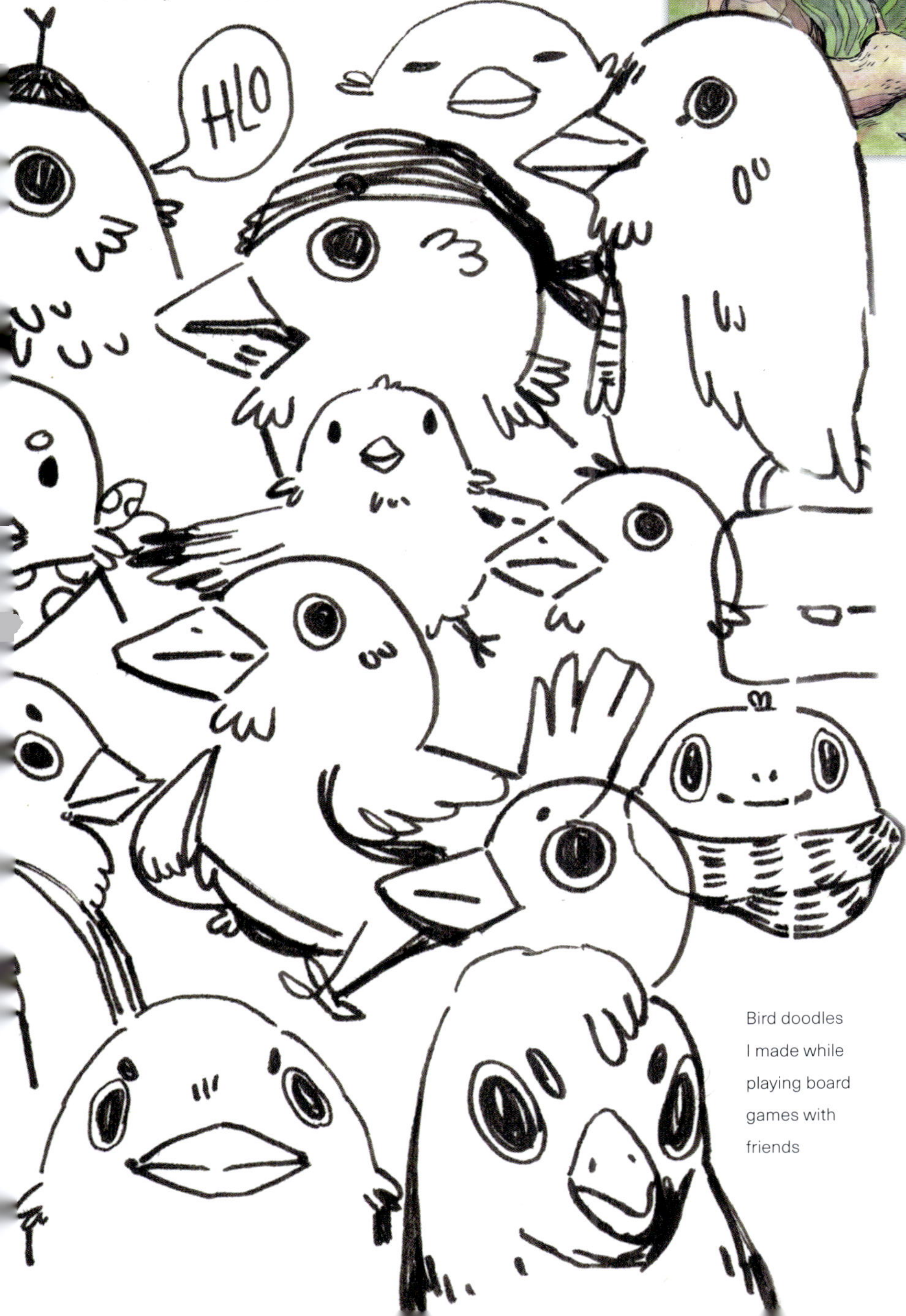

Fight against perfectionism

Like most artists, I feel the pressure to create something good – especially with social media watching on. The fear of 'ruining' a sketchbook with something less than perfect can be paralysing.

Remember: your sketchbook wants to be a creative playground for only you to see. It's the one place where anything is allowed. Don't buy a particularly expensive sketchbook, get something cheap. Start drawing in the middle of the book and cover unloved drawings with paint or sticky notes. Fight the fear of the blank page with one bad little doodle, the first thing that comes to mind, like a silly bird. Is it ugly? Good. Draw another bird that is a little less ugly right next to it. Now fill the whole page with birds – you will come up with one that has something you like about it.

Bird doodles I made while playing board games with friends

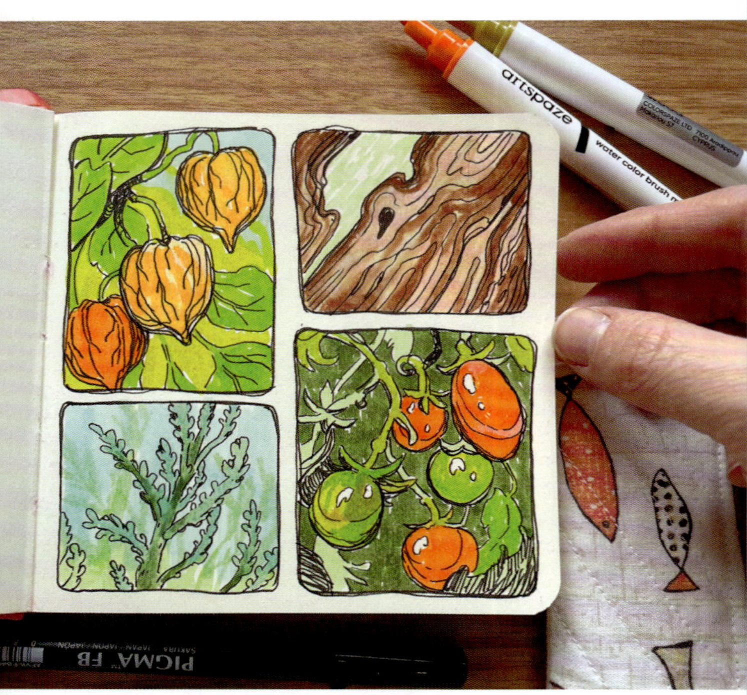

The mini sketchbook I use for travelling – it fits in any pocket!

Create more space for art in your life

A sketchbook can be the starting point for fitting art into a creative routine. Making time for drawing can be tough if you have a full-time job or someone to take care of, or both. I realized this myself when I had a child. If you don't make plans to sit down and create art for yourself, you will never have the time. So, integrate a sketchbook into your day, by drawing for fifteen minutes on the train or before going to sleep, for instance. I use three sketchbooks at the moment: one for pens, one suitable for watercolours, and a cheap, extra-small book to take with me wherever I go.

Framing thoughts

I love to start with little frames on a page and fill them with mock-ups for paintings, with themed mini-studies or textures. It is a great way to start small, to not get lost in detail, and to feel rewarded fast.

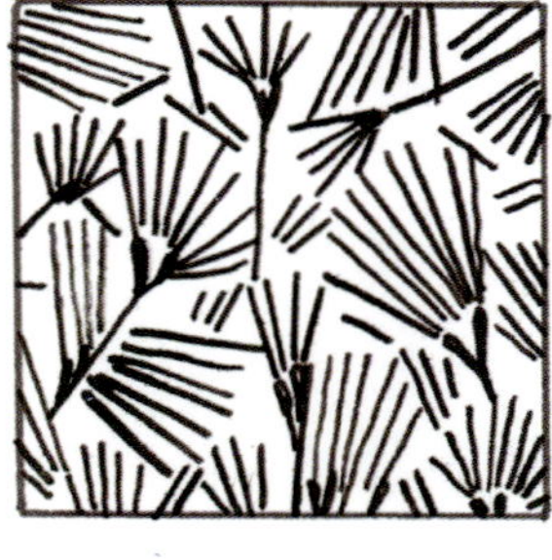
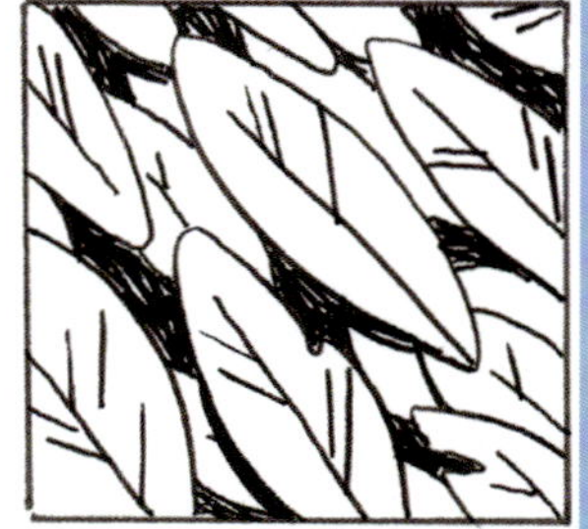
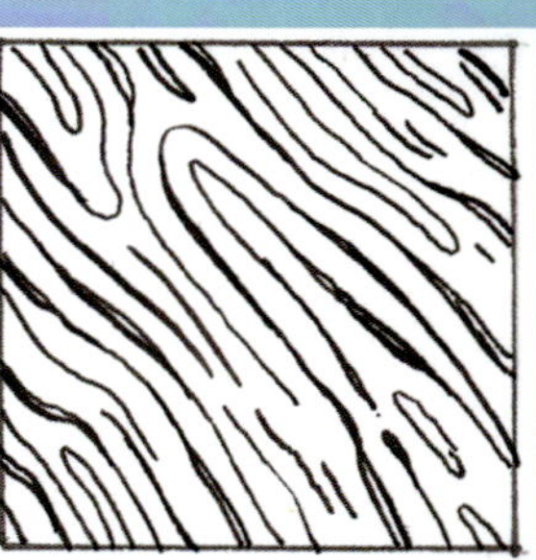
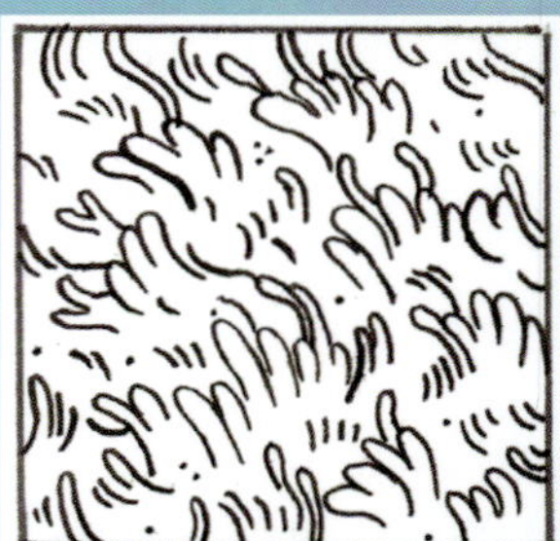
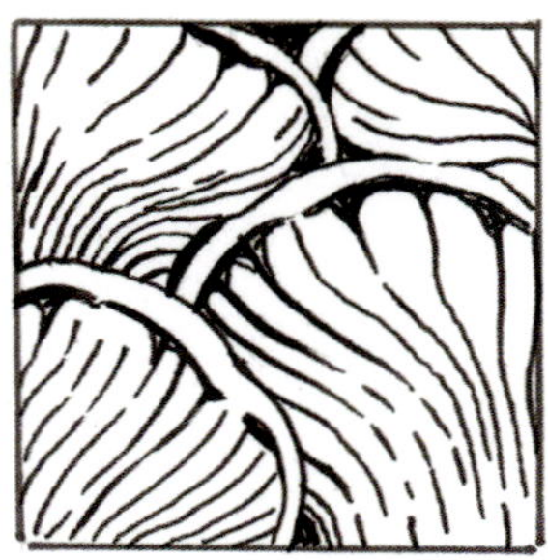
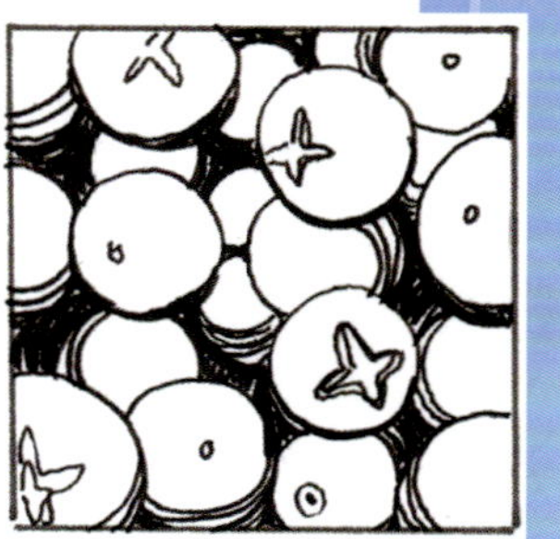
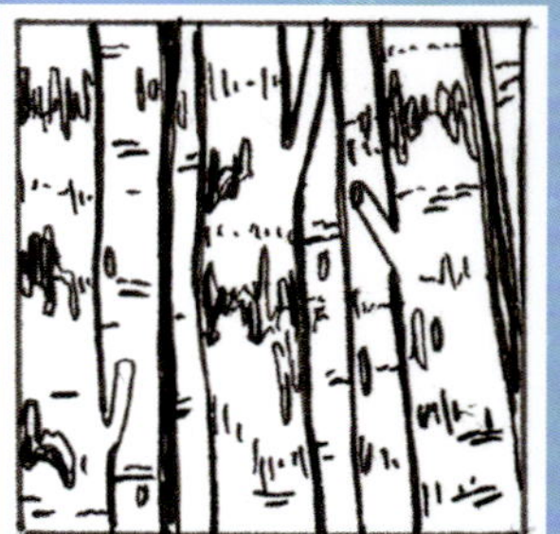
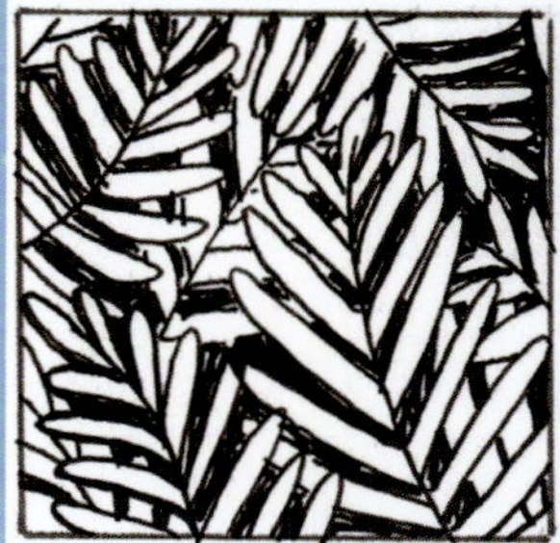
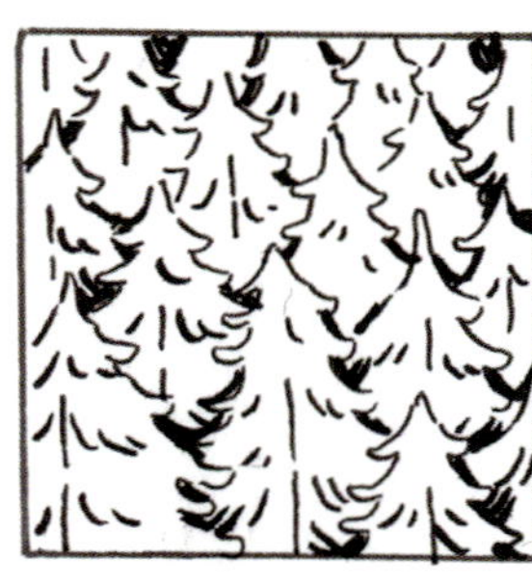
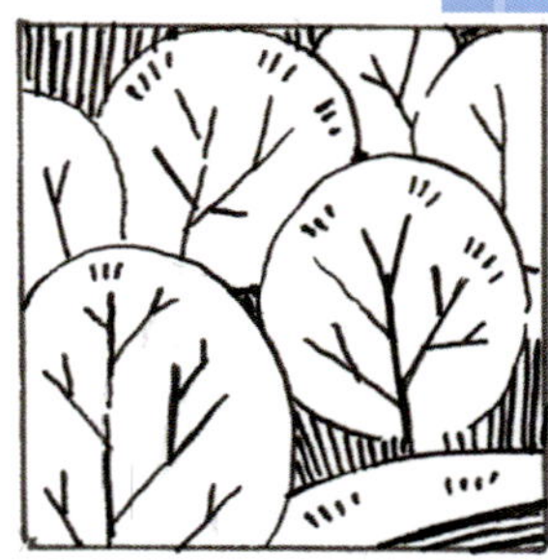
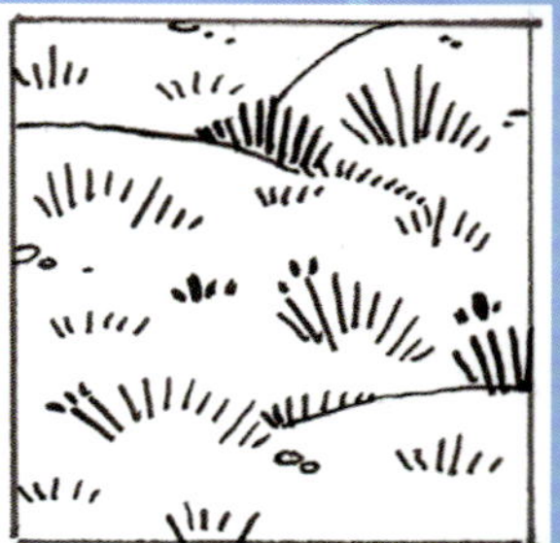
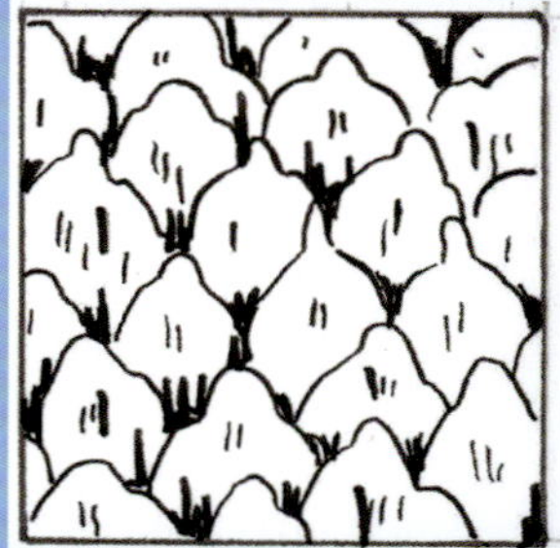

Working in small frames is a great way to focus your thoughts

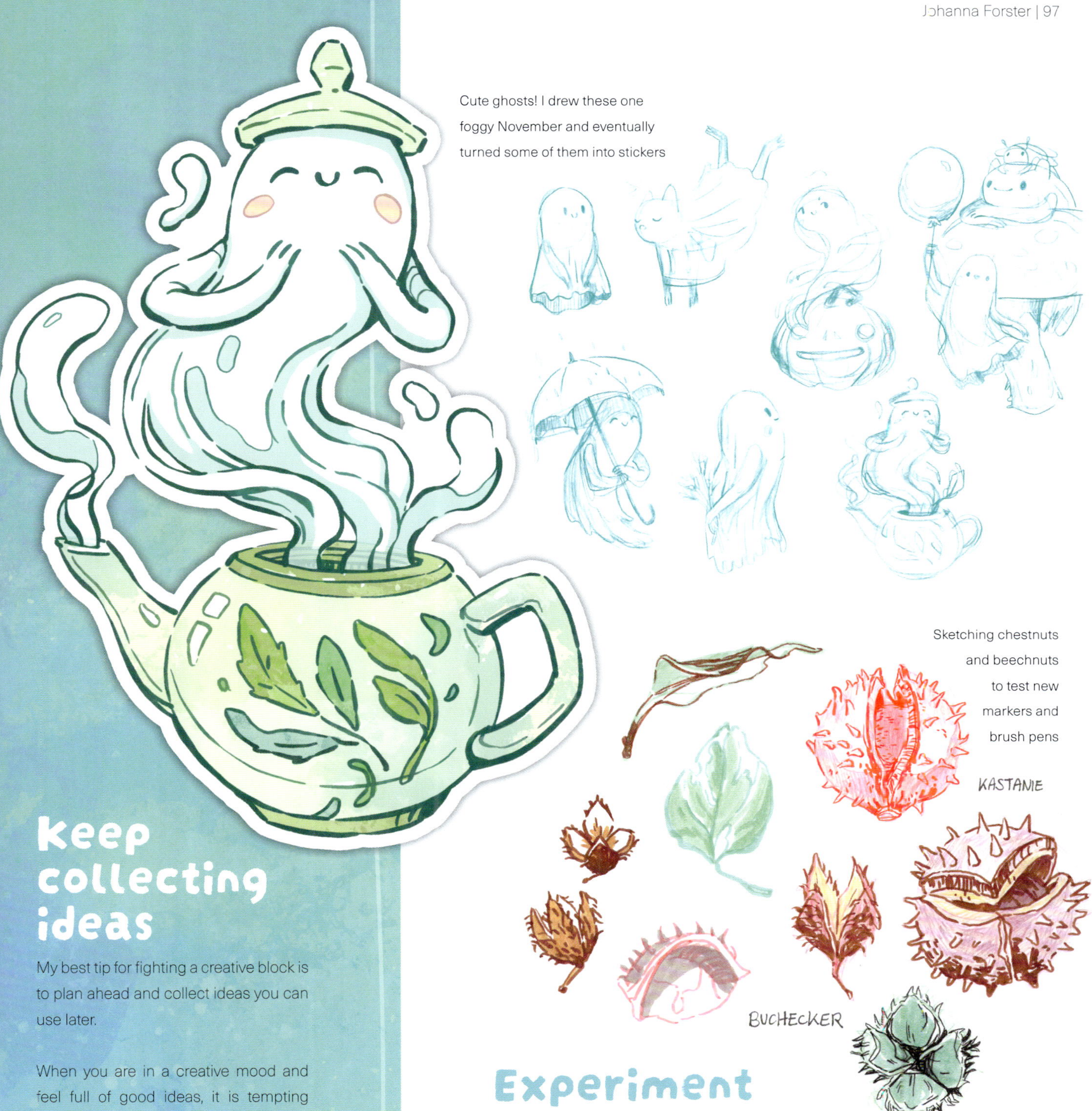

Cute ghosts! I drew these one foggy November and eventually turned some of them into stickers

Sketching chestnuts and beechnuts to test new markers and brush pens

keep collecting ideas

My best tip for fighting a creative block is to plan ahead and collect ideas you can use later.

When you are in a creative mood and feel full of good ideas, it is tempting to think that you will remember them all later, but you probably won't. That creative high can come when you don't have time to draw, but you can quickly put ideas into words, on a notepad or your phone, and explore them later. If you keep your treasure trove of ideas filled like this, you won't easily run out of ideas for your sketchbook.

Experiment with materials

One thing that can really fuel creativity is trying out new paints and pens. Use your sketchbook to experiment with materials you don't normally use. They might offer a new perspective and maybe you'll find something you really love working with. Have the materials ready at your workstation so that you don't have to prepare much when you come to draw, and keep your favourites ready in a pencil case for on the go.

Nothing is wasted

Working with something new can sometimes take you in the wrong direction. Neon green wasn't a good fit for these acorn characters, but I still like the rest of their design. I think there's almost always something that is likable in a drawing that we can keep in mind for future projects.

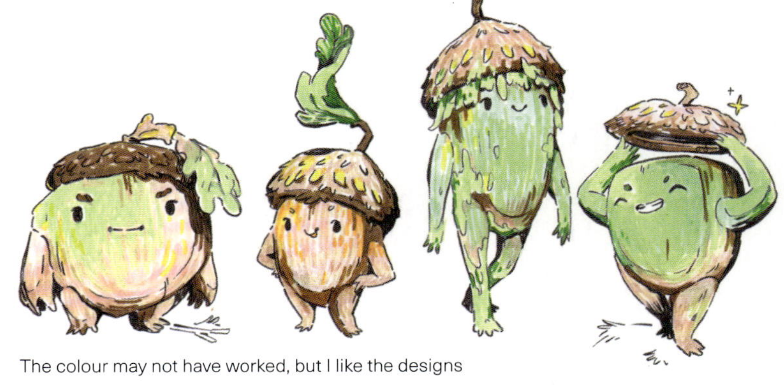

The colour may not have worked, but I like the designs

Practice your techniques

Your sketchbook is a great place to try out new drawing techniques, such as a new way to hold your pen or draw shadows. When you see a drawing you like somewhere, try to put into words what exactly you like about it. Then you can practise replicating that exact aspect in your sketchbook – maybe it will even become part of your drawing technique forever. If you want to improve on a particular subject, you can also do regular exercises (the 100 heads challenge, for example) or dedicate a sketchbook to just one subject, such as life drawings.

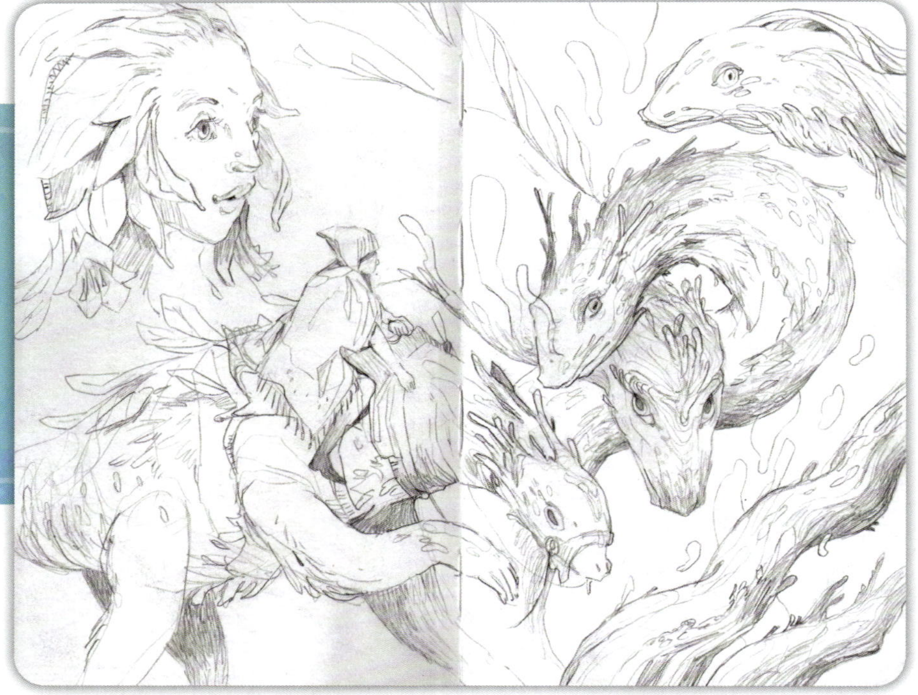

I gave pencils and shorter shading lines a try during a train ride

Experiment with style

There are so many different ways to express yourself. Just when I'm proud of the fact that my latest drawings have lots of outlines, I see a painting online that has no lines at all, and part of me wants to throw my previous technique overboard! In a sketch book you can experiment with different styles and simplifications, and find out what you like to do best. You can study and steal from the artists you admire without showing it to anyone.

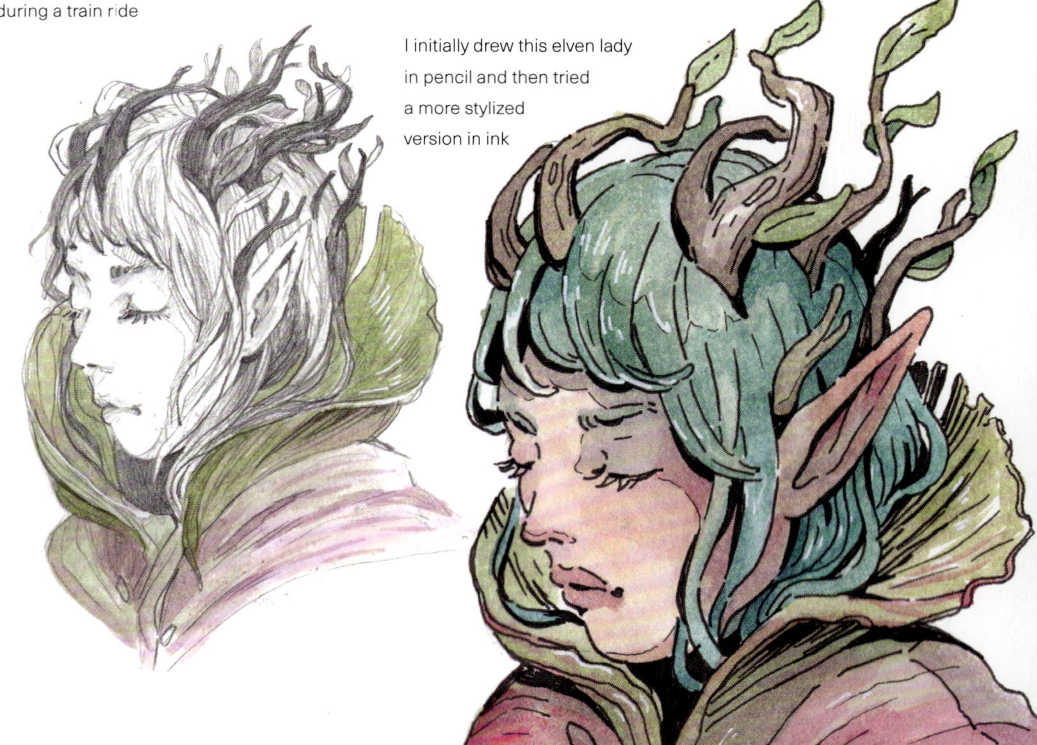

I initially drew this elven lady in pencil and then tried a more stylized version in ink

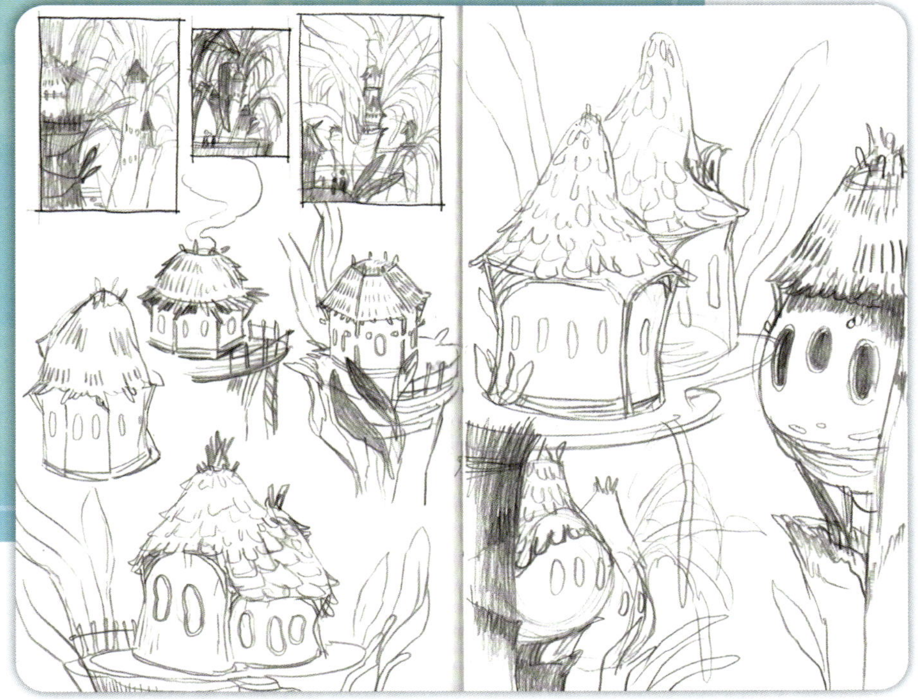

Possible designs for houses of a civilization hidden in my Yucca plant

More, more, more!

It may sound counterintuitive, but getting better at drawing means, in a sense, putting quantity before quality. The more you draw, the more natural it will feel. I used to focus too much on creating a single perfect drawing when I could have created ten sketches in the same amount of time that would have presented better options more quickly. I've noticed that this especially happens with digital drawing, because you can erase endlessly. A physical sketchbook can be the place to explore all of your ideas and put them down faster. If you are drawing something from the imagination, I would encourage you to allow time to create different iterations and then circle the best option for a design.

Shape inspiration

One technique that helps me to come up with ideas on a topic is to start with silhouettes in colour and then do the actual drawings on top. This way, you are forced to think in shapes first and get more variety in your designs.

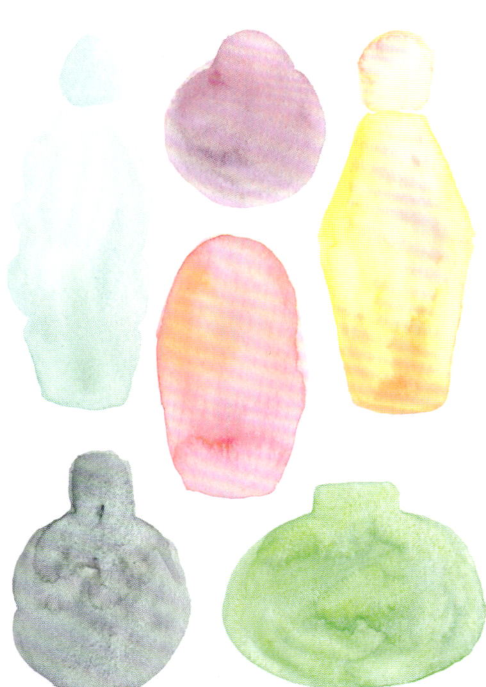

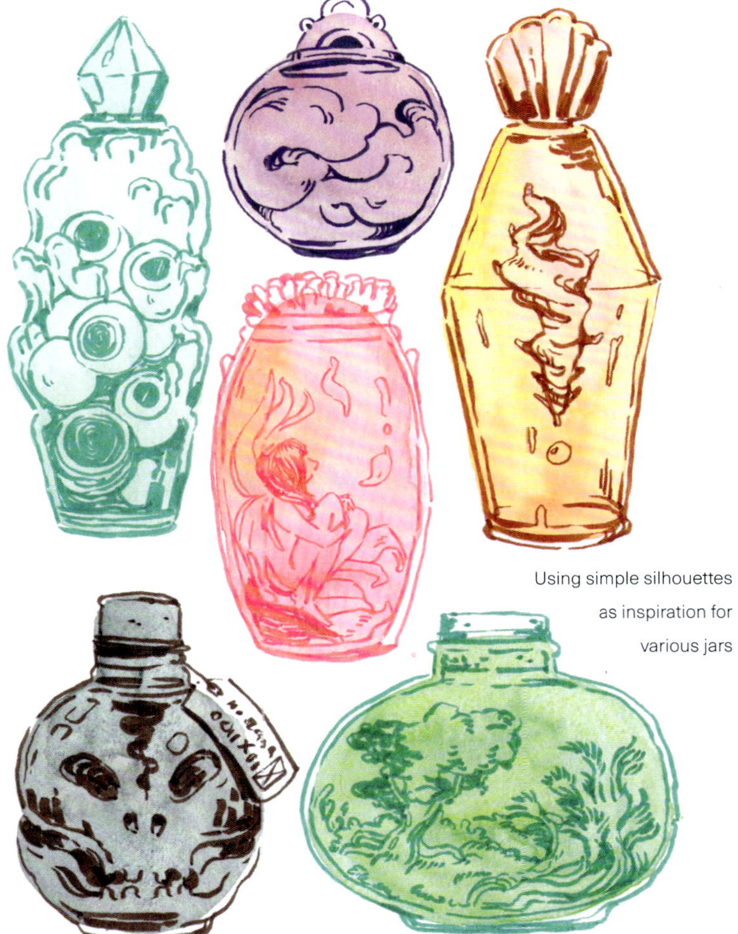

Using simple silhouettes as inspiration for various jars

Capture experiences

Use your sketchbook like a journal to capture beautiful moments in your everyday life. Drawing your surroundings is especially fun when you are travelling. Of course, you could just take a picture, but putting down on paper the details that are important to you in that moment is much more powerful. It can be difficult to fill a sketchbook like this, because you have to find enough peace and quiet to do it, but I especially look forward to revisiting drawings like this later on.

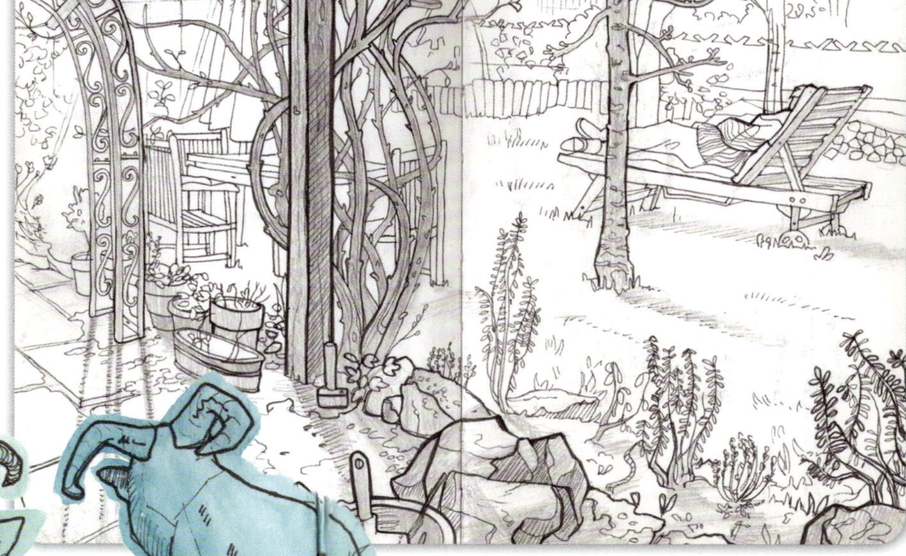

A sketch of the garden we no longer have. I can almost feel the sun when I remember that day

Take your creative playground everywhere

One of the biggest advantages of a sketchbook is that you can take it with you wherever you go. You can always have your own creative space with you to study the world or to put down a design idea quickly. Drawing outside is a great way to see your surroundings with new eyes, as if you were a tourist in your own city. If you need to wait for the bus, choose not to be annoyed and instead see it as an opportunity to fill your sketchbook. It can take a while to get used to people watching you draw in public, but they're just curious, and it really doesn't matter what anyone thinks.

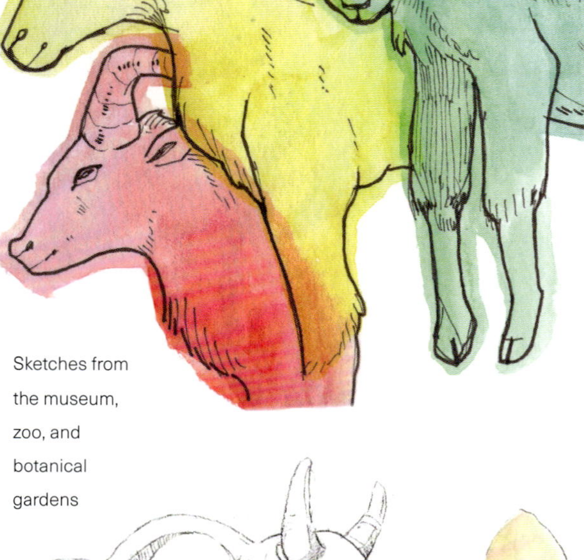

Sketches from the museum, zoo, and botanical gardens

Connect with like-minded people

I used to meet up with a local drawing group to explore the city, gardens, museums, or the zoo to fill our sketchbooks together. It was one of my greatest experiences as an artist. Connecting with other creatives online is great, but having a local art community can be even more motivating. You can stick to a routine together and motivate each other to improve. Maybe there's a drawing class in your area, or you could seek out local artists who might like to draw with you in person.

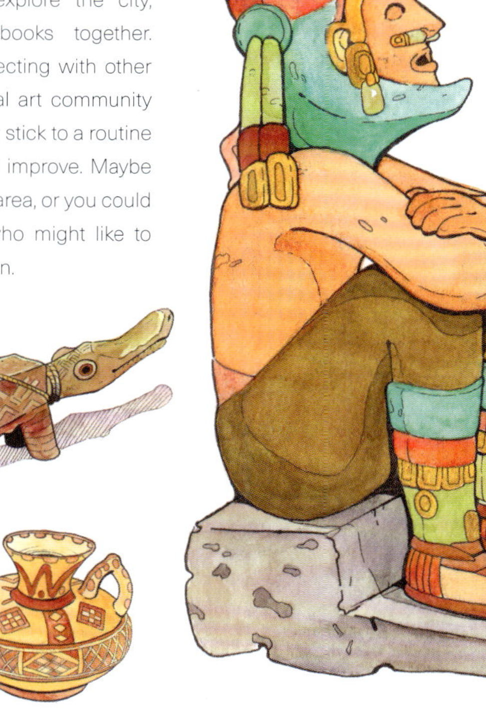

Museum drawings, sketched with pencil, and then worked out with watercolours and ink at home

Find interesting new ideas

In your sketchbook you can collect and combine all these experiences to create something new. For me, the best ideas come from a combination of nature studies and imagination. Use your sketchbook to find ideas that you personally find exciting and fun. They may inspire you to create your next great piece of art.

I hope my thoughts have inspired you to give your own sketchbook some attention. Now grab a pen and draw something just for yourself!

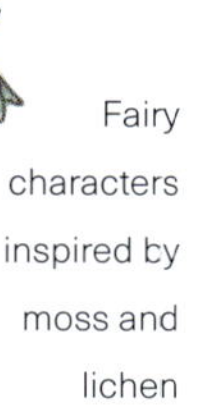

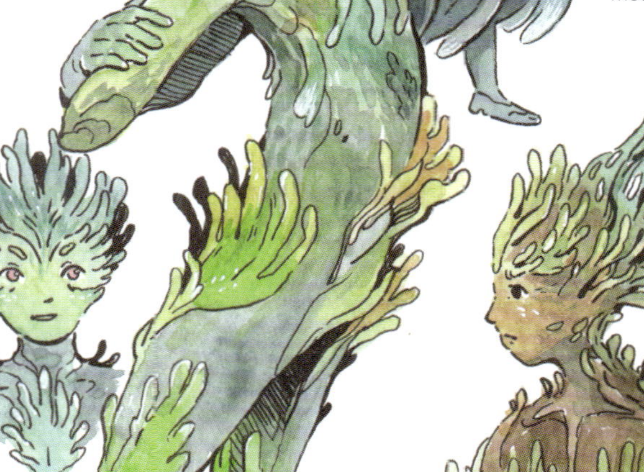

Fairy characters inspired by moss and lichen

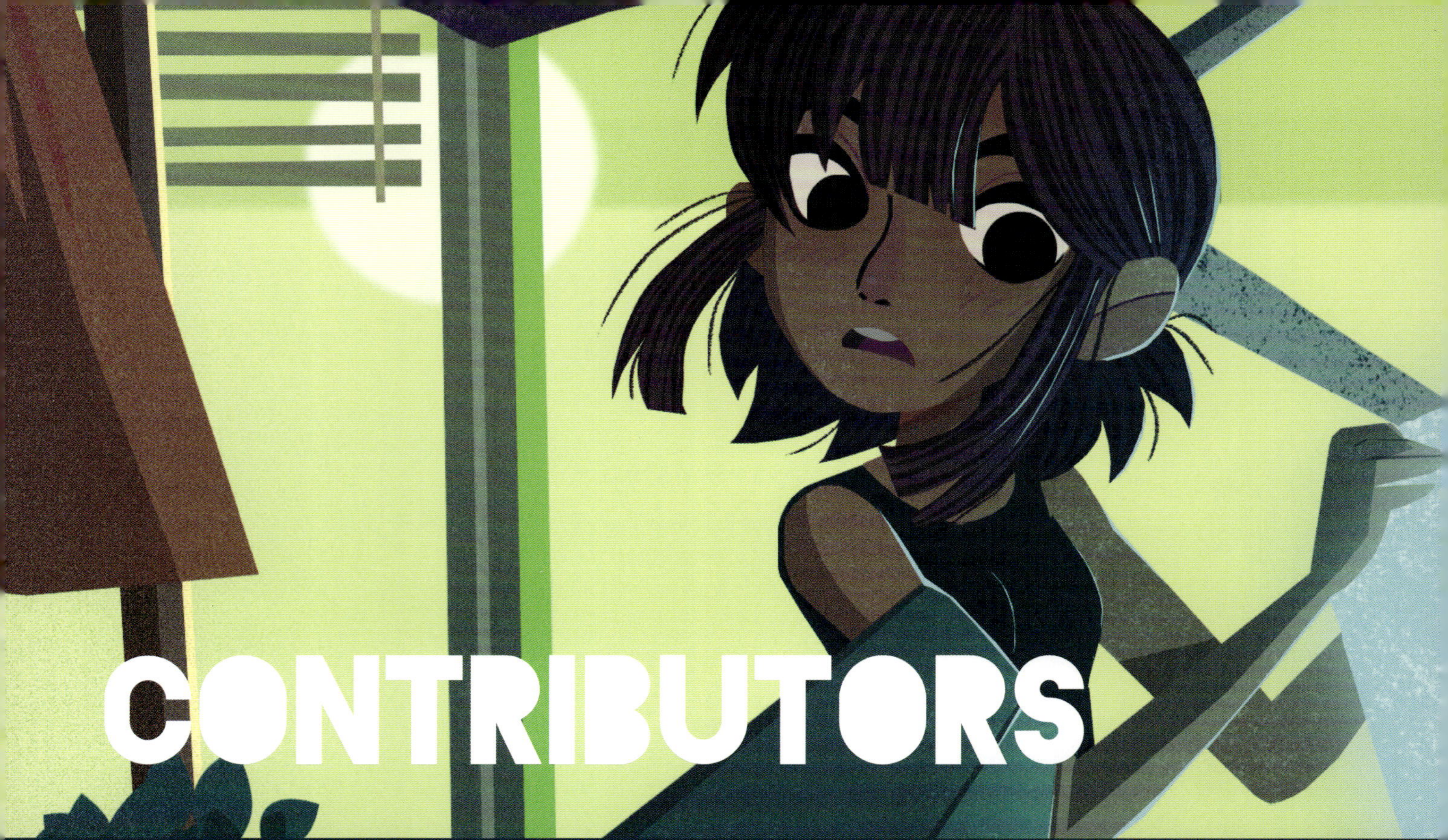

CONTRIBUTORS

YAROSLAVA APOLLONOVA
Illustrator & Character Designer
odnatamyara.com

Yara is a freelance illustrator and character designer based in Germany, Berlin. She is currently writing and illustrating her debut picture book.

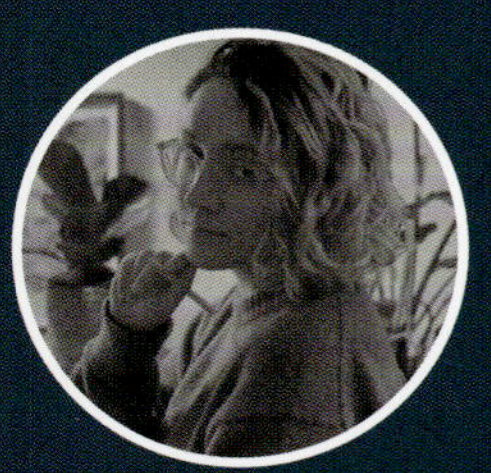

MARCO FERRARIS
Comic Book Artist
cara.app/marcoferraris1896

Marco is a cartoonist who mainly draws adventure comics for kids in France and the USA. He usually works digitally, but aims for a hand-drawn pencil look.

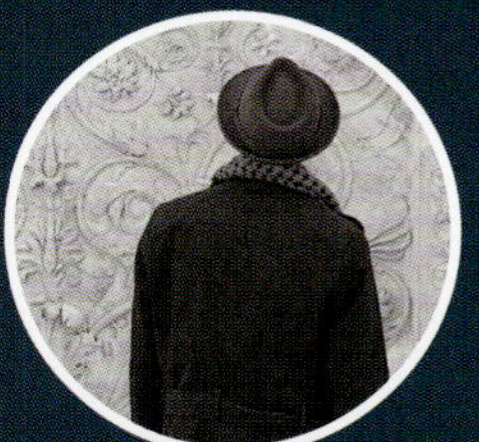

LINNEA KIKUCHI
Digital Artist
@feefal across the internet

Linnea is an illustrator from Sweden with a passion for creating artwork that is rich in dreamlike elements. She takes a lot of inspiration from science and biology.

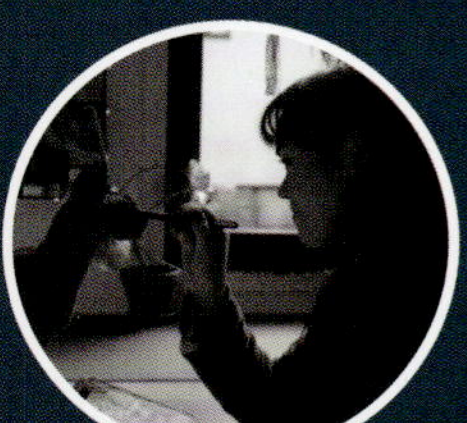

REX CROWLE
Freelance Artist / Creative Director
rexcrowle.com

Rex is a BAFTA award-winning designer and director of video games. He has led teams to create games such as *Return to Monkey Island*, *Tearaway*, and more.

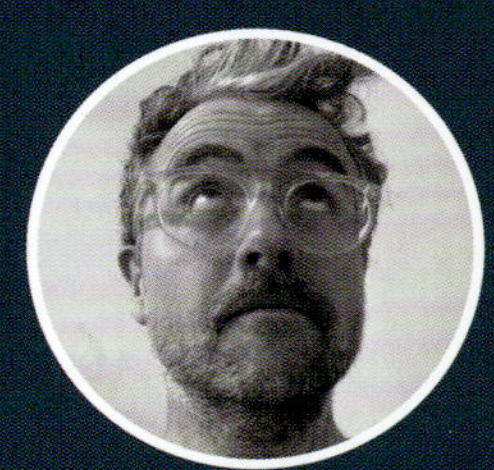

JOHANNA FORSTER
Independent Artist
johannaforster.com

Johanna is an artist and illustrator from Germany. After five years working for game companies she started her own business selling her art online and at markets.

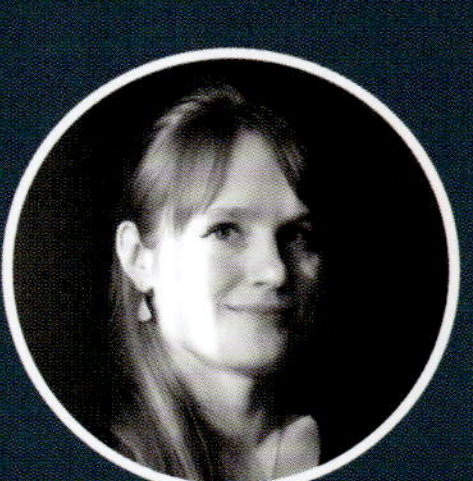

JUAN DIEGO LEÓN
Lead Artist at Bardel Entertainment
jotadeart.com

JD is a visual development artist based in Lima, Peru. Since 2008, he has worked for films, video games, and in advertising.

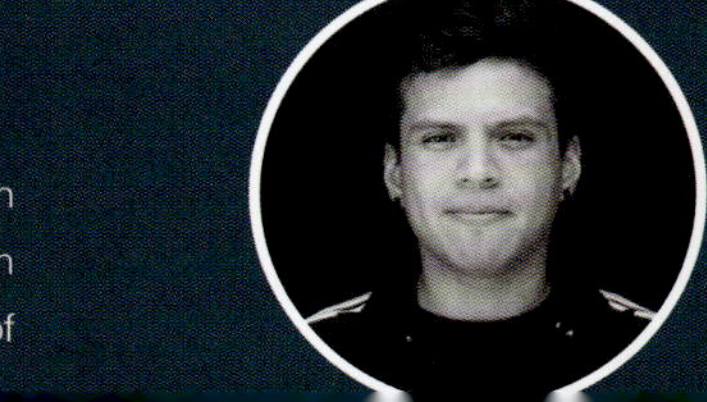

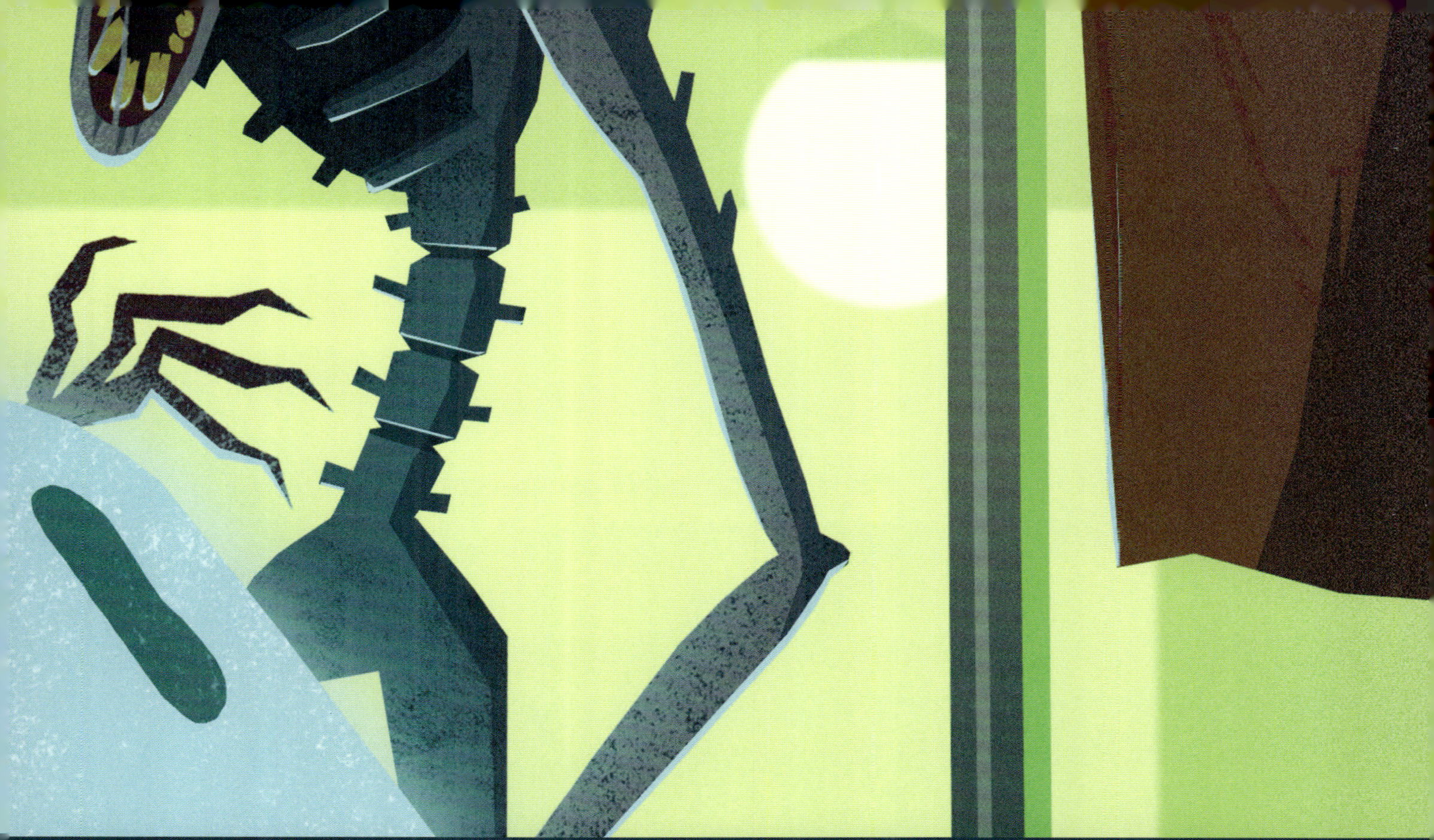

DAVID ARDINARYAS LOJAYA
Art Director at Stairway Games
david.lojaya.com

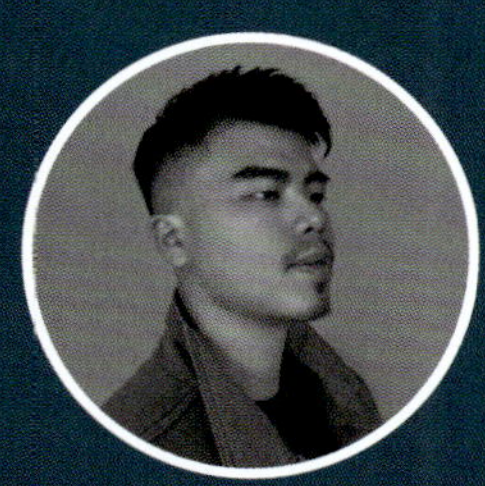

David is the art director for *Coral Island*. He has worked in animation and video games for over twelve years, for companies including DreamworksTV and DisneyTV.

LAURA PAUSELLI
Illustrator
instagram.com/fulemy

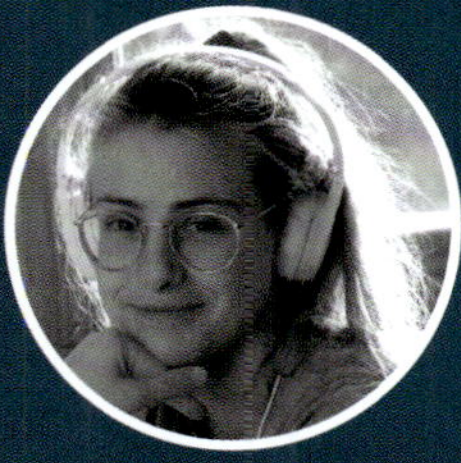

Laura is a character designer, visual development artist, and illustrator from Italy. She freelances for the animation industry and absolutely loves what she does!

ROGER PÉREZ
Character Designer
instagram.com/thealmightyjerk

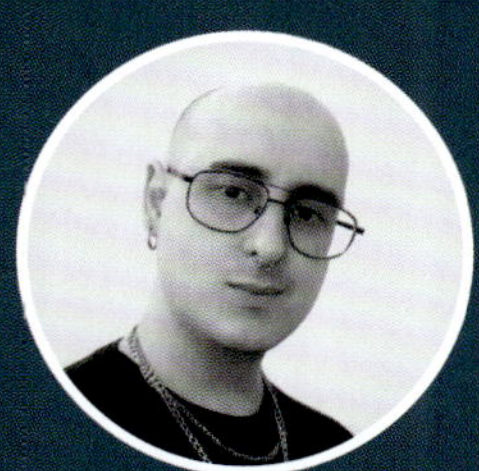

Roger has been working professionally for ten years, recently as a freelance character designer for several video game and animated productions.

TEO SKAFFA
Illustrator
teoskaffa.com

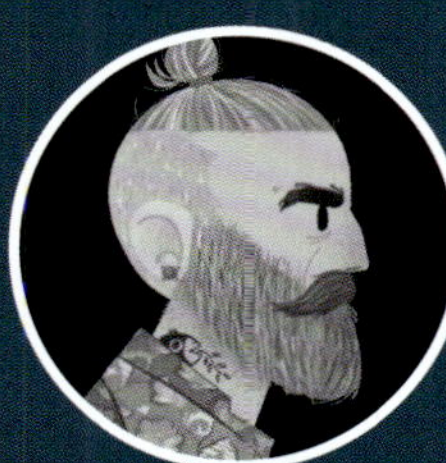

Teo lives in an abandoned school building in the outskirts of Groningen in the Netherlands. He likes to draw creepy-cute atmospheric scenes and characters.

HAIYANG SUN
Concept Artist at Tencent America
haiyangsun.artstation.com

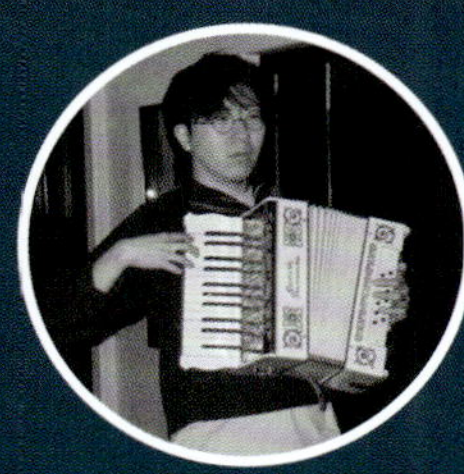

Haiyang Sun is a concept artist based in the LA area, working in the video-game industry. He is passionate about designing stylized characters and eating potato chips.